The Book Cover

I named this book "10 TOEZ DOWN" because I walked these streets and if I would not have made it to tell my story, I would be 10 TOEZ UP -- meaning, I would be cremated into a pile of ash and dust, or laying in some lowly graveyard.

As for the "Yellow Tape" -- it's still hanging on the sign post, a clear reminder of the drive-by that tragically killed my beloved niece.

The "Smile Now & Cry Later" faces are of mines showing the ups and downs of emotions while walking these precarious streets.

The 1976 caddie Coup deville was my very first car that I bought on my own. It had seen a lot of fun, excitement and dangers throughout the days and nights. It has been shot up and shot at -- I did my share of shooting out of it, too.

There is the neighborhood liquor store where Monty Earl and Darrel Sullivan were both killed. It's where we went when we wanted to get our 8 Ball, Silver Satin, or some Thunderbird with the red Bool-Aid.

Athens Park is the place we had our picnics and where the J-Block came together for unity and, at times, rivalry.

These are the streets that I walked and they have so much history on every corner, on each dead-end. It was a Killin' Zone and one better come with KAUTION if he or she is not flamed-up -- or you will find yourself 10 TOEZ UP.

10 TOEZ DOWN

All Rights Reserved

No part of this book may be reproduced or transmitted, downloaded, distributed, reverse engineered, or stored in or introduced into any information storage and retrieval system, in any form or by any means, including photocopying and recording, whether electronic or mechanical, now known or hereinafter invented without permission in writing from the author and publisher.

Both covers designed by Ojore Dhoruba Khafra Ajamu

10 Toez Down

ISBN 9798747282087

Author Albert "Ru-Al" Jones

"10 TOEZ DOWN"

by

ALBERT "Ru-al" JONES

The contents of this work including, but not limited to, the accuracy of events, people, and places depicted; opinions expressed; permission to use previously published materials included; and any advice given or actions advocated are solely the responsibility of the author, who assumes all liability for said work and indemnifies the publisher against any claims stemming from publication of the work.

DEDICATION

I dedicate this book to the Jones' family, my daughter Albanisha, my grandson Eugene, my granddaughter Emeire, and all my relatives, my homeboys and homegirls that walked these streets.

Thank you for that true Love.

CONTENTS

INTRODUCTION i

ACKNOWLEDGEMENT ii

THE JONES FAMILY. 1

MY HOOD 15

CENTENNIAL HIGH - MY FIRST YEAR 34

BIG VAL'S HOUSE 48

THE WEAK SIDE 60

SENIOR YEAR 65

JOB CORPS 92

CURB SERVING. 146

TOUCHED DOWN. 172

MY SEED 213

RU-AL GIRLS 220

THE DRIVE-BY. 243

DRESSED IN BLUE 280

THE L.A. RIOTS. 298

FIVE-DAY HIGH 315

RU-AL'S KARMA 348

RU-AL'S ANGELS. 350

PIRUS' and BLOODS' HISTORY. 352

B-DOG HOODS ROLL CALL 356

DAMU SAYINGS. 358

RU-AL STREET PRAYER 359

SUMMARY 360

MY REDEMPTION 364

THE LOST LOVED ONES (In Memoriam) 368

INTRODUCTION

I am RU-AL from Athens Park Bloods by way of Jarvis Street Mafia Pirus. When I got into this banging life I never thought I would turn out the way I did. But I turned out just fine. So let me invite you into my world. As you turn these pages make sure you put yourself into my Chuck Taylors. I'm sure you're going to say, "How can he be so crazy and heartless?" But then I'll show you I have compassion and, yes, I do cry. You will see that I don't just gang-bang, I had a love life too. I had time to be with girls, I treated some bad, but that's what they wanted. You will think that I'm an unpredictable person, but you will find out that these people got what they had coming. As you get deeper into my world your heart will start to beat fast. As you turn a page to see what's next, your hands will get all sweaty. You'll be hit with fear, then things calm down, but you will be looking for more and then I give it to you. Now the hairs on your arms and the back of your neck start to stand up. You keep reading until you're wondering, "How would it feel to be around RU-AL? Is his sex as good as he says it is? Is he a real bad boy?" I'll stop right here so you can read on to get the full effect of this gangsta known as RU-AL.

ACKNOWLEDGMENT

This book holds true stories of my life on these streets and my life in the Blood gang. Some of the names have been changed to protect them if they are still on the streets or in prison. All the shoot-out places and other incidents I have changed a bit so I don't incriminate myself. All of these encounters with Crips are true that occurred in high school, Job Corps and the pen. I used their real names but not their hoods. I left out their hoods so there would not be any retaliation on any of my homies. But their names are real and they know who they are. If they feel that I'm lying they know where I'm at and I'll just do it again.

It took me seven years to decide to write this book about my life and the way I gang-banged. There was a lot of people telling me not to write it. I think they was just haten because they can't talk about their own life. But there were many that said do it and getting their blessings means a lot. I'm only gonna say one name -- Sister Connie. I told her that this book will make a lot of people mad and upset. She said, "Write it and let the heads fall where they may, I got your back." That's all I needed to hear from her and a few Damu homies because there might be some funk once it gets out, and these homies I know got my back in a real way.

I did it my way and I kept it gangsta. There are many people that I want to thank who always showed me some love and never questioned me or asked why. My Daddy and Mama always kept me safe and tried to get me to do the right things in my life. But I was hardheaded. They were the best role models that I could ever have, but I wanted the street life more.

My four brothers and four sister, I love them all and I know they love me. When I needed to talk to either one of them they would stop what they was doing to listen and give me their opinion or advice. They accepted me for who I am and this meant the world to me. I love everyone of you.

All my homeboys and homegirls on Carlton, Jarvis, Cook, and Main streets, I love all of y'all and all the loved ones by the Park. If I left out anyone's name you know that the love is with you always.

Val, when you moved to the hood we became the best of friends. You're like a sister to me, you're such a beautiful person. I miss bringing my girls over and you giving me your approval. You have been a big part of my life, that's why you have your own chapter in this book. I love all the family members. I miss listening to my Honey Bee. Keep that lovely smile on your face. I love you, Big Val.

G-Man, my brotha, we came a long way together. We fought them Crabs side by side. I never told you, when those Crabs shot you in your stomach, I put in some work for you -- I know you did the same for me. The things we done on these streets! I am more proud of you for never going to prison. You somehow stayed out the way, you was there for your kids, and, to me, that makes you a good man. But I don't know how you got away because you was doing the same things I was doing and your ass is just as crazy. Keep raising your kids. I'll always love you, Miss Marie, B-Brown, Jerry, and my nigga Zell. You stay Ten Toes Down Gangsta.

The Johnsones, you have become my second family. And Judy, what a special woman you are. You have put up with my madness for many years and I know I left you with some sleepless nights. You knew I was a gangsta and I know that turned you on, but you also knew how much I loved you. I know if you read this book you're going to be upset and mad. I know you're going to say that you never knew me, but you did, you knew that I loved you. When you took me to church for the first time and you stayed by my side I really felt your true love. I fell in love with the church and Mother Reynolds, who is a very special person in my life to this day. Our son Vance, it took a while for us to click but we did and he's a good kid. I thank you Johnsones for the love only a family can give. As for you Judy, I pray the best for you. Loved always your stupid face.

Aunt Maple and Aunt Janice and all my relatives, I love y'all very much. And to my half-sisters and brothers, I love each and everyone of you.

My baby girl, my heart, Albanisha. When I first laid my eyes on you I fell in love. When your mama was pregnant with you, you would not kick or move for me. But when you were born that was a different story. You cried going out the driveway in my car. But once I got some music on, your mind was on Daddy. Baby, I'm so deeply sorry that I chose the streets over you. If I had spent more time with you I might not be here now. I know I love you with all my heart and I hope you know that too. I hate myself for not being the dad you always wanted. But I promise you this: when I get that chance to touch down again I'll be there for my beautiful grandkids. I know I can't bring back those lost years, but we can make new ones. Albanisha, I thank you for my three grandbabies. I love you, my child. I don't know how my life would be if me and your mama had become a couple, and I'm sorry I hurt her feelings too.

Wanda, you're my baby mama, and I knew I could always knock those boots. I want to thank you for keeping Albanisha and her big sister Nyea safe from harm, showing them all the love and affection you could.

I give my utmost love and respect to all Bloods that lost their lives on these streets. I do believe that gangstas do go to heaven because we have a forgiving God. You will always be missed but never forgotten. I know that our gangsta angeles are looking over us on them streets and pens. When you pour out that forty ounce in homage to the homies that left before us, make sure you look up because our loved ones is looking down on us.

I got to give it up for my nephew, Relly. He was getting his Crip on until his own people turned on him then killed him. I do miss him and his letters. He is loved by so many and will never be alone. So unkle says, "Crip in peace, nephew."

So, I say this: I give my props to all those that has my back because I got yours. And for the homies that is not with us anymore, P.I.P. (Piru In Peace) and B.I.P. (Blood In Peace) -- and you're still Ten Toez Down Gangsta.

CHAPTER ONE

(The Jones Family)

October 1979, it's a cool, damp and gloomy morning, it had been raining for the past four days. Today is the big move, my big brother Wayne came down from Compton to help us. Yvonne came with him, Anthony stayed at the new house until we get there. Last night we caught a big break, the rain had stopped long enough for us to load up Daddy's big, blue truck and his small one, and the two cars. Daddy asked Wayne if he tied down everything tight. "Yeah," he said.

Mama is in the kitchen cooking our last breakfast that we will be eating in this house together as a family. We lived here for seven months. We had some fun, joy, plenty of laughter, with very few bad days. It's all about to be left behind. Now it's time to hit the road.

"Let's go," Daddy said with his deep voice. He gave out orders on who was riding together. "Albert and Humphery is going with me. Honey (Mama), you, Kathleen and Katie, Connie and Yvonne, and Wayne and Paul is riding together."

Right before we are about to leave Daddy walked to Mama's car. I can see him in the mirror asking her if she is going to be okay. This is her first time ever driving on the freeway. Mama nodded her head to let him know that she was ready. Daddy leaned in the open window and gave her a reassuring kiss on the lips. I know Mama is scared.

Daddy gets into the driver's seat and says, "Boys, it's

THE JONES FAMILY

time to go!"

As we are driving off he pushed a button that made the windshield wipers sweep away the morning dew. I'm sitting in the middle of the seat with the shift lever in front of me. Each time the truck is shifted into a new gear, the shifting rod hits my legs. I always hated sitting in this position in any of his trucks, but I was stuck here for now.

Daddy is working that stick shift like crazy, we get to the freeway on-ramp quickly. I thought of Mama, I know her heart is beating real fast. I said a short prayer for her. I then said my goodbye to Palmdale and all my old friends, they will be missed. I'm only fourteen years old. I'll find many more new friends at our new home in Compton.

I couldn't sleep at all last night. I was so excited about moving. Now I'm getting tired so I lay my head on Daddy's shoulder and fall fast asleep. I know if I had laid on Humphery's shoulder he would have stuck something in my nose or played with my ear.

I woke up to the stick shift hitting my leg. I see we are on the freeway off-ramp, I wonder how long I been asleep. The traffic light is red. I took a look at the mirror on the door and see Mama's car, and Wayne's that Yvonne is driving. I don't see the other truck, I'm sure he's back there somewhere. I said to myself, "I'm glad Mama made it here safe."

The light turned green, we made a left turn on El Secundo Blvd. We drove right by a park passed Broadway then Main Street. We made a right turn on Carlton Avenue. The first thing that caught my eyes is this big building. We continued down the street and I don't see nobody outside or any kids playing. They must be in school. I looked at my watch to see it was ten o'clock in the morning.

Daddy pulled the truck in front of this house that had a big tree in the front yard; it had no fence like most of the homes I saw. Daddy said, "This is your new home." I smiled and we got out and I stretched. So did everyone else. That had been a long and tedious journey.

Out from the backyard came Anthony, saying, "The gang is all here!" Everyone started laughing.

Daddy is leading Mama to the door. He stopped and looked at her, saying, "Honey, here are the keys to your new home," then gave her a long, gentle kiss.

I can see her give Daddy that smile she do when she is happy. "Thank you, Jones," she replied. Mama always called him Jones, never by his first name Wilbert no matter what. It was always Jones.

She put the key in and opened the door. We walked in. It is a nice house with a big picture window. Mama and Daddy's room is to the left, the girls' room next to theirs, to the right was the boys' room. You can eat at the dinner table and look directly into our room. I didn't like that.

We went to the big backyard, which had a barbecue pit and a patio. "Oh, we are going to have some nice cookouts this coming summer and I'm going to be the family cook," Anthony said. Mama gave him a loving smile and wink of her eye.

There are three fruit trees in the yard; lemon, avocado, and pomegranate. Of all the houses we lived in before we never had these kind of fruit trees.

The sightseeing is over, it's time to unload the trucks and cars. Mama took over. She was an expert giving orders, telling everyone to put things here and there. Once everything was where she wanted it Wayne, Yvonne and Anthony said their goodbyes and left.

Mama started cooking dinner; you can smell the savory aroma of pork chops, mashed potatoes, green beans in the air. She know she can cook.

We have been cleaning and putting up things for hours. Mama got us working hard. I've been in the house ever since we got here. I never got a chance to see any kids coming home from school. I did see some walk by earlier, and they was looking over here to see who moved in. It's five o'clock, so I know I won't see anybody else the rest of the day.

I went outside for some fresh air and to make sure that we got everything out the vehicles. As I closed the door on the truck I see this kid walking towards me, he looked my age. He said, "Hey man, I'm Bruce. I live in that white house on the corner."

"Hi, I'm Albert," I replied. "We just moved in."

"Where did you come from, Albert?" he inquired more.

"Palmdale," I proudly answered back.

"Where is that, Albert?"

"I don't know. It took us two hours to get here."

I'm looking at Bruce. He got a short afro, a brown shirt, some black pants and he's wearing Chuck Taylors tennis shoes. He looked fresh. Here I am wearing a white T-shirt with some holes, green pants and some Pro Kids tennis shoes with three big white stripes on the sides. We talked for a while until Mama stepped outside and called me.

"Albert, come back inside, you still got work to do," she said while drawing nearer, seeing the new boy.

"Mama, this is Bruce. He lives over there," I said while pointing in the direction of his house.

"Hi, Bruce," Mama greeted him warmly.

"Hi, Mrs.? Mrs.? . . ."

"Mrs. Jones," I said, rescuing him quickly from his uncertainty and embarrassment.

"Oh, Hi, Mrs. Jones," Bruce said, relieved to get the proper words out.

"Okay, Mama," I'll be right in," I told her. I then turned to my new friend and said, "I got to go in now, Bruce. I'll see you tomorrow."

"Okay," Bruce said as he walked away. He had a cool walk about himself.

I then took a glance at my Pro Kids and said to myself, "I got to get me some Chuck Taylors."

It's six o'clock in the morning Wednesday, the next day.

THE JONES FAMILY

Mama got us all up so we can check into school today. I know I'll be the first because Vanguard Junior High is right around the corner. Me, Paul, Katie, Kathleen and Humphery all piled into Mama's blue four-door 1973 Chevy Impala. Connie didn't come with us because she graduated the year before at Palmdale High School.

I'm in the front seat when we pull up to the school. I'm looking fresh with some black slacks, brown button-down shirt, and some black croake sax shoes. I got a small afro. We walked into the office so Mama could check me in, then she left to get all the other kids to their schools.

The lady at the desk told me to sit down while she went to get my class schedule. A lot of other kids walked in and out the office looking at the new guy and I'm looking back at them. It seemed like forever before the lady returned and handed me a slip of paper.

"Mr. Jones, here are your classes and the times for you to be in them," she said.

I quickly glanced at the name tag pinned to your blouse, and said, "Thank you, Mrs. Taylor."

I'm walking down the halls looking for my first-period class when I see Bruce. He knew I would be checking in today. "Hey, Albert," he smiled, "did you get your classes yet?"

"Yeah," I responded, and held up the slip of paper.

"Let me see them, Albert."

I gave the slip of paper to him, he started laughing.

"What is so funny?" I asked puzzled.

"Man, we got all the same classes, all six of them!"

I'm happy that we got all the same classes, now I won't get lost looking around for them, and I have someone I can talk to. This is turning out to be great.

This guy walked up to us and said, "What's up, Bruce?"

"What's up, Kenny?" Bruce replied. "This is Albert, he just moved on our street yesterday."

Kenny looked me over then said, "What's going on, Albert?"

"Nothing much."

Bruce spoke. "Me and Albert have all the same classes, and four with you."

Kenny smiled and said, "That's cool."

While talking for some time this other guy approached us. He must have been the coolest dude I ever saw. He have a long perm in his hair and the curls is just hanging loosely. He's wearing a thick gold necklace, a black shirt, black silk pants and some sharp dress shoes. And to catch your eyes, he has on a bright red belt. This is one nice-looking brotha. "What's up, Bruce and Kenny?" he asked. They both acknowledged him with handshakes. Kenny introduced me to him.

"I'm John Boy," he said. "I live on Jarvis Street."

"What's up?" I said, then I shook his hand.

The bell rings and everybody is rushing to get to their prospective classes. Me and Bruce said our goodbyes to Kenny and John Boy then went to our first class.

THE JONES FAMILY

After school me, Kenny and Bruce walked home together. Bruce asked, "Albert, can you come over later?"

"Yeah, I'll be over there," I replied as we went our separate directions.

Just as I get inside the house and put my books down, Mama says, "Put on your work clothes." I know what that means, it's clean-up time.

I go to the backyard and see Connie already cleaning with a rake in her hand. "So how was your first day of school?" she asked.

"It was real nice. I got two new friends name Kenny and Bruce."

She smiled, she was happy for me being so easily accepted in a strange new place. Me and Connie has always been close. She has been my protector from knee high when the other kids would mess with me. I go get Connie and she would keep them from killing me. She is a real cool sister.

I can hear Mama talking to Kathleen and Humphery, they came to the backyard to join us. Connie asked them how their first day of high school went, and they both said it went well.

Mama came outside and said, "Your daddy will bring home a saw so that tree in the front yard can be cut down. Don't make any plans for Saturday." Mama ran her household with an iron fist. She love to yell at us. She got this voice that would intimidate you to the core, and she knew it, or she would whip that butt! Because of that, I won't be bringing too many friends over to get embarrassed. She got no problem doing that to them or me.

The yard is clean and everyone went their own ways.

I walked across the street to Bruce's house and knocked on the door. A girl answered. When I saw her I said to myself, "Wow, she's fine." She's light-skinned, brown eyes, silky-black hair, she's tall with a sexy body and she's about one or two years older than me. This girl is FINE!

"Hi," she said. "Can I help you?"

"Yeah, is Bruce home?" I said with my deepest voice.

"Come on in and have a seat. I'm Red, Bruce's sister."

"Hi, I'm Albert. I just moved in that house across the street."

As she walked away into another room I was looking at her firm, tight butt. Then an older woman came out the room first and said, "Hi, I'm Bruce's mother, Mrs. Ezell."

"Hi, how are you, Mrs. Ezell?" I greeted her politely.

"So you're the new kid that Bruce has been talking about?"

"Yeah."

"Bruce, come out here, somebody is here to see you," she yelled, and then said to me, "Welcome to the neighborhood, Albert."

"Thank you, Mrs. Ezell," I said with a smile.

Here came Bruce with three other kids. "Hey, what's up, Albert?" he said.

"Nothing much."

THE JONES FAMILY

"This is my brother Crip, my little brother Puncho, and Rose, my baby sister."

"Hi," I said to them all. They waved then went back into their rooms. Bruce suggested we go to the backyard. I was cool with that because I was getting nervous inside the house.

He had a big backyard, a lot of fruit trees, and a picnic table where we sat to talk. "Say, Bruce, where do your Pops work?" I asked him.

"He's a brick mason," Bruce proudly admitted.

"Where do your father work, Albert?"

"My Pops is the supervisor of the trash truck company. You see that blue pickup truck over there? He drives that."

"Yeah, I seen that truck many of times. Say, Albert, you want to go to the store?"

"Yeah, let's go," I said, knowing I don't have a dime in my pocket. As we are walking Bruce is telling me who lives in each house as we pass them.

We get to the top of Carlton Street and I asked Bruce what that big building is that I noticed earlier arriving here.

"That's our library."

I noticed a lot of grass. I asked Bruce, "Do you know how to tumble?"

"Nope. Why, do you?"

"Yeah, you want to see me get down?"

"Yeah, do some because we got a lot of guys that can flip," Bruce informed me.

I did a round off, flip, flop, flip, flop, back, back.

Bruce stared at me and said, "Damn, you can tumble. Blood, I think you can tumble better than everybody around here."

That comment made me feel good about myself.

We started walking down El Segundo then to Jarvis Street. Bruce said, "John Boy live on this street."

There are a lot of guys hanging out. I see fancy cars, three motorcycles and I notice a lot of cars driving up, parking, then someone is walking up to them. I asked Bruce, "What's up with them?"

"Oh, they are serving customers."

"Serving them what?" I asked.

"Weed," Bruce answered plainly. "The name of our hood is Jarvis Street Mafia Pirus and this is what we do, we sell weed."

As we walked to Cook Street Bruce named some homies down there. "Albert, we got about twenty guys and girls on each street, and there's more on Main Street. The alley behind your house homies sell there, the dead end they sell weed there, too."

"Damn, Bruce, we got weed spots everywhere!"

"Yep, we sure do," Bruce replied with joy.

We get to the dairy and he started grabbing stuff off the shelves, while I am just standing there. He looked at me and said, "Albert, are you getting anything?"

"I don't have any money," I let him know candidly.

"Get whatever you want, I'll pay for it," he offered.

I got some Funnions, a Snicker bar and a cherry soda. He got Cheetoes, an orange soda, and some other candy. I put all my stuff on the counter with his. He pulled out a large wad of bills, it had to be fifty dollars in ones and fives. My eyes got big as saucers. He paid the tab and collected his change.

We walked down San Pedro Street on our way back home. I noticed a liquor store across the street, I see guys hanging out drinking from a brown paper bag, enjoying themselves on this warm, sunny day.

Walking beside Bruce I had to ask him, "Where did you get all that money?"

"I sell joints at school. I'll buy a bag of weed for ten dollars and roll up fifteen to eighteen joints then sell them."

So that's how he got them fresh clothes and tennis shoes.

"Do you smoke, Albert?" he asked me.

"Hell, yeah, I do!"

"Cool, we will smoke one when we get to the empty shopping center, it's just down the street."

As we finished our snacks we turned off into the shopping center. "Say, Bruce, how long this place been closed down?" I asked.

"About two years. I hear they are going to build some apartments here. That would be cool, we will have our own little projects," Bruce said.

We walked halfway inside, it's dark and there is no walls, just an empty shell. Bruce handed me a fat-ass joint to light. I hit it twice and passed it to him. I'm holding the smoke in as long as I can and then I started coughing. "Damn, this weed is good," I said. I see Bruce trying to hold his breath in but he couldn't and he started coughing too. I can hear the echo throughout the empty building and we both began laughing at each other. This is some good weed. After we finished it I asked Bruce, "Have you ever smoked a sherm stick before?"

"Hell no, blood. I heard about what that shit do to your brain and we got homeboys that smoke it all the time. Why, have you ever smoked one?" he asked me.

"Yeah, I did about four months ago, and I was so high I got lost on the way home from school. It was a cool high for me, I only hit it two times and, blood, I was high for awhile." I noticed I said "blood" for the first time.

"Man, you're crazy to smoke that shit," Bruce said.

"I only did it that one time. I do prefer to smoke weed though, and drink beer."

"Yeah, I drink also but not too much. I don't want my mama to see me drunk," Bruce admitted openly.

"I'm the same way on the drinking. If my mama found out she would beat my ass."

"Albert, you still get whippens?" he asked.

"Hell yeah, blood, my mama don't play. She is real

strick. What?! You don't get whippens?" I asked.

"No, I don't. My baby brother and sister do, but not me."

"You got it good, Bruce. It's getting late, I got to get home," I mentioned finally.

We walked down 132nd Street. Vanguard is right across the street from the shopping center. I got to see the whole neighborhood, we got everything we need in this square block, and now I'm a member of the Jarvis Street Mafia Pirus. I like my new hood.

When we get to the corner of Carlton, I said, "I'll see you in the morning for school."

"Okay," Bruce answered.

We both walked our separate ways.

I get in the house and Daddy is already asleep. Mama is washing dishes, Paul and Katie is watching TV. Connie, Humphery and Kathleen is in the other room talking. I'm high as a kite. I get out my homework and sit at the table. Today was a very good day for me. I found my new best friend, Bruce.

*   *   *

CHAPTER TWO

(My Hood)

Eight months has passed and I've graduated from Vanguard. This is my first summer in my new hood, I'm looking forward to having lots of fun. Over them eight months I've met everyone and their parents. I liked the way I have been accepted by everyone with lots of love and hugs. I'm so amazed at how, just in that short time, my life has changed from a kid that liked to play table games or shooting marbles, to joining a gang and running the streets day and night. Growing up in Compton as a youngster I never knew anything about gangs or if there was any back in the early '70s. Now I'm here and I'm about to travel down a life-changing road.

When I seen everybody dressing fresh I wanted to have that fresh look too. When I seen them original gangsters (O.G.'s) with all them fancy cars, I wanted the same things. Moving here has changed my whole way of thinking about life. And all them things I will get in time.

After that walk around the hood with Bruce months ago I notice we got everything a person need; a dairy, liquor store, Steven's Hamburgers, a full shopping center just up the street. Someone in the hood is always having a barbecue, a house party, or just hanging out in the front yard. On these four streets is a lot of love and we're one big family.

MY HOOD

Today is going to be a hot one. Bruce came over and asked me if I wanted to go swimming. "Hell yeah!," I said, "I have been wanting to go swimming for the longest of time."

We walked down El Segundo to Broadway and there it is, Athens Park. This is my first time leaving the hood. I'm excited and a bit nervous but I know that Bruce know what he is doing. He says, "This is blood park and the homies up here are cool." I was happy to hear that.

We get in the pool. I'm swimming back and forth while Burce is trying to keep up. He said, "Albert, let's get on the high dive."

"Okay," I said. Little do Bruce know I can really flip off the diving broad.

He went first. All he did was a one and a half front flip. Now it's my turn. I got a good bounce and did a two and a half front flip and I hit the water clean.

When I came up Bruce said, "Damn, Albert! You got skills." I know I can get down. Mama used to send all the kids to Mona Park every summer and I would sneak to Lynwood swimming pool. They got the highest diving board I ever been on. So this one is small compared to that one.

We got on the diving board about ten more times before we are ready to leave. We get dressed and walk to the ice-cream truck. I get a cherry bomb pop, Bruce got a sidewalk sundae ice cream.

As we are walking up the hill to watch everyone else

swim, two dudes approach us, the short one says, "What's up, Bruce?"

"Nothing much, just hanging out with my new homeboy, Albert." He glances at me then continues, "Albert, this is Mel and Rob. They are from Athens Park Bloods."

I reach out my hand and said, "What's up, Mel and Rob." Rob shook my hand first and I notice that he made some kind of movement with his fingers. Then I shook Mel's hand and he did the same thing. I had to ask what that was. "Say, Rob, what was that you did with your fingers when we shook hands?"

Mel spoke first. "Oh, that! Bloods do that when we greet another blood and we can tell what hood they are from. Bruce never told you about the blood handshake?"

"Nope," I replied.

Mel said, "I seen you on the high dive, you can really flip. I'm surprised that they have not asked you to be on the Park Diving Team."

Bruce said, "Y'all want to smoke some weed? I got a few joints, let's go over there by those trees." When we sit down he gave one to Rob, he and me lit the other one. We're hitting them twice and passing them around until they was gone. Ten minutes later Rob started telling these corny-ass jokes, he had us busting up laughing. We hung out for an hour and a half enjoying our high.

Mel said, "Bloods, I got to get home. I got to do this check-in thing with my moms, so I'll see y'all later on, okay?"

MY HOOD

"Yeah, I got to check-in too," I told him.

We said our goodbyes with that handshake and I got it right with the finger thing the very first time. Me and Bruce walked the way we came. I said, "Blood, that was alright! We got to do this again."

"Yeah, we did have a lot of fun. So what do you think of the homies?"

"Oh, I thought they was cool," I answered.

I thought to myself, there's a lot we can do outside of our hood. I'm sure they have four to five streets that they call home, it's like a small box. I can't wait to get back to my box.

As we are walking I ask Bruce, "Why didn't I see them guys at our school?"

"Because if you live on this side of El Segundo you're in South Central, L.A. On our side of El Segundo you're in Compton. They are not in our district to go to our schools and we can't go to theirs."

"Damn, that's messed up!" I said.

"That's the way it is," Bruce said getting the last words.

I got the taste of something new. I met some new bloods, went to the park, got a good walk, that was cool. Now I need to make some money before the summer is up, and I know how I'm going to do it, too. I want to be fresh when I go to high school. Bruce must have been thinking the same thing. He suddenly said, "I need to make some money for school."

10 TOEZ DOWN

We made it back home with a lot of sunlight left in the sky. We're sitting on the porch talking. I said, "Bruce, the first three weeks of July my Pops job have this clean-up campaign."

"What's that?" he asked with a wondering gaze.

"Every summer my Pops job picks up trash, anything people don't want anymore. It don't matter what it is out there on the curb, it will get picked up. We work five days a week and the pay is real good. So if you want to work, ask your mama and see what she says. I'm going to ask some homies if they want to work."

I see Rudy walking down the street, so I say in a loud voice, "Rudy, my Pops is having this clean-up campaign and I'm seeing how many homies want to work."

"Do it pay good," Rudy inquired. "Because last summer I worked for Mr. Watkins that live up the street. He's the head man for Watts Labor Community Action Committee (W.L.C.A.C.), they hire kids from all over Compton, Watts, and South Central to work for them. They clean up vacant lots where houses used to be and a lot of other work sites that they have, but they don't pay that much. If your Pops pay more I'll work for him."

"You can make up to two hundred and fifty dollars a week. I got to find four or five more homeboys. And I'll tell you this, you got to get up real early in the morning, like at 4:30 a.m., and my Pops is not going to wait on you if you're late. So if you want to work, you know what time to be here."

MY HOOD

Only four of the five guys showed up and Rudy was not one of them. While waiting on Pops to come we smoked two joints. When he came outside we jumped into the back of his truck. To be so early in the morning it's a bit warm, that means it will be a hot day.

After a twenty-five minute ride we get to the yard. When the others seen it and all the trash trucks they eyes got big, there got to be at least twenty to twenty-five trucks. We all got out.

Pops said, "Okay, young men. I want y'all to start all the trucks so they will be ready to go when the drivers come."

Cars and trucks started pulling up and kids is jumping out of them. I see Mosses' son Lenard and Jerome. We grew up together, our Pops gamble with each other every weekend, they live in Fruittown piru neighborhood. I see other guys that's here every year.

Pops said, "Okay, men, each truck gets two kids so pair off." Me and Bruce stayed together. Kenny and Gil is together. Crip and Humphery is together, and off we all went. The sun is not up yet, it will be hard work and hot later.

I'm glad we got our first week out the way and our first check was two hundred and twenty-two dollars. I gave my money to Mama so I don't blow it. All the homies was happy with their pay. When Rudy heard how much we got paid he went to work with us the last two weeks. Everyone that worked said they would be back next year.

10 TOEZ DOWN

Mama gave me four hundred dollars for school shopping. This is my first time ever going shopping on my own. Last year Mama took me to National Dollar Store, Zody's Store, and Montgomery Wards. She got my tennis shoes from Vons grocery store. So this is a big moment for me, I'm doing my own school shopping. I feel sorry for Paul and Katie.

Kenny's older brother Jerry took me, Bruce and Kenny to the Hawthorne Mall to do our shopping. I never been to a mall before. I'm glad I let Mama hold my money earlier because I know I would had blown it if I had it. Now I can look fresh for my first year of high school.

We walked into the mall, it looked liked a whole 'nother world. There are stores everywhere.

Kenny said, "Let's get some Stacy Adams."

Me and Bruce said, "Okay." We went inside the store and the first pair I see are some all black ones, a mixture of black leather and black suede. "I got mines," I announced proudly to the others.

Bruce got the black and white leather ones, and Kenny got the all-brown ones.

Bruce is all excited, "We're gonna be decked out for our first day!"

We bought some Nike kickers, white Chuck Taylors, and some red shoestrings. We spent one hundred and ten dollars on our shoes.

Walking through this big-ass mall, looking all around, I

said, "Let's go get our dress clothes."

Bruce said, "Let's go in here, I see some nice slacks I want to get."

We went in and each of us bought three pairs of slacks and three shirts. Next door is Dickies Store. I got four pairs of khakis and four Ocean Pacific shirts. I like the O.P. logo on the front of the shirts, I say it's for Original Piru.

Bruce said, "Let's get one khaki suit alike."

Kenny said, "Let's get burgundy ones." We all agreed.

I wanted to get a jacket, something like a wind breaker.

"We will get some black ones and put our names on the back of them," Bruce said. "First, let me see how much money I have left because I want to get some weed when we get back."

We all checked our money, we got enough to get some weed.

Kenny said, "Let's go to the print store and get our names put on the jackets, it shouldn't cost that much."

I asked Kenny what name he's gonna get.

"Albert, I'm thinking of using the first letter in my last name Griffin and I came up with G-Man."

Bruce said, "Yeah, that sound cool and it fit you. I'm going to use my birth sign Leo."

"That sound good too," I said, "but I can't think of a name for me, and I'm not going to use Al or Albert. I want a good name."

G-Man said, "Okay, how about RU-AL. I took the "RU" from

Piru and used the "AL" from your first name and came up with RU-AL. So, do you like it, blood?"

"Yeah, I love it."

"You know that name will carry a lot of weight, right?" Bruce questioned me.

"Yeah, I know and I'm going to represent my name to the fullest for the hood and all bloods," I said with a strong conviction.

Everybody is happy with their new names on their jackets. Now all our school shopping is out the way.

I woke up about 7:20 a.m. and took me a hot shower. Last night at G-Man's house we got fucked up and now I have a hangover. Today I will be buying my first quarter-pound (Q.P.) of weed. I'm happy about that. I have been going half with Leo and G-Man, so today I will be getting my own. I got three dime bags left. I know as soon as I get outside they will be gone.

I'm going out the back door, everybody is still sleep. As soon as I walked halfway to G-Man house a car pulls up and they want four bags. I tell them I only have three. They bought them. Now I got some money for breakfast.

I get on the J-Block and see the homie Silk. He's one of many O.G.'s in our hood. He stood only five-feet six and weighed one hundred twenty pounds, with a long perm.

He sees me and said, "What can I do for you, young blood?"

"Let me get a Q.P." I handed him the hundred and twenty-five dollars and stood there while he counted every bill.

"It's all here," he said, "wait right here I'll be right back in a few minutes with your stuff."

While waiting on Silk his brother Derick is out there serving customers. He got this brown paper bag full of dime bags and cars is coming and going like a fast-food drive-thru. He had to have made three hundred dollars just that fast and now they was buying five to six bags at a time.

Silk came from the backyard and hands me this brown bag. I looked in it and it's a Q.P. "This is some better weed," Silk said. "RU-AL, make sure you're careful because Slim went to jail for two pounds of weed."

"Good lookin' out, Silk, I'll keep my eyes open." I put the Q.P. in my pants and walked through the Senior Citizen's parking lot to Carlton Street. That's one of our shortcuts if the pigs chase us. I learned all the in and outs of my hood and every yard and who got dogs. I know I can go in any house and most without knocking. So I would be out of line if I got caught if I allow the pigs to catch me on foot if I took off first.

I get to G-Man house and walked to his window like I do every time I need him. This morning he won't wake up, I can see him through the window. I know where everything is in the garage so I step in and see he didn't do any cleaning after last night. I'll do a little touch-up since I helped make some of the mess too. "Damn, at least he could have tossed out the empty Ole English bottles, put the dominoes up, and fix the sheet on the couch," I said in a low voice to myself.

I got the Ziploc bags and Tupperware bowl out and start sacking up my weed. I got the music on low in case I hear somebody coming. I do hear something, so I get up and go to the door. I see G-Man and he gives me wave. I returned to sacking up my dime bags.

Fifteen minutes later he came into the garage. "What's up, RU-AL? You already got your Q.P. sacked up?"

"Yeah, and I got the ten joints already rolled up for the day. So what's up with you? Are you going to get your Q.P. today? Did you hear what happen to Slim last night on the J-Block?" I asked.

"I got to sell five more bags to get my Q.P. And yeah, I did hear what happen to Slim last night. He might get a lot of time but I'm sure Silk will get him out. That's their relative. You got the breakfast money today?"

"Yeah, I got it . . . so let's go so we can get back and make some money."

We ate our breakfast at Steven's Burgers and it was a good meal. On the way, G-Man sold six bags, just enough to get his Q.P. He went home to sack his up.

I stayed at the rat cage so I can be first in line. In about an hour the rat cage will be full of homies waiting their turn. I like the name we made our hangout spot. We cut a hole in the gate so we can run to the next street when the pigs come. So like a rat hole in the wall, we got a hole in the fence.

I told G-Man to bring me ten bags since I left some weed in the garage, I only had five bags on me. People are starting to come. One thing about our street everybody can come and make some money. We can't sell weed on the J-Block. The dead end sells out of their house and they got that special weed. And in the alley gangsta Mike and the Bell Boys got that spot going on like crazy. So Cook Street homies sell on our street. The good thing about our hood is there's enough money for everyone and everyone is happy.

In the three hours I stood out here I made one hundred and ten dollars. One thing about the J-Block, they make the most money out of all the spots in the hood. They been doing this since the sixties and it's still rolling. G-Man and Leo made about the same amount as I did and it's only 12:35 p.m.

"We need to get out the hood," G-Man said.

"Where are we going, and how are we going to get there?" Leo wondered.

"We can buy us some beach cruiser bikes and ride to other bloods' hoods. I can ask my Pops to take us to Pep Boys."

The next day Pops took us and we got our bikes. We hooked them up with truck lights and a bike rack. We rode down the street and everyone looked at us.

"So what hood are we going to first?" Leo asked.

"Let's go the Campanelle hood first," said G-Man. "Then

on the way back we can go to Enterprise Park in Westside Piru
hood, and then to Village Town Piru before we come home."
Riding through all them hoods we were always in a blood hood.

"Let's go to the liquor store first and get some malt
duck," I said. "I also want to get that burgundy golf hat and
I need a pack of cigs."

"I'm going to get that black golf hat," Leo added. "What
color hat you gonna get, G-Man?"

"I'm gonna get that all-white one. I got just about
every color anyway. So do you, RU-AL," G-Man mentioned.

We got on new golf hats, the malt duck is in the racks,
G-Man got the boom box on his bike. It's 11:45 a.m., the sun
is out, today is going to be a hot one. We hit all the back
streets and it took us about forty minutes to get to Camp
Hood.

"Blood, I see some homies over there by those benches,"
Leo observed, pointing in their direction. We rode over to
some vacant tables.

G-Man spoke first. "What's up, bloods. I'm G-Man. This
is Ru-al and Leo. We're from Jarvis Street Mafia Pirus."

One of the guys spoke. "I'm Jay Dog. This is D-Mack and
Ray," he said with a voice too deep for his face. We shook
hands and I did the blood handshake and they did it back. This
time they formed a "P" for Piru with their fingers instead of
a "B" for Blood -- but that was cool, it's all the same.

We all sat down, G-Man plugged up the boom box and I'm

rolling up some joints.

Leo said, "Do y'all smoke weed?"

"Hell yeah, we do, blood," D-Mack replied enthusiastically.

We passed around about four joints and popped the tops on the malt ducks.

The homeboy J-Dog said, "Blood, this malt duck taste good. I always seen it in the store but never bought none. I will buy it now. And this weed, damn, homies, this shit is good, too."

Ray said, "I like it because it's red."

We all start laughing. I'm feeling good, we got music going on real loud. We are making true alliances. They will be going to high school as freshmen too. This is what we came to do, meet other bloods.

Leo said, "Blood, I'm hungry, let's go get something to eat."

"Okay," G-Man said. "I could go for some McDonald's, it's one on Central and Rosecrans."

"Blood, y'all be careful up there," D-Mack cautioned. "Just last week two homeboys got jumped on by some crabs with bats. They got them good, put them both in the hospital, so watch out, okay?"

"Good lookin' out, blood," I said. "Say, D-Mack, why did you call them crabs?"

"Oh! That's what bloods call crips. If you see how they walk it look like they just came out the sea like real crabs."

I had to laugh at that. I'm learning so much about this new life I'm living as a blood.

"Ru-al," said G-Man, "we got to get us a gun. I don't want us to get caught slippin' going into these other hoods and not be ready."

"Okay, bloods, we are about to leave, we'll see y'all in school in a few weeks," I said. We will address the gun issue when we are in a more private setting.

We got our eat on and those big macks was good.

"It's 2:15 p.m. We are not going to make it to those other hoods, so let's just go to Enterprise Park then home," Leo said.

We get there and it wasn't nobody there. We stayed about an hour then left.

"Blood, it felt good to leave the hood," I said. "I know everybody is wondering where we went. We'll build up our alliances later on."

G-Man said, "Now we got bikes to leave the hood when we want to. It do feel like we live in a box until you come out it and there is so much out here we was missing. A lot. Let's go home, bloods."

"Say, bloods, I know this spot in Watts that hook-up jeri curls if y'all want to go. It only cost forty dollars. I'll be calling my relatives in the morning to make my appointment so if y'all want to go with me, cool. It's in crabhood, but nothing is going to happen to us over there," Ru-al said.

MY HOOD

"My mom's friend do mines and my brother's curls so I'll pass," said G-Man.

"Yeah, Ru-al, make an appointment for me, I'll go with you," Leo spoke. He went on to say, "G-Man, I seen how you, B-Brown and Zell hair turn red after a month you get it done." We all started laughing at that comment.

"Leo," I said, "we are going to catch the bus."

"What! The R.T.D. -- the rough, tough, dangerous bus," G-Man said being surprised.

We're hanging out on the corner by Gene Timmons' house, we can hear the loud music playing. Leo said, "Junior must be feeling good today when he got that music blasting like that."

Gene's brother came to the door. "Say, Albert, come over later on, I got something for you, okay?" Glen said.

"Okay, Glen, in about ten minutes," I said.

"Say, bloods, I got to go check out the homeboy from Miller Gangsters tomorrow. Do any one of y'all want to ride with me?" Ru-al asked.

"I got something to do," Leo said.

"I will be busy also," G-Man replied. "Do you know the short way there?"

"Yeah, I'll go down El Segundo to Avalon to 120th and turn right and I'm there. I know, blood. Say G-Man, don't forget I'm going to look for us a gun in the morning."

"I'm not spending over fifty dollars," G-Man said.

"Okay, blood, I'll get at you when I get it."

Leo walked off before we started talking about the gun so it will be mines and G-Man's. "Let me go see Glen. I know all he want to do is smoke weed and play dominoes, which he know he can't beat me."

It's 8:00 a.m. I know that Albert Sullivan should be woke. I knock and hear a voice behind the door. "Who is it?" the muffled voice asked.

"It's Albert. Is Albert home?"

The door opened up, it's little Timmy. "Who do you want to see?" he asked with his kid voice.

"Is Albert home?" I asked again.

Then his sister Denise came to the door, she said, "Boy, I told you don't be opening up this damn door, boy! Now get your butt in your room." Then she looked at me, asking, "What's up, Albert?"

"Can you go get your brother Albert?"

"Come in and have a seat while I go get him."

Albert came walking from his room, it look like he had a rough night. "What's up, Ru-al? Blood, I'm sleepy as fuck."

"Blood, do you got a gun I can buy? I need one bad."

"No, I don't have one," he responded while rubbing his eyes, "but Cookie got a thirty-two pistol, he want one hundred dollars for it. I'm sure he still got it."

"Okay, thanks, blood." I left.

I walked down the street selling three bags on my way.

Cookie live in the corner house with his fine-ass sister

MY HOOD

Lay Lay. I see him in the backyard. "Say, Cookie, blood Albert said you got a gat for sale. If so, I want to get it."

"Shhhhh, Ru-al, my Pops is by the garage. Yeah, I got one I want one hundred dollars for it. Come back in thirty minutes, me and my Pops is doing some work right now."

"Okay, Cookie."

Melven came from behind the house. "Hi, how are you doing, brother Melven?" I asked him.

"Ru-al, where are you going to be?"

"I'm going over to Carolyn's house because her brother Goat owes me ten dollars for some weed he got from me three days ago, so I'll be up there."

An hour passed and Cookie didn't come up here, so I went to see if he's done working. When I walked up to the gate he had a broom in one hand and with the other hand motioned with a finger to his lips for me to talk quietly. "You got the money?" he asked in a hushed tone of voice.

"Yeah," I replied in a whisper.

He took the gun out his pocket, it is a thirty-two, black with a brown wooden hand-grip. He spun the cylinder like he was playing Russian roulette then handed it to me. I gave him the money, he counted it and was about to walk away.

"Say, Cookie, do you have any extra bullet?" I whispered in the same low, hushed voice.

"Yeah, I have a whole box of them. Hold on while I go get them." He walked to the other side of the garage then shortly afterwards returned with a box of bullets, handing them to me. I tucked the box under my shirt and jogged across the street to my house. I went to the backyard and hid the gat and the bullets by the chicken coop. Mama got ducks and chickens, and Anthony had also built a pigeon cage he's raising his birds here. So it's a great place where nobody would expect a gun and bullets to be hidden.

I see G-Man later on that day, he wants to see the gat. I show it to him. He smiles and says, "This is perfect, it fit right in the pocket. Who did you get it from?"

"I got it from Cookie," I said, "and he gave us a box of bullets. I paid one hundred dollars for everything. I'll always hide it right here so you can come get it anytime you need. And when you got it, let me know where you're going to hide it. Now we are ready for any misunderstandings."

G-Man said, "Okay, you keep it because I don't want B-Brown or Zell ass to find it."

"This is just another day in the hood, blood," I said.

* * *

CHAPTER THREE

(Centennial High - My First Year)

The night before my first day of high school I went to bed early so I can be well rested for a long day. I got all my clothes laid out, ready to be put on early the next morning. Just like when we was about to move out here, I couldn't sleep because I was too excited about the next day. I tossed and turned most of the night thinking about my first encounter with a Crip. I know they are going to be there looking at me and I'm looking back at them. What do I do? Walk up to him and say, "Blood, what the fuck is you looking at?" Or do I keep walking? I know this much, if a crab say anything to me out of line I'm going to sock him in the eye first.

Somehow I had finally fallen asleep.

At 6:15 a.m. I awoke feeling fresh and eager. I went to the bathroom to wash my face, brush my teeth, and took off the plastic curl bag I had on my head. I looked at my Jeri curl, it's tight. I got curls everywhere. I smiled at the imagine staring back at me in the mirror. I went back to my room and got ready. I put on my black dress pants and red belt then slipped on my Stacy Adams. I'll put on my shirt later. Like Pops, he always put his shirt on last so it don't get dirty. I got my red flag in my right back pocket just high enough so it can be seen. I remember in Vanguard when John Boy had on these same kind of clothes, I liked it so much I had to make it my style for my first day. But as far as I was concerned, it fit me much better.

Mama got up and cooked a breakfast of oatmeal. I hated oatmeal and grits, so I told her that I would get something from the dairy. Paul and Katie was also getting ready for their first day of school, the bus will pick them up in front of Mrs. Timmons' house. They look nice, Mama had took them to a good store to buy their clothes.

I called Leo to see if he was ready. "Hello, is Bruce home?" I asked.

"Hi, Albert, let me go get him," Red replied with an attractive tone to her voice. Damn, she sounds so sexy!

"What's up, Ru-al? I'll be over in about ten minutes, okay?" Bruce responded before hanging up the phone.

Then I called down to G-Man's house. Zell answer the phone. "What's up, blood?"

"Let me talk to G-Man, Zell."

"He's in the shower . . . here's B-Brown."

"Yeah, what's up, homeboy? Is you ready for school? B-Brown said come on down, he'll be ready."

"Okay, me and Leo will be there soon."

I hear a knock on the door. When I opened it, it's Leo. "Come on in, let me go put on my shirt," I told him.

Mama come out the kitchen. "Hey Bruce, you look nice

this morning. Where are your folders and pencils?" she asked.

"Oh! Hi Mrs. Jones. We don't have to bring that stuff in today, but I do have a lot of school supplies at home."

"Okay, Bruce," Mama said, then turned to me to say, "Here is five dollars for your lunch." I took it knowing it was from money probably earned when I worked with Pops. I said thanks and we walked out the door.

On our way to G-Man house Crip caught up to us. "Say, blood, why do y'all call him Crip?" I asked perplexed.

"Leo said, "My mama gave him the name when he was two years old, way before there was Crips. But we usually call him Erecket."

"Oh, that's what y'all been calling him," I said.

"We stopped in front of Sergio house to see if he want to walk with us. I called his name and his mother came to the door. "Hi, Mrs. Andraies. Is Sergio ready for school?"

She spoke in broken English. "No, Albert, his father is going to take him later."

"Okay, thank you," I replied then moved on.

Sergio had got into a Mexican gang while in Vanguard called the Compton Varrio, CV-131st. We'll see him at school.

We get to G-man house and Jerry opened the door. "Come in, blood, he is in his room," Jerry said.

We walked in, Grump and Skinny is in there waiting to leave. They are twins and they are pumped up for school too.

"What's up, Ru-al? Is you ready?" Grump asked. He is

the bigger of the two, and they don't look like twins at all. G-Man is going with their babysitter, Tosida. She is one of the finest girls in our hood.

Everybody is looking their best. Once we start walking, others begin joining us: Denise, Carolyn, and Tilda who's John Boy's fine-ass sister. We picked up everybody off of Cook Street.

At the dairy I got a chocolate milk and a honey bun. After everyone got their breakfast we walked through the Westside Piru Hood all the way to the Ten, which is the short name we called our school. We got to Central to see so many buses lined up dropping off kids from all hoods in Compton. Painted on the side of the wall is a big mural of an Indian, and over the top it read: "HOME OF THE APACHES" in big red letters. I said to myself, "This is going to be fun."

"Let's go to the office and get our classes," Leo said.

There was a gray-haired lady at the desk who wrote all our names on a pink piece of paper then told us to wait. After fifteen minutes she returned with a stack of paper. She called off everyone's names and gave them their class schedules. I looked at mines, G-Man's and Leo's, we didn't have the same classes like we did in Vanguard. I only got one class with G-Man and that's gym at first period.

Our locker numbers is also on the papers. We walked down the hall and found Bruce's locker first. We opened it then wrote the number for ourselves on another piece of paper. We found mine's, then G-Man's. Now we got all the locker stuff out the way.

Rudy walked up and said, "Let's go to the Senior Square."

We get there and it's packed with groups of people all over the place. It seem like every one is smoking a cigarette so I took out my Benson & Hedges and lit one up. I'm looking around in amazement at how many people is here. I notice the crabs is on the other side of Senior Square. I see one crab all in blue doing all the talking in his group. The homie did say that we are on one side and the crabs is on the other side. I see the snack bar and it's right in the middle and the other one is by the lunchroom on the crab side.

The bell rings and it's time to go to my first class. I'm nervous as hell but no one can see it. I hope none of them crabs say shit to me because I'm jumpy, and when I get this way I got to make my move first.

G-Man said, "Let's go, blood, we got gym."

"Yeah, blood, let's do this."

The gym is in the back of the school. I looked around and said, "Damn! Blood, do you see all them crabs over there?"

"Yeah, blood, I see them," G-Man replied. "This must be their hangout spot. Look, they are coming from Pamelee Street and over the canal."

I'm looking at these crabs. The one I seen earlier, he got them dudes laughing at something. He got this walk with his blue rag hanging almost to the ground. He got on his blue Chuck Taylors while doing his crab walk with his hands swinging from side to side, looking all up in the sky. I know my relative Willie now carry the name Blue from 117th Street got that walk, but he don't do all that arm swinging stuff. I can kick it with him, but now it's all a different story. "Let's check into our class before we be late," I said breaking my own train of thought.

We been to two classes and now it's snack time, we got thirty minutes to eat. I got a soda and some chips.

Sitting on a bench talking to the homies, Leo said, "Blood, look at them bloods all dressed alike in brown khaki suits with some writing on the backs. Let's go over there and see where they from."

When we approach I said, "What's up, blood? I'm Ru-al. These are my homeboys Leo, G-Man, Grump, Skinny, and John Boy. We are from Jarvis Street Mafia Pirus and we have more homies and homegirls over there if y'all want to come hang out, it's cool."

They not only had on the same clothes, they all got long perms with a brown and gold striped "P" on their hats and wore black Chuck Taylors. These are some sharp looking bloods.

The tall one spoke first. "What's up, bloods? I'm Zapp and these are my homeboys. We are from Fruit Town Pirus Invaders. We are cool kicking it over here. I heard about your hood, y'all sell weed. I've been to J-Block a few times. You know we got the water, and sherm sticks (PCP) that's the two-hitter-quitter shit. So if y'all want some let me know. But I would like to buy a dime bag if you got one."

"We didn't bring none today," I said, "we had to check out the guards first. We will have some tomorrow for sure. I'll make sure I get at you or your homies will get it."

The bell rings, it's time to go to our next class. We all shook hands. Some of the guys did the "P" thing with their fingers while others did the "B" thing concluding the handshakes. That was cool.

After two more classes it's lunch time. Senior Square is packed, it got to be well over two hundred people there. I see the homies from Fruit Town go to the snack bar on the crabs side, it's about five of them going.

"G-Man," I said, "let's go to the snack bar. Let Skinny and Grump know so they can go with us."

Walking passed them crabs I can feel them staring at us. I looked over at them and see that guy with all that blue on, we catch each other's eyes. He stopped talking and just glared at me. My heart is pounding, I'm glad he can't see it. I did a head nod and he nodded back.

We get to the snack bar and I buy a rubber burger and some fries. On the way back to our spot the blue guy is gone. I'm looking all over for this crab, he went somewhere. While eating on this burger I see why they call it a rubber burger. I will never buy this thing again.

"Say, G-Man, I gave that crab a mean look on the way to the snack bar and now I don't see him."

"Ru-al, what's up with you and that crab, blood? You been talking about him all day."

"Yeah! I want to fight him, he got that crazy walk and he think that he is too hard. That is the one I want if we ever get into it with them. Blood, it's time to get that high-school reputation."

Leo said, "I see the one I want too!"

"Blood, you two niggas is crazy," G-Man said. "Say homie, is that the homeboys from Camp Hood sitting over there?"

"Yeah, that's them," I confirmed. "I seen D-Mack earlier, let's go holla at them bloods."

After spending some time with the homies from Camp Hood we got about ten minutes left for lunch. Grump said, "Blood! Have y'all noticed that most of our classes is on the crabs' side?"

"Yeah, I see that," Leo said. "But check where all the electives are. Wood shop, auto shop, metal shop, cooking and typing classes are on our side."

"It's a setup so we can get into a big-ass riot. It's a death trap," Skinny said. Everybody started laughing, even he thought it was pretty funny.

So far Westside Piru Hood got the most bloods, our hood is next. Some homies from Village Town Pirus is here. I seen Snake, I told him that I will be stopping by his house soon.

CENTENNIAL HIGH - MY FIRST YEAR

A lot of people has been asking us do we have any weed. I know tomorrow I will bring a lot of joints to sell.

The bell rings, I got two classes left. It seem like forever before them two classes ended. On the way out we left through the side gate and, just like it was when we came, lots of buses and parents were there picking up their kids. We walked home together.

I see Sergio walking with his Mexican homies, most live in our hood. "Say Sergio, I didn't see you none today. Where was you, man?" I asked.

"Oh! We got this spot over by the bleachers and we had a nice time. I only went to three classes, I met some other S.A.'s (Spanish Americans), they are cool with our set and I got a girlfriend too."

"Damn, Sergio! You got a girl!" I remarked with joy in my voice for him.

I see everybody had a good first day.

I scoped out the crab that I want to fight. I got three years to get it done. I could fight some other dudes in the meantime but it won't be like beating his ass.

When I arrived home and walked through the front door, Mama said, "How was your first day of school?"

"It was nice. I got all my classes and I met all my teachers, and they are nice too. I will be taking all my school supplies in the morning."

I couldn't wait to take off my shoes, my dogs were hot

and barking. I put on my work clothes because I know Mama got some stuff for me to do. But first I'm going to make me a bologna and cheese sandwich to go with some chips and a big cup of Kool-Aid. I went into my bedroom and turned on the TV to watch some Loony Tunes Cartoons, seeing Elmer Fudd chasing Bugs Bunny with his shotgun. He got on his red hunting hat and was shooting like crazy, but not one buckshot hit Bugs Bunny. I'm cheering Elmer Fudd on to shoot that rabbit. I love my Loony Tunes.

Paul and Katie haven't made it home yet. Over the summer Mama kicked Humphery, Kathleen and Connie out the house. Humphery and Kathleen didn't want to do Mama's program so she told them to get out. Humphery went to stay with our childhood friends in Watts. Kathleen moved to Mead Valley, a hicktown just outside Riverside. Connie moved across the street to France's house. France has three sons; Albert, Freddy, and George Lay. France let Connie stay with her because she was pregnant, that's the reason Mama kicked her out. Now it's just me, Paul, and Katie. Pops let Mama do all the discipline and she cleaned house.

Later on that day G-Man came over. Mama liked him and Leo. "So how was school for you today, Kenny?" she asked.

"It was good," G-Man replied, "a lot different from junior-high school, but I liked it. Is Albert home?"

"Yes, he's in the backyard."

I was raking up the last pile of fallen leaves, it was a

CENTENNIAL HIGH - MY FIRST YEAR

lot today. I like the fruit trees, but they drop so many leaves on the ground.

G-Man come walking out the back door. "What's up, blood? Here is the gat. I know you want it when you ride to the village and to Miller Gangster Hood. Ru-al, you be careful. Word is out that some crabs have been jumping out of cars and beating homies with bats," he let me know with a lot of concern because this was the first time riding without him or Leo.

"Okay," I answered and offered nothing more.

I went to the dairy first and got a quart of Eight Ball, they always have the coldest beers. I rode with my eyes watching every car that I passed. If someone jumped out on me it's going to get ugly for them.

I get to the Millers Apartments, I don't see anyone hanging out in the front yard. I stopped my bike and pushed out the kick stand then knocked on his door. He opened it up. "What's up, Kasper?" I greeted him with a smile on my face.

"Ru-al, I thought you wasn't going to come," he replied.

"Let's go to the back, we can kick it there. I know you brought some weed, I see the Eight Ball."

"You know I got the weed, blood, and this is some bomb-ass stuff I got from the dead end. Here, light this," I said. I'm watching him hit the weed. He started coughing on the first hit. I'm drinking on the Eight Ball laughing at him, trying to keep the beer from shooting out my mouth.

10 TOEZ DOWN

"Damn! Blood, what kind of shit is this?" he asked with tears coming out his bloodshot eyes.

"Oh! You never had some chocolate Thai stick weed before? Homie, you only get five joints out of a ten-dollar bag, this what we are smoking on now. So how was school? I know that Locke High School got some crabs too."

"Hell yeah, we almost got into it with some at lunchtime. It was crazy," Kasper said with a lot of excitement in his voice. He hit the joint and took a big swig of the Eight Ball while holding in the smoke from the weed. He is trying to get fucked up. He coughed and beer came squirting out his nose. We started laughing, I never got high with someone like blood. Kasper is a tall slender guy, dark-skinned and he got a long Jeri curl and a big-ass smile.

We kicked it for about an hour and a half when some of his homeboys came in the back. I never seen them before so I put my hand inside my pocket where my gat is just in case.

There are three of them. The tall one said, "What's up, Kasper? Who is this, blood?"

"This is Ru-al from the J-Block. I met him while I was over there last week." Kasper turned toward me to introduce the other guys. "Blood, these are my big homeboys G-Wine, Joint, and their older brother, Artis."

I got up and shook their hands, and just like all the other handshakes, I put a "B" with mine. After a few minutes of small talk they left.

CENTENNIAL HIGH - MY FIRST YEAR

I told Kasper about my first day of school. I looked at my watch, it was 5:35. "Say, blood, I got to go. Next time I come I need you to take me to the homie Snake house, okay?"

"Yeah, I'll take you there. Say, blood, when you see the homie Cyclone, tell him I'll be over in a few days. Be careful on the way home. I'm gonna go lay my ass down, I'm high as a fuckin' kite," Kasper said with a slurred voice and bloodshot eyes.

I got on my bike and rode home. Not once did I tell them about my gat. I didn't have to.

I rode down Carlton Street, I see a lot of people by the rat cage. I get in line but I don't have no bags on me, so I ask Eirk Baker "E.B." to let me hold five of his. He went to Hawkeye's fence right across the street from the rat cage and came back with the five bags. I also walked with him to hide the pistol.

My Pops is coming down the street, so nobody sold anything until he passed. That's the respect thing we got for the parents that drive up and down our street. They start calling Pops "Hands" because when he passes he waves with one big-ass hand every time.

My first year at the Ten went by so fast. I almost got into two fights with some crabs but not the one that I wanted. I still got two more years to get that high-school reputation and I'm going to get it before I leave. I met some real down bloods from a lot of hoods out of Compton and I hope to visit their hoods over the summer.

Even though I missed eighty-five percent of my classes, the teachers still gave me a passing grade even though I didn't learn shit. Mama was cool that I passed to the eleventh grade.

I won't be working with Pops this summer because most of the pick-up routes are in crab hoods. And I know from this year at the Ten they will spot my face and it won't look pretty because I will take my gat. So I told Pops I won't be helping him anymore. He didn't ask me why, he just said okay.

I can say that my first year at Centennial High was a good one. Next year I'm hoping to see more action with some crabs. But, for now, I'm gonna enjoy the summer of 1980.

*   *   *

CHAPTER FOUR

(Big Val's House)

The new apartments has been built and people are moving in. They also built a four-story apartment building for the senior citizens; that building is facing Cook Street and the other apartments is facing San Pedro and the back is on the J-Block and 132nd Street.

I'm hanging out talking to Red and she is telling me about this young family that had just moved in. I said, "I have not been in there to meet anyone, I want to wait a few more days so they can settle in."

"Oh! I met Val at the dairy yesterday. She's cool, she asked me to come over. So do you want to walk up there with me?" Red said with her sexy-ass voice.

"Yeah, I'll go up there with you. First let me go get some weed, they might smoke." I ran into the house and got two dime bags from my stash.

We're walking up the hill on 132nd to Jarvis Street, the second door from the corner is the one Red knocked on. No one answered. She knocked again a little harder. The door opened and this light-skinned guy said, "Can I help you?"

"Yeah, do Val live here," Red asked politely.

"Yes, she do. What's your names and I'll go let her know you're here," he replied humbly.

"I'm Red and this is Al. How are you doing?"

"Hey, I'm Val's husband. Come on in and have a seat, I'll go get her, she's upstairs." Looking around we see they fixed their apartment up real nice. Red looked at me and smiled.

Two minutes later Val came into the living room. She's a big girl about one hundred fifty pounds and very pretty. She's wearing a gown as if she was in bed. She smiled at Red and said, "I thought you wasn't going to come see me. I had to put my baby to bed. I got a two-month-old son name Little Willie, but we call him Fudd. This is Big Will -- who is that?"

"This is my friend Albert, he live on Carlton by me."

I looked at Val and smiled, then said, "Hi, Val. You have a nice place here."

"Thank you," she replied. Big Will had left during the conversation because Fudd had started crying.

"Say Val, do you smoke weed? I got some if you want to get high," I freely offered her.

"How old are you, Val?" Red asked. "You look so young." After a quick glance around the room Red wanted to know, "How much is the rent here?"

"I'm eighteen and I pay ninety-six dollars a month. As you may know these apartments are all Section Eight. Yes, I smoke weed, I was about to go down the street to buy some."

Big Will came down the stairs with their son, who looked just like his father. He smiled at me and I shook his little hand. He got a strong grip too.

I'm rolling up a bag of weed, I made seven fat joints. I gave one to Will because he had to leave for work. I gave one to Val. She first took Fudd back upstairs and returned shortly after he fell fast asleep. She lit the joint and took two hits, then said, "Wow! This weed taste good! It's been a while since I last smoked one." I can tell she's really feeling it because she started laughing, then so did me and Red. "Al, sell me some joints. I need some while I clean up."

"Here, you can have this bag for free as a welcome-to-the-neighborhood gift," I said as I handed her the bag.

The front door opened and this short dark-skinned girl came in. "I smell it! I smell it! Now somebody let me hit it!" Her voice is very loud to where it hurt your ears.

"What's up," I responded with a big smile. "I'm Al and this is Red. We live down the hill. And yes, you can hit the weed, here you go." She eagerly took my joint and immediately inhaled deeply twice.

"Al, this is my crazy-ass sister, Wee-Wee. She live with my mama and my sister Von and my little brother June Bug. We got another sister that have a apartment, her name is Lady Bug. And Will got a sister and his mama got one apartment. Yeah, we brought the whole family here."

"It's getting late, I got to go to work," Red said.

"I got to go too, but if it's okay, I'll come back over in a few days once you get your house in order."

"Y'all can come over anytime, and thanks for the weed Al."

Three days later while on my bike taking a shortcut to the store -- I'm learning all the getaway spots just in case I got to run through here -- I see Val walking down the sidewalk. "Hey, where you going?" I asked her.

"Hi, Albert. I'm going over to my mama house. Do you want to come and meet her? She is cool."

"Sure, I like to meet your moms. I was on my way to the store."

We walked together while I pushed my bike beside me. Val grabbed the door handle and gave it a turn, the door was unlocked, so we just walked in. I looked around and the house is hooked up real nice.

"Mama! Mama!," Val yelled, "where are you?" Her voice echoed loudly throughout the house.

This other voice came booming from upstairs, "Girl, you better stop that damn yelling in my house!"

I hear someone coming down the stairs and then I see this short, stocky lady come into view. She said, "Val, why is you yelling? I heard you plenty the first time. Now that you're here I need you to go pick up my prescription from the store."

"Okay, Mama," Val replied, then motioned her attention toward me. "This is my friend Al. He live around the corner from me."

She stood every bit of five foot three and got the same dark skin as Wee-Wee. She said, "Hi, Al."

BIG VAL'S HOUSE

I said hi and smiled warmly at her. Then I hear another female voice upstairs. She came walking in with rollers in her hair like she is getting ready to go somewhere later.

"Al, this is my sister Von," Val said, then changed her tone. "Von, why you won't go get Mama medication? You ain't doing nothing!"

"I got to be somewhere in thirty minutes," Von replied.

Val got the money and we left back to her house. Before we get there she went into this other apartment. I see this lady sitting on a couch, she got on some black shorts and was wearing a blue cotton shirt without a bra. I can see her nipples protruding from her ample breasts.

"Lady Bug, this is my friend Al. Al, this is my sister Lady Bug. We both said hi to each other. While her and Val is talking I'm looking at her perky nipples and I think she sees me looking because she put the pillow over her chest.

I hear a voice that I heard before, it was Wee-Wee. "Hey, y'all," she greeted happily.

"Hi," I said back. We all talked for about ten minutes then we left to Val's house.

Big Will is holding his son, he look so happy. Val said, "I got to go to the store for Mama to get her prescription, so me and Al is going to pick it up. Do you need anything?"

"Nope," Will replied, "I don't need anything."

I put my bike in her patio then we left in their brown 1975 Bonnieville.

10 TOEZ DOWN

We arrive at Clark's Drug Store and Val bought what she needed. I just bought some cigarettes for myself. Val went off to the ice-cream stand.

I remember when I was a kid Mama used to bring us here to shop and she would give us four kids one dollar each. I would steal some kind of toy then buy some candy. This store still have that same sweet smell of candy and popcorn.

"Al, do you like mint & chocolate chip ice cream? Because I'm going to get a gallon and some beer nuts to pour in it, it's going to taste good," Val reassured me.

"Yeah, I'll try it."

After dropping off her mama's prescription we went right to Val's house. She got two big-ass bowls and filled them with ice cream then poured beer nuts on top. I eat the whole bowl full and it was delicious. After that we smoked a fat joint.

Over the summer me and Val has become the best of friends. I'm at her house more than on the streets.

Four months have passed and another school year has arrived. The summer came and went so fast. I've met so many new people in the apartment, I also know all the ends and outs of them. Val is about to throw her first house party this Saturday night and everybody in our hood is going to be there. Me and Will has been moving all the furniture upstairs and setting up the turntable. She got a rent-to-own hookup with two big house speakers which we put in the corners of the

BIG VAL'S HOUSE

living room. This is a bring-your-own-drinks (B.Y.O.D.) party. Val and Wee-Wee is cooking chicken wings and there will be all variety of chips, cookies, and alcohol-spiked punch. We got everything set up for the big party.

June Bug, Daren, Will's brother and their friend Andre came over to check out the sounds because Andre will do the music. We was told that he can DJ. But this is his first time before this crowd and Val is a little nervous because she want her first house party to be good.

I brought my party clothes earlier so I got dressed. People started coming over and the music is sounding good. This party is already jumping, the rhythm and beat of the music is pumping hard. I see Val over there dancing with Will.

I stepped outside to smoke my first joint of the day, it's that good Thai bud. Wee-Wee came out soon after, I tell her, "This party is going well. I see all the people that came, they are really enjoying themselves." I hand her the joint after taking another hit. "Here, hit this weed."

After inhaling deeply she started coughing, then said, "Yeah, this party is jumping, I'm drunk as fuck and high as hell!" We laughed at each other as our high intensified.

I hear Andre on the microphone, saying, "I'm Dr. Dre and I'm going to make you sweat. This is a party and I don't want to see anybody sitting down."

Me and Wee-Wee went back inside. This dance floor is packed and I'm floating around dancing with everyone. The party finally started to fade out about 3 a.m. and everyone went home.

"Val, this is the best house party I ever went to," I told her. "Last year the Lucans had a house party but not as good as this one. People will be talking for weeks about this."

"Yeah, it did turn out just fine, didn't it!" She was obviously proud and relieved at the result.

I slept on the floor until morning. After I got up we cleaned the house and yard, then I went home to take a shower.

This is June Bug, Daren, and Dr. Dre's first year in high school. They are not the gang-banging type of people. They are dancers and did some rapping. Andre changed his name to Dr. Dre after Val's house party. While at the Ten, Centennial High, the J-Block had their backs and nobody fucked with them. Every two months the Ten have a talent show. In two weeks there will be a dancing talent show and they got into it. For the passed week they have been practicing at Val's house. Me and Val has been helping them with their moves and we picked out their music that they will be dancing to. Planted rock is the best type of music for their routines, and they got some good moves. Now we got to find a unique name for the group.

June Bug said, "How about the Emerald City Boppers?"

Dr. Dre and Daren both said, "That's it, we are the Emerald City Boppers!." We liked it.

Val is hooking up their outfits. They will wear long, green socks, black khakis which she cut at the knees, and a shiny, long-sleeved green shirt, a black tie, a black derby hat, and black Chuck Taylors with green shoestrings. The outfits were stylish and fit perfectly, Val did an amazing job.

It's now Friday and every Friday it's Red and White Day, the Ten's colors. The crabs don't like that. The Ten is the only high school in Compton that's red and white. All the other schools got some kind of blue in their colors.

I got on my red sweatshirt, black khakis, and white Chuck Taylors. All day we been talking about the talent show and how our homies are gonna turn it out. I see Dr. Dre, Daren, and June Bug, they don't have on their dance clothes yet.

G-Man said, "Dr. Dre, are y'all ready to represent the J-Block in the talent show?"

"Hell yeah! We got this!"

The bell rings, it's 2:30, everybody is headed to the gym. All of the bloods is on one side of the gym and the crabs are on the other side. The bleachers are packed with students.

The M.C. got on the mike and said, "There will be six acts and the winner will get a Ten sweatshirt, a five-dollar snack bar coupon, and a first-place winner trophy. So are you ready for some competition dancing?"

Everyone yelled and screamed "Yeah!" as loud as they could in a thunderous din as they stomped on the wooden bleachers.

The first four acts was nice and the fifth one was real good. Our homies got to put on the show of a lifetime because the crowd went wild. The M.C. said the upcoming act was last and they got to really bring it because the previous act was really good. "So let's welcome the Emerald City Boppers!" he loudly announced.

The lights went out and the crowd grew quiet. When the lights came back on there was a black box in the middle of the floor. June Bug was sitting on one side and Dr. Dre was sitting on the other side. People were wondering what they were going to do next. Planted rock music began booming over the speaker system while June Bug and Dr. Dre started their dance routine. Suddenly the top of the box popped open, shiny green and black confetti flew high up into the air almost to the ceiling. Then all sides of the box opened up and Daren jumped out dancing in sync with the other two. The crowd went crazy with amazement and excitement. The lights unexpectedly went out again and when they came back on, the dancers had vanished into thin air.

"Was that some great talent or what!" the M.C. yelled into the microphone as he glanced around still looking for the missing dancers. The roar of the crowd was deafening and finally it began to fade. The M.C. was ready to make his announcement. The crowd grew quiet, you could hear a pin drop. My heart is beating so fast. "Emerald City Boppers!" he announced loudly.

We all went crazy in a frenzy of wild emotions and pride. I can see homies jumping up and down in a celebratory fashion. We are on the bleaches stomping and giving it up to them while they are waving and cheering back at us.

BIG VAL'S HOUSE

After receiving their gifts and the trophy they went back to Val's house. She is so happy that they won. She had put in a lot of work for them. They graciously gave her the trophy and Val accepted it with gratitude and a big smile.

Dr. Dre DJ-ed about five more house parties for Val by the time he mastered his craft of mixes on her rent-to-own turntable. My next-door neighbor Lonzo, who was opening up a club called "Eve's After Dark" in Westside Piru Hood, had heard about him and wanted an introduction. Once Lonzo got Dr. Dre in his garage with all that music equipment he worked all day and night. When the club was about to open they moved all their equipment there. Dr. Dre stopped going to school and started performing in other clubs. The homie Fat Fat was their equipment man, going from city to city with them, until he caught a murder case banging too hard. It was easy to get caught up in this banging life. Dr. Dre stayed with the club scene. When the club opened up we made sure no crabs came in. Dr. Dre had put the club on the map and when people came from all over L.A. we was able to sell more weed, so everybody got something out of it. The club had gotten a nickname "The Sweat Box" because it got real hot inside.

Big Val still gave the best house parties, but now June Bug and Daren are doing all the DJ work.

Lonzo and Dr. Dre had started this group "The World Class Reckon Crew" who put out some good hits. It's cool to see someone come from the hood and do something real good. Lonzo and Dr. Dre did that.

We got two nice spots to party at -- "Eve's After Dark" and Big Val's house.

*   *   *

CHAPTER FIVE

(The Weak Side)

    I walked to G-Man's house to kick it with him for a bit. I went straight to the garage because I can hear voices and the radio playing in there. I walked in to see Grump, Skinny, and Gil is sitting at a table slapping some bones and smoking some weed. Skinny got a bottle of Night Train in his hand and passes it to me as I entered. I took a few refreshing swigs, it's good and cold. I took out a joint I got from the alley and passed it around to the guys.

    G-Man turned the boombox down and said, "What's up, Ru-al? We got to find something to do today."

    "Let's play some basketball," I offered, "we have not played none this week. Blood, it's Saturday, we ain't got shit to do, so let's get the rest of the homies and go to Vanguard."

    "Let's see if the homies on the Weak Side want to play," Gil added as he blew out a puff of weed smoke he was holding in.

    "Blood, you know them niggas can't fuck with us on the court or in any other sport. That's why we gave them that name, Weak Side," I said, taking my turn with the joint.

    Last summer we played them some tackle football. Their hood got as many streets as our side. They are at the end of the Westside Piru Hood. We walk through their hood to go to

THE WEAK SIDE

school, all of us went to Vanguard together. We hang out on their side and they hang out on ours, but when it comes to playing any kind of sports, we can get very competitive and we know we got to win for the bragging rights.

We called them out for a football game and they accepted. Today is the big game, we got our homegirls cheering for us and they got their cheerleaders on their side. This is going to be a hard-hitting competition. There's hundreds of people here to play and watch the action. There are cars and bikes lined up and down 132nd Street and in the school parking lot. We flipped a coin to see who get the ball first, and we won. G-Man is our quarterback, he is one of the best athletes. I'm a wide receiver.

On the first play G-Man threw me a bomb and I caught it right over my shoulder. I can hear everyone yelling, "Oooh! Oooh! Touch down, Ru-al!" We scored first.

Now they got the ball. We already know who they are going to throw it to. Lonney plays pro ball for the Los Angeles Express team in the USFL League. He is a wide receiver -- he wasn't that tall, about five-ten -- but he had the talent to catch anything thrown his way.

Grump said, "Let me stick Lonney, but you, Ru-al, play off us so he don't get by me." Grumps **dating** his sister Avis and she is fine. She got these short bowlegs and have a sexy-ass walk.

They threw the ball to Lonney two times but he didn't

catch either one, they didn't score. We got the ball again. We are talking big-time shit to each other, but we didn't score either.

G-Man said, "Blood, let me get Lonney, he just hit me with a cheap shot and I got to get him back."

They threw the ball to Lonney and G-Man did just what he said he was going to do. Lonney jumped high for the ball and G-Man hit him so hard he flew into the tree. He got laid out. The people on our side went crazy after seeing the hit.

G-Man said, "I told you, blood, that I was gonna hit that nigga hard." We all started laughing and the opposing team and their fans didn't like that.

"Y'all know we got to keep hitting them hard because they are coming after us after that hit," Rudy let everyone know.

Lonney finally got up and staggered gingerly to the sideline and sat heavily on the grass. He had been down for about ten minutes. Now he is mad as hell because he could have lost his pro career by getting injured in a street game. Once again they did not score.

We got the ball back. I said, "G-Man, let's go deep again but this time throw the ball more over my head so I can run under it. The last two passes I got hit hard, blood." Leo started laughing because he has been getting clobbered a lot too while running the ball.

Vic hiked the ball to G-Man and I took off running as fast as I could. I got Joe sticking me tight. I did a fake

THE WEAK SIDE

stop and when he stopped, I took off sprinting again. G-Man threw the perfect pass. Just as I said, I ran right under and caught it for our second touchdown. That made the score fourteen to zero. They are getting   us because they can't score any points while we keep making fun of them.

The homegirls on our side started a cheer: "We are the strong side and y'all are the weak side!"

The others didn't like that so they began repeating the same chant back to us.

Lonney started talking shit to Skinny. Before he could get out another word Skinny socked him in the eye. When that happened it was on, everybody was trying to find someone to fight. Me and Joe started mixing it up and I got the best of him, but he did get in a few good hits. Our homegirls even started brawling their homegirls. This went on for twenty minutes. When it was over we won the fight and the football game, so that's why we call them the Weak Side.

Time passed since that football game and we made up with them, but we still call them the Weak Side. G-Man said, "Let's go to the dairy with the rest of the homeboys to get some juice and tell the Weak Side to meet us at Vanguard."

Once everybody got to the school we had about twenty people on our side and they had about the same. Everyone was sitting together on the bleachers. It's me, G-Man, Grump, Whoop, and Gil. Gil is our big man, he stood six foot five and can dunk on anybody. We got our reserve players Chuck and

Carlyn's sister, Levita. She's our tomboy that will play any sport with us and she got mad ball skills.

We started playing, going to thirty-six by twos. We won the first game real easy. Me and G-Man sat out the next game and our team lost. The Weak Side is talking shit and I don't like it. "Say, Joe, let's play for five quarts of Ole English and a bag of Thai bud from the dead end," I wagered him.

"Bet, blood," Joe accepted freely without hesitation.

The game started, we got the team that won the first game. The score is much closer than the first time but we got a two-basket lead. They got possession of the ball and was dribbling down the court. We only need one more bucket to win. Joe shot and missed. Gil grabbed the rebound with those big-ass mitts he got then threw the ball to G-Man, who passed it down to me because I had been hitting my jumper all day. I got a good look at the rim and let it go. The ball hit the front of the rim and bounced out. Gil jumped up, grabbed the ball and slam-dunked it hard. Everybody went wild, cheering loudly and celebrating. "Ooooh! Wooo-whoooo! Yea!"

We won again. The Weak Side can't hang with the Strong Side in nothing. Later on that night they all came over to Carlton Street with beer and weed so we all got high together.

"That was another brutal beatdown for the Weak Side," I said with pride in the tone of my voice and a big smile on my face.

*   *   *

CHAPTER SIX

(Senior Year)

This is my last year of high school. The previous years went by really fast. I didn't have no fights, but I almost did. Maybe this is the year that everything will finally get crazy. I've been anticipating some action eventually.

Somehow all my teachers passed me. I know every time a new semester started I would check into class but then never go back. That was our thing; we would check-in that first day and the teacher might see us twice during the year, but they still passed us. However, the class I would always attend was my cooking class. The homeboys and girls loved it when I baked cookies. So three times a week I would bring out cookies for lunch. Our ditching spots are Enterprise Park, Golden Bird Chicken, Taco Pete's, or we will go to Willowbrook Park next to Eugima Village. The crabs had their spots at Momanaka's Diner and El Segundo Park.

While hanging out shooting dice at Taco Pete's I'm hitting good, I got almost one hundred dollars. There are about ten of us there having a good time. Not everyone is gambling, the ones that was to keep watch got caught up in the enthusiasm of the dice game.

Out of nowhere these two dudes walked up and said, "Nobody move and you won't get shot, cuz." They got some big-ass guns but were not wearing any ski masks.

I'm thinking to myself, "Oh shit! We are getting robbed and they could kill us all."

The dark-skinned one said with a sinister voice, "Pick up all the money and put it on the table. And if one of y'all try to play hero, it's going to be blood everywhere." He pointed the gun at John Boy to pick up the money.

Another crab said, "Empty your pockets and put the money in this bag. I want to see everyone pockets turned inside out. I want rings, necklaces, and watches too. Hurry up, damnit!"

They got about four hundred dollars and all our jewelry. They ran off to the back of the building where, a few minutes later, a green Datsun came by burning rubber. They was gone.

"Blood, I thought y'all was keep watch," I said. "Well, at least they didn't shoot any of us because they had us dead to right to kill us all."

This other Blood spoke, "Yeah, we got a pass because I know if I was to rob so many people, somebody would have got that ass shot. But hey, that's just me. But we did get very lucky today."

I see G-Man later that day, and said, "Blood, we got to bring our gun to school."

"Why, Ru-al?" he asked surprised.

"Because we got robbed at Taco Pete's today and if I had the gat I could have shot at them for the shit they did. They got us good too, blood," I let him know.

SENIOR YEAR

"Ru-al, where are we gonna keep it? You know those three guards is always pulling people over and searching them. And if you get caught with it we could go to jail."

"Yeah, but we got caught slippin' today and I don't like that shit, blood. It made me mad."

The Ten got three dirty-ass guards paroling that place. Harper, he's fat, and weighs about two hundred and sixty pounds. Mary is every bit of five foot four, a hundred ten pounds, and really ugly. For a woman she can talk a lot of shit, and she got a mouth on her like a truck driver. Crawford stood six foot five, very slim, and is the one that like to put people on the wall to search them all the time. These guards would take our money and weed, then say, "You can get suspended and have your parents come up here to pick you up, or you can just walk away." I knew their game because there was many times when I got caught then let go without my money or weed. All three of them carried big pistols too. Mary was a freak who liked to feel up on the homegirls' titties and pussies, saying she heard there might be drugs hid on them.

They really had a thing for the homies from Fruit Town Piru Hood, they would always fuck with them at every chance they got. Then it happened, they caught Harper in the back of the gym, took his gun, and beat his ass good. He had walked up on them and that's the blind spot you don't want to get caught in. The assailants all got away scot-free. Three weeks later the homie Knob from Westside Piru Hood slapped the shit out of Mary. He only got suspended for two weeks.

For three years these dirty-ass guards had been stealing from us and getting away with it. Now they aren't walking around the campus anymore, they got these golf carts they ride around in. Harper and Mary ride together in one and Crawford rides by himself in the other. We like that they are in the carts because now we can hear them coming and they aren't creeping up on us like they used to do. I can see this is going to be a crazy and exciting year.

It's fourth period wood shop when I asked the teacher if I can go to the rest room. He said yeah. So I got a hall pass off his desk and left the room.

The rest room is in the middle of Senior Square. I see some students walking about, then I suddenly hear a scream. It sound like a girl screaming over by the classrooms on the Crip side of the school. I walked over toward the screaming and see homie Vick fighting with a crab. Then G-Man, Grump, Skinny and Dr. Gibbs come out the same class fighting with these other crabs. When I ran over to help I saw the Crip I've been wanting for the last three years coming out the class too. He came out with his crazy walk and his pants hanging off his ass. He's sagging hard today for some reason, his pants looked like they were about to fall all the way down.

I remember when I first saw him behind the gym walking all hard and the homie said, "Blood, that's why we call them crabs. Look how he walk, like he just came out the sea like a

SENIOR YEAR

crab walking sideways."

He wasn't the only one walking like that but his walk was different than the others. That's what made me want him so bad by his crazy-ass walk. It was distinctive. And you can tell a Blood and Crip by the way they walk. We Bloods got a smooth walk and if we sag it's not like them either. I never sagged though. Pops once said, "Son, never wear your pants down like that, it make you look like you never had any home training." So I never sagged to avoid disappointing my Pops.

When I seen that crab my eyes got big -- this is my moment! I ran right to him and socked him in the eye. He swung back but missed. I caught him with a combination left then a right -- I was trying to knock his head off his shoulders. I can hear girls screaming more now, but my mind is on the crab. He got one in, the punch caught me in the jaw. I felt the blow and it backed me up, but that made me even madder. When I rushed him he backed up, then his pants fell to his ankles. I really came at him with full force and got him in the nose. He fell to the ground where I jumped on him swinging away, busting up his face real bad.

Out of nowhere I got socked in the back of the head. I was hit so hard I felt my eyeballs about to pop out the sockets. I got off the crab to see who punched the shit out of me, but I couldn't see nothing, my eyes had watered up and then that crab socked me in the jaw again.

I jumped up real fast about to do more damage when I hear

G-Man yell, "Come on, Ru-al." After wiping my eyes I can see him, I got a full view of everything happening around me.

I turn toward the crab and kicked him square in the balls with my full force. He didn't expect me to do that.

"Aaaaw! Cuz, you kicked me," he screamed through clinched teeth. He was on the ground writhing in pain, flopping around like a fish out of water.

I looked over where Dr. Gibbs is fighting with this other crab. They call **Lee**. G-Man is fighting C-Bo. Grump and Skinny is tag-teaming Moose. All these crabs are some of the hard-core Crips at the Ten.

I ran over to help G-Man. I see so many students out of their classes watching the melée happening.

Out of nowhere there was the distinct sound of gunshots. BANG! BANG! Bang! Everyone hit the ground and it got real quiet. I can feel it in my bones that one of the homies got hit. I knew that we didn't have the gat up here. Damnit!

While laying down four to five crabs jumped up and ran. One said, "Come on, cuz, let's get the fuck out of here!" As fast as it all began, it ended and all the crabs had ran off.

I got up and heard somebody say, "Blood, Dr. Gibbs is shot. Somebody get the nurse over here, blood is shot in the head."

Harper came and told everyone to get away from him. I watch Mary pull out her gun at the crabs but didn't shoot or chase anyone down. When I got to where blood is laying he is not moving and blood is coming out of the side of his head. I never seen nobody shot before, or dead. I hope he don't die. I can hear the whining of the ambulance approaching from a distance, it is taking it a long time to get here. Killer King Hospital is only ten minutes from the school.

Dr. Gibbs just moved his legs. The nurse said, "Don't move, you're going to be okay, just stay still."

The ambulance finally pulled to a stop and took out the stretcher, then place him on it. Once he was strapped down they placed him inside and drove off to Martin Luther King Hospital, lights flashing brightly and sirens screaming loudly. I hope blood be okay because that hospital will kill you for a broken leg or a runny nose.

Me and the homies started walking away when we heard a voice say, "Hey, you guys, come here." But we kept going until we got to the hallway, then we ran and jumped the fence then ran to the park. Right after we left the principal dismissed the entire school for the rest of the day.

As we're walking home, I said, "I got that crab Lue-C. It took three years but I finally got him. He was trying to hang, but he got that ass beat down."

G-Man laughed and said, "Blood, I had to help you get to your feet when you got hit from behind, but you did fuck him up, and I did the same to C-Bo."

"I hope homeboy make it," Grump said. "Did you see all that blood coming out his head? Y'all know them crabs set us up, and they did a good job. They waited for most of us to be in our classes on their side of the school."

"Say, Ru-al, how did you know that we was getting down because you was not there right when it started?"

"I was going to the rest room and heard this girl scream. I came to see what it was about and saw Vick fighting, so I jumped in and, just my luck, I got to get at Lue-C. I'm glad that I did come because that shit was fun."

When I walked into the house, Mama said, "Boy, what is you doing home this early? And why is your eye red like that?"

"It was a big riot at school and I was in it. I had a fight with this Crip dude and so did everybody else. They shot our friend Eric in the head while we was fighting. You don't know him, he live on the Weak Side."

"Boy, you're to go to school to learn, not fighting and shooting each other. Is that boy okay?" she asked with anger then concern in her voice.

I shouldn't have told her nothing and let her find out somewhere else. She don't know anything about Crips and Bloods and, so far, she don't know I'm in a gang either.

I went outside to set out the trash cans and see Leo, he didn't go to school today. "Say, blood, you missed out on a big fight at school," I informed him, excited to tell him details. "I got that crab Lue-C and we got them other ones too. But the homie Dr. Gibbs got shot in the head."

Leo is looking at me with his eyes wide open, then he

deflected to my eye. "I see your eye is getting puffed up. Was that crab I wanted there?" he asked.

"Yeah, Grumpy and Skinny got Moose. Blood, it was a lot of fun, you missed out. Say, blood, I got to talk to Connie across the street at Frances' so get at me later on," I said.

I walked through the gate and see Connie through the window. I hated that Mama kicked her out the house but I'm glad she is just across the street. "Hi, Frances. Hi Connie," I said. They both said hi back to me.

"Albert, what are you doing home this early?" Connie wanted to know.

"It was a big riot at school and Dr. Gibbs got shot in the head. And I beat up this Crip dude. It was fun until the gunshots rang out." I had to light a joint and get mellow.

Freddy walked in the house with a tall can of Eight Ball. He asked me if I wanted some and I told him no thanks.

I see my two-year-old niece come running to me, I know what she wants. She likes when I blow some weed smoke into her face. And after I do, she like to do her little dance.

"Come on, Ludis," I said as she jumped into my arms. She like the nickname I had given her. I took a drag then exhaled.

Connie turned her head just when I blew smoke in Ludis' face then she started doing her little dance. "Albert! Stop getting my baby high!" she yelled at me.

I don't know what it is. Either she is happy to see me or she just want to get high.

10 TOEZ DOWN

    I walked down to G-Man house and everybody is in the garage talking about what happen in school today. Whoop's little brother Rabbit spoke with a lot of excitement. This is his first year at the Ten and he is as wild as they come. He missed out on the action because his class is way on the other side of the school. He will get his turn eventually because it has been many times we had to stop him from going off on them crabs.

    I hear somebody yelling. G-Man said, "Rabbit, you hear your sister T.K. calling you."

    She is still yelling for him so he left, but he didn't want to.

    G-Man Pops bought them a pool table, so we are shooting pool and smoking weed when Zell come walking in. He pulled out his Q.P. and started sacking up his weed.

    Zell said, "Blood, it's customers rolling hard." We all left and went to the rat cage. He wasn't lying, it was the Friday rush going down.

    B-Brown come running real fast, we think he's being chased by the police. G-Man said, "What's up?"

    B-Brown is trying to catch his breath before he talk. "I was walking on the J-Block and this customer asked me for five bags of weed and I had some on me, so I sold them to him. Dereck seen me and started talking crazy to me so I socked him in the face and his brothers came after me!"

SENIOR YEAR

"Ru-al, is the gat in Hawkeye's fence?" G-Man asked.

"Yeah," I confirmed to him.

"Blood, I'm sick and tired of them thinking that they are the king of the whole hood. We let homies come from Cook and Main streets over here and make money, it's enough to go around. Let's go see what their problem is."

It's about ten of us walking through the Senior Center and there's about eight guys out front of Silk's house. Most of them standing out there are O.G.'s and Dereck and Bodean. They see us coming.

In the middle of the street we start fighting. We are holding our ground then Slim grabbed a bat and went after G-Man. He is swinging it at him so we all backed up into the Senior Center. I said, "Shoot him, blood!"

G-Man pulled out the gat but Slim kept coming. Next thing we know we hear a loud POP! One shot and everybody ran. I seen the bullet hit right at his foot but it didn't hit him. We looked at him and seen the fear in his eyes and we started laughing. We went back to the rat cage, and I said, "You know that we got to watch our backs now."

"Damn, blood," Vick spoke. "Today is full of drama. It took our senior year of high school to get it up with those crabs and now we got to deal with this shit in our own hood."

Later on that night Whoop and Chuck drove up and asked us was we going to Eve's After Dark tonight. Chuck said, "They are having a Hump Shaking contest tonight and it's going to be a lot of honeys there too."

G-Man and Grump said they are going. "Ru-al, is you going?" Vick asked.

"Nah. I'm going over to my big sister Yvonne house to babysit my nieces and nephew. She had asked me early in the week and I said yeah. She is going out with one of her girlfriends, plus she got Select Cable TV. I'll watch movies with the kids. I need to get out the hood anyway, it's super crazy right now."

"Homie," G-Man warned, "be careful over there in that crab hood."

"I know. The apartments she live in don't have any crabs live in them, but they do hang out across the street so I will be taking the gat with me. I'll stay inside most of the time and let Nasha, Tiff and Relly play in the driveway. It's this girl I like I'm hoping to get some pussy tonight. I told her the next time I come over I want some. She said okay. The last time I was about to get some her little brother was cock blocking. So I got two days to get me some pussy."

I had a nice, peaceful weekend at Yvonne house and I was able to get that pussy, and I watched some good movies too.

It's Monday morning and we're walking to school. We stopped at Dr. Gibbs house to see how he is doing. His Pops is in the driveway working on a washing machine because they own a washing machine business downtown Compton. I said, "Hi Mr. Gibbs. How is Erik and yourself doing?"

SENIOR YEAR

"Well, I'm doing just fine, thank the Lord. Erik, he got real lucky, the bullet hit a nerve in his ear. If it was a bigger gun he would not be with us today. My son is very blessed, he will be home in a few weeks. I don't understand why a child would bring a gun to school," he finished with a sad, broken voice.

I spoke again attempting to be humorous, trying to lighten the mood. "When you go see him tell him that the guys on the Strong Side said hi, and to get well soon."

"Strong Side?" Mr. Gibbs said looking confused.

"He will know what we are talking about," G-Man added. Then we said our good-byes and left for school.

"When Erik hear that he's going to laugh," Leo said.

We only made it to the park. By that time we had already missed two classes. It's about twenty people hanging out, so we are all talking and planning how we are going to pay them crabs back.

Baby Huey was there. He hardly come to school and I know why he's here today. He said, "Blood, those crabs is going to pay. But if something will happen too soon they are going to get y'all. So wait, give it some time to calm down, and then we hit them. What they did was well planned so we got to do ours even better." What he said made a lot of sense.

We get to the campus, it's snack time. It's quiet, you can feel the tension in the Senior Square. I looked on the crab side, there is none that we had a fight with. I only see some of their homegirls, that's it. The guards are sitting in their carts by the snack bar watching all movement, but they know that nothing is going to happen.

This Friday is the big football game. The Ten is playing Compton High, our school rival, we have not beat them in five years. We know they are going to bring a lot of crabs from their school, there is not one Blood there. But if you're on a suicide mission there is Dominguez High, they are like the Ten, half Bloods and half Crips.

"Ru-al," G-Man asked, "is you going to the game?"

"Hell yeah, I'm going. This is our last good game of the year. Even though we are going to lose, I'll be there."

We got an assembly today, as we do at all home games to pump up our team. It's Red and White Day and just about everyone is wearing some kind of red color. We're pumping up the football team even though we know they are going to get that ass beat. We are one and four and Compton is five and zero. They are putting up big points. The game starts at 8:00 p.m.

"G-Man, should I bring the gat? Because you know the last two times we came close to fighting with crabs," I reminded him.

Grump said, "You know we get searched at the gate and, if you get caught, you know you're going to jail."

"Yeah, that makes a lot of sense, I just don't want to get caught slipping. It happen too many times already. Okay, I'll leave it behind this time," but I was disappointed.

SENIOR YEAR

When we get to the school the lights got it all lit up. I see the homeboys from the Fruits and Westside is also here. Camp Hood is here. All the Compton Blood hoods are here for this game. We are on one side of the field and everything on the other side is all blue. I see their school brought their crabs too.

The game started and they scored on their first play. We went three and out, they scored again. Damn, our team is sorry.

"Man, we're getting our ass beat," G-Man said. "That's why nobody who came from this school made it to the pros."

"We had a good baseball player, Darrel Strawberry, before he transferred to Crenshaw High," Leo said. "But I can see why he left because our school got nothing but gang-bangers."

G-Man spoke with noticeable anger in his voice, "Yeah, Ru-al, you're right, our school is sorry in all sports and, just think, the coach wanted us to get on the track team."

Halftime is over now. Starting the second half, we get the ball first and, once again, we went three and out and they scored another touchdown. We finally get on the scoreboard with a field goal.

Now the ball is at their two-yard line about to score. Leo yells out, "If y'all don't score a touchdown, I'm going home!"

Then I suddenly hear BANG! BANG! BANG! BANG! -- four loud shots. I looked over on the crab side and see the flash from the gun's muzzle before the last shot ended. Everybody started running for the gates. We see the crabs running toward our side, so we started running toward them, while both football teams bolted to the locker rooms. We met the crabs on the track and the fight was on. I got hit in the head. I turned around and see the dude that hit me, so I rushed over to him and got him back. We are fighting, this crab can really fight. But I got the best of him when I kicked him in his balls. No one thinks they would ever get kicked during a fist-fight. I had to do it, though, because he was winning. Now he's on the ground all balled up in the fetal position like a little bitch. I took off on another crab and see the other homies getting down too.

A helicopter suddenly lit up the field like daytime, it was so bright. Compton Police, Carson Sheriff, and the school guards arrived and had their guns out.

The fight stopped and everybody ran in all directions, not wanting to get caught. We already had our escape plan by running through the school, the hallways are very dark and spooky. We then jumped the fence and went to Golden Bird parking lot. It's a lot of Bloods here from all hoods.

I said, "See, blood, we should have brought our gat, we could have put it in our locker. Next time I don't care, I'm going to bring it. If I get caught, I get caught. But this is not going to happen again, it will be in my pocket."

"Yeah, you're right, Ru-al. This was the time to have it with us," G-Man admitting he was wrong.

SENIOR YEAR

While in the parking lot the homeboy from Westside said, "That's for what they did to Dr. Gibbs and all them crabs are going to catch hell."

We been in school three months and we had more action then the whole two years. I like this shit! It's all about getting that high-school reputation as a down Blood.

One month has passed since Dr. Gibbs got shot. He's at home now, we went to see him. The bullet had hit him in the ear and got stuck between the meat and the skull. It didn't hit his brain but it did some nerve damage, now he got this twitch on the left side of his face. But he seem happy to be alive. He said, "Blood, they caught us slipping. When I was laying there I could hear everyone, but my eyes wouldn't open. I heard about what y'all been doing out there for me, I can't wait to get back on my feet. And yeah, I got the message that y'all gave my Pops." We all laughed together with him. It was Dr. Gibbs who is the first person to get shot in school throughout Compton. Now everybody is packing a gat. I got mines.

Two weeks has gone by and we have not seen any of the crabs that was in the big fight when the homie got shot. We have been waiting on them to come back to school, but they never did.

It's third period and the principal got on the office intercom to all classes and said, "Students, I have some very sad news to tell you. Norman Johnson was killed yesterday on his way home from school. So I would like for everyone in every class to have a moment of silence on his behalf."

The room stayed quiet for a moment until the homie from Fruit Town exploded. "Fuck that crab! He got what he had coming!"

"Yeah, fuck him! That's not right, the school didn't do a moment of silence for the homie Dr. Gibbs when he got shot and almost died."

"So fuck that crab!" me and Leo yelled loudly.

"Mr. Jones, you and Mr. Brown go to the principal's office. I'll call up there to let him know why I'm sending you both there. I'm very disappointed at the both of y'all," the teacher said.

We never made it. We skipped out, jumped the fence, went to the park, and got high with some other Bloods that was already there.

Leo came over early this morning for school, as always we walked down to G-Man's house. I knocked on the door and Jerry answered, "What's up, Ru-al?"

"Is G-Man ready for school?" I asked.

"Oh, you didn't know he went to jail last night for some weed? My mama and B-Brown went to go pick him up," Jerry informed us. We were surprised to hear that news. We left for school wondering what had happened to him.

"Damn, that's fucked up," Leo said. "I thought he went inside when I left him last night."

It was boring and felt funny not having our homeboy at

school with us, so we went back home. By the time we get to G-Man house he is standing in his front yard. I went up and gave him a hug, then said, "What the hell happen? How did you get caught?"

"Right when I was going in the house a customer rolled up and, right when I was about to give him the five bags, the police hit the corner real fast and the customer pulled off. I was left in the middle of the street with all five bags in my hand. And guess who it was? It was Samson. When I seen him I was like, 'What the fuck is he doing working the late-night shift?' That pig has been trying to get me for years. I got some bad news for you guys, my mama signed me and B-Brown up to go to Job Corps. We was on our way home from the substation when she took a detour and signed us up."

"Hell, nah! Blood, your moms did that?" I said with obvious shock and disbelief.

"Yeah, and she's going to tell all the mothers to sign all y'all up to go. We leave in two weeks," G-Man said.

"Is that the Job Corps that Tony Nicholes went to in Utah?" Leo asked. "If so, I hear that one is cool, they got girls there also."

"Yeah, that's the one homeboy Snoop went to," G-Man added.

Three days later Leo, Gil, Lucan and Sergio's moms signed them up and they all leave on the same day. Mama asked me if I wanted to go and I said no. I don't want to leave the hood.

The time flew by so fast. We are standing in front of

G-Man house, everybody got their bags packed and was ready to go. Three cars is taking them to the train station. Now it's time we embraced and said our goodbyes. They got into the cars, rode up Carlton to El Segundo, turned left, then they were gone.

I went home and Mama seen how sad I was, so she said, "Albert, you should have went with them. Them police are trying to put you away for a long time if you keep on hanging out like you're doing. You better get your act together."

I thought about what Mama had to say, but I was having too much fun here to leave.

Now me and Rabbit is hanging out together. He changed his name to G-Rab and started claiming Miller Gangster Hood. We have been ditching school every day. We began selling weed at the O.G. homeboy sister house Nicki. She asked us if we wanted to make some money, we both said yeah. Now we don't have to sell on the streets and she only live two blocks from the school. For weeks we been making good money.

Nicki is cool, she stood five foot one, light-skinned and hair that went down to her butt. Her mama live right behind us so I know her family very well. She is fine, but she got a cool husband name Sam who like to smoke a sherm stick before he went to work. He would leave me and G-Rab there in the garage until Nicki would find us stuck, then she would bring us a glass of milk that would bring our high down where we can function again.

SENIOR YEAR

Me and G-Rab had been smoking a stick everyday for two weeks. On my way home I got pulled over by the pigs and I forgot I had two bags of weed in my pocket that Nicki gave me to try out. In the back seat of the police car I thought about what Mama was going to do.

I get to Carson Police Station and I made my one call. Mama picked up the phone. "Mama, hi. This is Albert and I'm in jail. They found some weed on me and I need you to come get me out."

"Boy, didn't I tell your ass that you would end up in jail? I should leave your hardheaded ass in there and let your daddy come get you. Give the phone to the officer and let me speak to him," she said, very frustrated with me.

A few hours later the police came to my cell and said, "Mr. Jones, your mother is here to pick you up. And I want you to know that if I see you out there selling drugs again, we're going to get you again."

Sitting in the car leaving the police station nobody is saying anything. I know Mama is mad at me. Finally she broke the silence. "You're going to Job Corps," she stated matter-of-factly with no hesitation.

I didn't say shit because I knew she would backhand my ass. We arrived at the Job Corps office and she wasted no time filling out all the paperwork and giving them her permission. I'll be leaving in two weeks, right after Christmas.

When I get home I went straight to my room, I don't want

to be nowhere in Mama sight right now.

Somebody knocked on the door, Mama answered and I can hear G-Rab say, "Hi, Mrs. Jones. Is Albert home?"

"Yes, he is, he's in his room. How you doing, Derrick?"

"I'm doing fine," he said, then made his way to my room. When he entered, he asked, "Blood, how did you go to jail?"

"Man, I got caught with some weed on the way home last night. Now guess what? Mama signed me up to go to Job Corps and I'll be gone in two weeks."

"Damn, that's messed up. Let's go over to Nicki house and make some money," he offered to cheer me up.

"I can't go right now, I got a few things I need to take care of first, but I'll be over later."

After we said our goodbyes and G-Rab left I walked across the street to tell Connie what happened. She had another baby, Rinesha, who is only two months old. But here comes Ludis so happy to see her uncle. I spent some time with them then walked up to Val's house to tell her what happened. She was sad for me. "Yeah, I heard you went to jail. You know I got to throw you a going-away party before you leave, okay?"

"Thank you, Val. No one had never done anything like that for me before," I said to her.

I get to Nicki's house, G-Rab had already told her that I would be leaving. She said, "You're gonna need some new clothes and shoes, so let's make some money this week and get you ready."

SENIOR YEAR

"Okay!" So all week me made good money. Then Nicki took me and G-Rab shopping. The first place we went was Kenny's shoe store. I got some white Chuck Taylors, some slip-on and tie-up Vans, and ten pairs of socks. G-Rab put me up on the footies with the colored balls on the back, they went with the Vans. I got all the colors, except blue.

We went to the Carson mall where I got my dress clothes and fresh khakis. She spent two hundred dollars on me alone. I got two more golf hats and a Pittsburgh Pirate hat, I liked the gold "P" embroidered on the front of it.

I got my suitcases packed and ready to go, now it's time to party.

This morning Mama and me is going to the Ten to check me out and get my grades so I can take them with me to Job Corps because there I can still work on my high-school diploma. Once the gray-haired lady gave Mama all the paperwork and transcripts I knew this was the end of my high-school journey. But, I must say, my senior year was the best.

It's party time. I walked in Val's house. Everybody has not arrived yet but it's going on. June Bug is doing the music. I see Val talking to this light-skinned girl. I walk over there and said, "Hi, I'm Al, and this is my party. What's your name?"

"Hi, my name is Angie. I'm Val's cousin and yes, I know this is your party." She looked at me and I smiled at her, then she started rubbing Val's stomach, who is five months pregnant.

"Say Angie, can I get a dance later on?" I asked.

"Yeah, I see no problem with that since this is your last party. Just let me know when you're ready."

Now the house is packed with people and it's all for me. I danced with just about everybody but I'm waiting on a slow jam so I can ask Angie to dance.

Wee-Wee is going out with John Boy's little brother Briece, they came over to me and wanted to smoke some weed. I said, "Cool, let me go see if your relative want to smoke some." We get outside and smoked a fat joint, I'm feeling good.

I go back in and asked June Bug to play a slow song. Shortly thereafter the perfect slow jam "Always and Forever" by Heatwave came on. Me and Angie are slow dancing and she smell so damn good. We are pressed tightly against each other and she started rubbing her pussy against my dick. I got hard as a rock. She can feel it swelling and throbbing against her. We are getting our slow dance on and lost all concept of the world around us. The song had ended but we kept dancing. Everybody started clapping then we stopped, I can see she is blushing shyly. "Thank you for the nice dance," I said. "I hope to get another one before the night is up."

"I would like that Big Al," she said in a soft voice.

I gave her a seductive look, licked my lips, and walked

away to make my rounds at the party.

The night went by real fast. I got that last dance and it was even better than the first one. It was time for her to go so I asked, "Say Angie, I leave next week on Monday. Could we get together before I go?"

"I got to work that day, but I can make it that Sunday for a while," she said with a beautiful grin.

The week went by so fast. I got three days left before I go to Clear Field, Utah. Val hooked up my perm for the last time. We sat around the house talking and then Val said, "Al, I'm getting sleepy and it's late."

Right as she said that Wee-Wee and Briece walked in with Angie. I'm so happy to see them. Wee-Wee said, "Let's go to my house so Val can go to sleep."

We get to Wee-Wee house, it's dark and quiet. We walked upstairs and Wee-Wee went into her room, saying it was cool for me and Angie to go in Von room. We went in and never turned on the lights. We sat on the floor and started kissing. I'm feeling on her big-ass titties, so I take off her shirt and bra. It was so dark I couldn't see them but they sure feel soft. I went to take off her pants but she stopped me and said, "No Al, somebody might come in. I want to but not right here."

"Okay, baby, it's cool," I reassured her with a gentle kiss. We kissed and touched each other intimately for two hours before it was time to go.

"Say, Angie, I really like you. I hate that I met you so

late and now I got to leave town. But when I get back, if you don't have a boyfriend and I don't have a girlfriend, could we get back together?" I said in a very hushed voice.

"That would be okay. You be careful out there, Albert."

We said our goodbyes then she gave me a lasting kiss that will always be on my lips and my mind.

It's my last full day in the hood. I'm spending most of my day with Nicki and G-Rab. She gave me a half-ounce of Thai bud weed and three hundred dollars. In the garage me and G-Rab smoked one more sherm stick together. We was stuck for two hours then, right on time, Nicki brought us some milk.

G-Rab had to finally go and said, "Blood, I got to work. I'll catch you in the morning before you leave."

"Okay," I said as I embraced my homeboy goodbye.

Nicki is in the car waiting on me to come. On the way home, I said, "Nicki, drop me off at Val's house, I got to see her before I go, okay?"

She dropped me off and I said my goodbye to her. I seen a small tear coming from the corner of her brown eye. We hugged tightly then she waved as she drove away.

I walked inside and saw Val looked like she was about to go to bed. I said my goodbye to her and the rest of the family. Fudd is still woke, he said, "Uncle Al, when is you coming back?"

"I don't know but it will be soon, okay?"

Val had the radio on low and the "Dubble Dutch Bus" song

came on. I did my little dance on the way out and they started laughing as I closed the door behind me. I said to myself, "I'm going to miss them now that I'm really stepping out the hood."

When I get home everybody is sleep. I know Mama got one ear open for me to come in, though. I put my red flag on my head to hold my blue rollers, then I went right to sleep.

*   *   *

CHAPTER SEVEN

(Job Corps)

"Albert! Albert! Get up! Your daddy will be here in an hour . . . Albert! I said get your ass up! I'm not gonna tell you again, you got to be at the train station at 8:30," Mama yelled with obvious urgency.

I could hear her voice, but my body won't move. I felt a strong shake and that voice I heard for seventeen years. "Boy, get your ass up! Nobody told you to come in at the wee hours in the morning," she growled angrily.

I finally rolled out of bed, slowly. The moment I stood up my head started spinning like crazy. I got a mad hangover, it seem like I slept with my head in steel jaws of a vise. I still feel the sherm stick, weed, and the short dog of Silver Satan. Shit, I don't even know how I got my blackass home. I got a stomach ache from that Silver Satan I dranked. This is not like the other two times I got excited about something new that was going to happen, but this I'm not happy at all. I'm glad I packed all my stuff yesterday. All I got to do is take my shower. I took my rollers out, Val got my perm looking real good. I got curls that are hanging down to my shoulders.

Thirty minutes has passed since I woke up from my foggy state of mind. I'm still high off that wet one, the sherm stick, and the shower did not help at all. I put on my green

JOB CORPS

slacks, new Stacy Adams, I got two hundred dollars in my pocket and a half-ounce of Thai bud weed in my shoe. Nicki looked out for me.

Mama cooked a big breakfast of scramble eggs, three pork sausages, two pieces of toast and a tall glass of milk. I got my eat on, that was good, and the milk helped on my sherm-stick hangover.

I hear Pops voice so I stepped out the room and Uncle Leon is with him. Pops' brother look and sound just like him. Pops looked over at me and said, "Are you ready, son?"

"Yeah, I'm ready." I didn't feel it though.

Uncle Leon said, "Hey, young man, I hear that you're going to Utah. I hear it gets real cold out there."

"Yeah, I heard the same thing, I do have my big jacket."

I said my goodbyes to Paul and Katie as they walked out the door for school.

Sitting in my room waiting on Pops and Uncle Leon to finish their breakfast, I hear a knock on the door, then Mama said, "Albert! Derek is here to see you."

When he entered my room, he said, "What's up, blood? I thought you would be gone by now, but I'm glad you're not. Hand me that suitcase, I'll help you put your stuff out on the truck."

I said my goodbye to my homeboy and he walked up the street towards Val's house.

The homie Snoop had just came back after sixteen months

and Gil came back also, he only was there three weeks.

Pops and his brother came walking out the house. "Albert, do you have everything you need? It's time to go."

"Yeah, I got everything. Let me go say bye to Mama." I walked into the house and she is cleaning up the dishes. I told her, "Well, this is it, I'm going to miss you, Mama."

Tears started running down my cheeks and I can see some about to come from her eyes, too. She hugged me and said, "Albert, you be good out there and take advantage of this opportunity, okay?"

"I will, Mama. Bye-bye, I love you." I walked out.

When I got to the truck I seen Connie and Ludis, I hugged them then we parted ways.

Once again I'm sitting in the middle and Pops is working his stick shift, it's hitting my knees. He got his White Owl cigar in his mouth and he's wearing his black captain's cap. He seem to be enjoying spending time with his only brother. I know he feel sad for him, Uncle Leon had just got some of his foot cut off due to sugar diabetes. I hope it don't spread.

We arrived at Union Station. It's very crowed, people are walking everywhere. We get to the ticket counter and this young lady said, "May I have your ticket, please?" I gave it to her and she stamped it, then said, "Take your suitcases to that door over there and you will board the train through the door next to that one. Train 537 to Utah will be leaving in twenty minutes."

JOB CORPS

Uncle Leon took my suitcases to the door and we followed knowing that he shouldn't be carrying anything that heavy to unbalance him with his unstable foot, but we let him.

Pops said, "Son, you take care of yourself and anytime you want to come home, you do so. I don't think your mama would like that though . . . ha-ha!"

We hugged and he handed me two fifty dollar bills. Then I hugged Uncle Leon. I started walking towards the door and looked back to see Pops was still looking at me. I gave him a wave and he waved back with a smile.

"Train 537 to Salt Lake City, Utah, will be leaving in ten minutes," was announced over the loudspeakers. I boarded the train and got me a good seat next to the window. Looking out I see people giving their loved ones their last hugs and kisses before departing. I still got a little buzz going on, then it hit me, I'm about to leave for a long time. Well at least I'll be with some homeboys when I get there so this might not be that bad after all.

Right before the train started to move this girl and this dude came walking toward the back where I'm sitting, they take the two seats in front of me. The girl is tall, slim, brown-skinned with braids in her hair, and she is wearing a blue "L.A." hat. She smiled at me before she sat down. The dude is real dark-skinned. He got on some 501 blue jeans and some black Chuck Taylors. The first thing came to my mind was, he's a crab. I'm not gonna trip if he is.

The train conductor came walking down the aisle stamping people's tickets. Five minutes later the train pulled out of the station. The journey begins.

After the train had picked up running speed the girl in front of me looked back and said, "Hi, I'm Janice and this is Carl."

The dude turned to say, "You can call me Crazy Duke."

"What's up, I'm Ru-al. Are y'all going to Job Corps in Utah?" I asked them both.

Crazy Duke answered, "Yeah."

Janice added, "Me, I'm coming back from my three-week home pass, and I'm glad to be going back." She is not a bad looking girl.

They seemed to be cool enough, so I asked, "Say, do y'all want to smoke a joint?" They both said yeah.

Crazy Duke suggested we walk to the back. When we got there Janice opened up one of the doors and it was a room we went in, it was nice with nobody else there. I took out my weed and rolled up two fat-ass joints. I know they looked at all my weed and want some for themselves, but I got to take the homies some. I gave one joint to Crazy Duke to light up and as soon as he did, he started coughing harshly. I lit the other one and passed it to Janice and she did the same thing.

"Damn, this is some good-ass weed," Crazy Duke said between coughs. "You got to sell me some."

"No, I can't. This is for my homeboys that's already up

there. But I can roll you and Janice a joint."

Janice asked, "Ru-al, what's the name of your homeboys? I might know them."

"They are G-Man, Leo, B-Brown --"

Before I could get another word out Janice said, "G-Man is my boyfriend, he's waiting on me right now." She was happy to talk about G-Man and I can see in Crazy Duke face he is not liking that. "You're a Blood?" Janice asked politely.

"Yeah, I'm a Blood," I answered proudly.

Crazy Duke said, "I knew you was when I seen your red flag in your back pocket when you was talking to them two men back at the station."

"Yeah, them was my Pops and uncle, I knew you was a Crip when I first seen you," I told him.

The door opened unexpectedly. The weed smoke was so thick and strong it hit the conductor so hard he put his hand up to his mouth. He said, "Okay, kids. Y'all come out here and get back into your regular seats. And there is no smoking on the train."

We get back to our seats. Now Janice is sitting with me and I can see that Crazy Duke really don't like that. He got a look on his face that showed his disapproval. But I don't care about him or what he thinks.

Me and Janice went to the kitchen car to eat dinner using my food voucher they gave me with my train ticket. I ate a nice, filling meal then went to the bathroom and smoked a cigarette.

When I get back to my seat the conductor was passing by, I asked, "Sir, how much more time do we have to get to Salt Lake City?"

"We are just getting started, we should get there in sixteen hours. What's the rush? Enjoy the ride and take in the wonderful scenic views. Have either of you been on a train before?" he asked. Janice and dude responded, I didn't.

I'm sitting there and I can tell Crazy Duke want to tell me something, then he spoke, "I have a few homeboys and a brother up there in Utah. I have not seen them in a very long time."

"That's cool," was all I had to say to him.

I'm leaning back in this big cushion seat and quickly I fell asleep. It was something I really needed after that rough night I had last night.

When I woke up I looked at my watch, it's 6:26 a.m. I looked outside to see a thick blanket of white snow on the ground. Overnight I came from sunny Compton, California, to some cold snow. It do look beautiful though, but still cold.

The conductor's voice over the loudspeaker broke the silence, "We are six hours from Salt Lake City. There will be one more stop in Provo for twenty minutes." I had wondered what other stops I missed that I had slept through.

When we got to Provo I got off the train to stretch my legs. It is real cold, I could see my breath and I began to shiver, so I got back on the train where it was warm.

Five hours later we're in Salt Lake City. I got off the train and walked into the station to retrieved my suitcases.

Janice said, "A van with two guys will pick us up, so be looking for them."

I hear a voice real loud saying, "Is there anybody here going to Job Corps? I'm looking for three individuals."

"We are over here," we said at the same time.

A tall, white guy walked over and asked our full names and dates of birth, then he checked that information with his list to make sure he is taking the right people. We walked outside and put our suitcases in the back of the van.

While on this two-lane highway I see the great Salt Lake I heard so much about. It has this silver sheen on the surface that reflects the surrounding landscape like a mirror, that must be the salt in the water. We pass a sign that reads "Clear Field" one mile. We are near.

The van pulled up to the gate and it opened. We drove right into this big garage next to an office. We all got out and went inside. This huge security guard told us to open up our suitcases so he can look through them. I got nervous because I think he's going to search me and find the weed in my shoe. But all he did was move a few things around then closed the lids. I took a deep breath in relief.

Me and Crazy Duke was told to sit on one bench and Janice to sit on the other one. A slim guy said, "Janice, you're coming off your home leave. I can get you back to your dorm in five minutes." Looking at us, he said, "You two, I got to find a place to put you, but it won't take long." I was assigned to E-dorm and Crazy Duke was assigned to D-dorm.

"Gentlemen, let me tell you some of the rules here. You got to do three weeks in orientation so there is no leaving the grounds before then, no school or jobs. You will get fifteen dollars your first three weeks. When you get out of orientation you will get thirty-six dollars on the first and fifteenth of every month. Once you get to the orientation class they will tell you more about the things you can do. So, do you both understand so far?" he asked, glaring very intensely at us. We both said yes that we understood.

The man walked us to the door and, as soon as it opened, I see G-Man, B-Brown, Leo, Sergio, and three other dudes. It was literally a breath of fresh air to see them, everybody off Carlton Street. I felt like I was in the hood again. B-Brown grabbed my suitcases and we started our trek to the dorms. I didn't see nobody come to greet Crazy Duke, but he seen all my homeboys, and Janice is with us -- she's hugged up with G-Man.

B-Brown said, "We called home last week and was told that you will be coming up here."

"Ru-al, this the homie K-9 from Denver Land Gang, and this is the homie Vern from Neighborhood Twenty, and I know you remember the homeboy Heroin from Westside Piru," Leo introduced them to me.

"What's up, bloods? Yeah, I remember you, Heroin, you was at the Ten. Say, blood, get me to my dorm so I can take off these shoes, they are killing my feet."

"Is that a crab that came with you?" Leo asked.

"Yeah, he's a crab, his name is Crazy Duke. So, what's up on the crabs up here? Y'all know me, it's all about getting that reputation and I'm down for whatever," I let them know.

"Ru-al, you're crazy," G-Man said. "Nope, the crabs up here don't want any problems, but we are outnumbered, so be on guard anyway."

"I know you brought us some weed," B-Brown couldn't wait to say. He was ready to get high.

"You know I did, blood. Let me get to my dorm and put my stuff up first, okay?"

When I get to E-dorm the homies can't come in with me because it's one of the rules, if they don't live here they have to stay out. I get to the office, set my suitcases down and I see this short, black man sitting behind the desk. He stopped working and looked up at me. He had to be five three with a short afro and goatee mustache. He stuck out his hand and said, "Hi, how are you doing Mr. Jones? I'm the E-dorm counselor, Mr. James. We will be having a dorm meeting tonight at 10:00, don't be late. You're in cube eight, go unpack your things and take this lock for your locker. You can buy a new one from the store and return this one back to me later. I'll give you some time to settle in and, if you have any questions, ask me at anytime, okay?"

When I walked into my cube I see three bunk beds. The top bunk is empty with two sheets and one thick blanket folded at the foot of the bed. I made up the bed and put all my clothes in the locker. I changed into a fresh set of clothes, my burgundy khaki suit and white Chuck Taylors. It felt good to wear something fresh and clean after the long trip here.

When I walked outside the homies had all been waiting on me. We strolled down the ramp, I see girls hanging out on the other side, those must be the girls' dorms. B-Brown started yelling this girl name and this short and thick girl walks up. "Ru-al, this is my girlfriend, Jessie. Jessie, this my relative, Ru-al."

"Hi," I replied.

"Hi, Ru-al" she answered back with a coy smile.

G-Man got the boombox and said, "Let's go to the park and hang out." He plugged it up and the music was bumpin' loud.

I took the weed out my pocket and gave it to B-Brown, who rolled up five joints. Then he passed them out to get lit. K-9 hit the joint one time and started coughing nonstop. "Blood, this shit is good," he admitted.

"Yeah, you got this from Nicki, didn't you?" Leo asked me.

"Yeah, you know I did." I hit the weed but I don't feel anything although I know the weed is good. "Say, blood, why I'm not feeling the weed like y'all?"

B-Brown answered, "Oh, your head and lungs is not used to

the very thin air up here, so it's gonna take you a while to get used to it. So I'll just keep the weed for you, ha-ha!" He was joking, but I let him have the weed anyway.

Lucan just got off work and is telling me about the program. I asked him, "Where is your girlfriend?"

He laughed at the question while hitting the joint. "Man, me and Leo is just fucking these bitches. We don't need a girlfriend, do we Leo?"

"Nope," Leo answer back with certainty.

Me and Leo is brothers. G-Man and B-Brown is brothers. And Lucan and the rest of the homies are relatives.

Janice walked up to me and said, "Ru-al, this girl in my dorm want to get at you. She seen you and she said she got to have you. So what do you want me to tell her?"

"Tell her that I will meet with her later on."

We kicked it in the park for two hours then it was time for us to got back to our dorms to get ready for dinner. G-Man said, "Blood, we meet in the middle of the ramp and we wait for everyone to walk together because you will see the crabs at the front of the ramp. I'll see you later."

Walking down the ramp with the homies I hear somebody calling my name. I look on the other side towards the girls' ramp and it's Janice waving me to come over. I get to the end of the ramp and walked over to where she got this girl with her. The girl look nice -- tall, brown-skinned and a plump butt, her hair is short. "What's up, Janice?" I asked.

"This is my friend, Kim. Kim, this is Ru-al."

"Hi, Kim."

"Hi, Ru-al. I want to know if I can talk to you later in T-dorm?" she asked.

"Okay," I said. Then I said goodbye to the girls so I could catch up with the guys.

When I was asked what that was about, I said, "Blood, she want to get at me in T-dorm. What's T-dorm?"

G-Man said, "That's the dance room. It's like Eve's After Dark, on Friday and Saturday they play black music. Oh, you're going to like it."

"Blood," Leo added, "you ain't seen nothing yet. This place got a swimming pool, movie theater, bowling alley, full-sized basketball court. This is the biggest Job Corps in the U.S., so you will find something to do everyday here."

After dinner we stayed at the park until it was time to go in, so I never got to see the crabs. That was cool because I wanted to spend time with my homies, it's group time. I said my goodbyes to everyone. Today was a nice day.

I get into the dayroom and see all kinds of guys. I see two Crips sitting together . . . Leo had already told me about the crabs in my dorm. I'm not gonna trip unless they do. The dayroom is full with about sixty guys.

Mr. James walked in and everybody got real quiet. He said, "We got someone new in our dorm and I would like everyone to welcome him here today. So Mr. Jones, tell us a little

JOB CORPS

about yourself."

Everyone is looking at me and I'm nervous as hell. I clear my throat and said, "Hi, I'm Albert Jones, but you can call me Ru-al. I'm from Compton, California, and I want to get into the welding class."

This white guy quickly spoke up, "Good luck in getting in that class, it has a long waiting list. I'm Zack, the dorm president, let me tell you a few rules we have. Everyone has a chore to do here, but you won't get yours assigned until your three-week orientation is over. This is a cool dorm and we all get along. So if you have any questions, you can ask me or the vice-president, Tom, over there. And if we can't help you, talk to Mr. James. If that's it for group, this meeting is over. Thank you gentlemen."

I go to the bathroom to roll my hair up. Once back in the cube the other guys had already went to sleep. I'm laying on my bunk thinking that this place can be a lot of fun, I'm glad Mama made me come now. I closed my eyes and right away I was asleep.

Next thing I know all the lights came on. I look at the clock and it's 6:00 a.m. "It's early" I said to myself. I went to take a shower and it was full of others cleaning themselves. I should have took my shower last night. Once out the shower I took my rollers out and combed my hair down so I can wear my "P" hat. I put on my black khakis, black sweatshirt, my black Vans with white footies with the red ball on the back.

10 TOEZ DOWN

I hear Leo calling me so I look out the cube and he says, "Come on, Ru-al. Let's go eat breakfast, everybody is waiting on you."

I walked outside and they were all there waiting. Walking down the ramp I see the crabs, they got us outnumbered two-to-one. But when we passed by, nobody said anything. Leo said, "We ain't trippin' on them. We made this pact that we wasn't going to trip on each other because we're from L.A. You see them east coast dudes we got to watch them. We are state tripping. Most of them dudes are from New York, Kansas City, and St. Louis -- so we all agreed to ride together on the state thang."

"Oh, don't get it wrong," B-Brown interjected. "We will still take off on them crabs if they get out of line."

"Y'all know me, I'm not trying to be buddy-buddy with them crabs in any way. But if y'all made that pact with them then I got to roll with y'all."

Standing in line for breakfast everybody is talking to somebody, B-Brown and G-Man got their girls with them. It's cold and there's snow covering the ground.

Then it happened, I got hit in the back of the head with a snowball. I looked behind me to see these crabs laughing at me, and I see Crazy Duke, he's laughing the hardest with his brother Darko. It's about fifteen of them there.

With a loud voice, I said, "Which one of you crabs hit me with that snowball?"

JOB CORPS

No one said shit. I'm mad and the homies know what I'm about to do. "Fuck it then. Since none of you bitches want to be a man about it, I'll fuck you up." I pointed at Crazy Duke, but he just stood in line, his laughing stopped.

Then this tall light-skinned crab stepped out of line and said, "I'll fight you, cuzz."

He burned my ears with that word, that made me even madder. I walked toward him but G-Man grabbed my arm and said, "Don't trip, Ru-al. You just got here and they will send you home immediately, blood."

"I don't care, blood. This crab can't just hit me and I don't do shit -- I'm no punk!"

I stared at all them crabs and gave them my sinister smirk before getting back in line. "Blood, whatever that pact is y'all made with them is off now as far as I'm concerned. The next time one of them crabs get out of line it's on. You can roll or not but they just crossed the line."

K-9 said, "I'm rolling with you, Ru-al. I never did like that tall crab anyway."

We got our breakfast and there's a lot of food that look good. When we walked into the dining room it's all red, I like that. They have blue, brown, and yellow rooms. The crabs eat in the blue room on the other side.

After we ate the others had to go to work or school. I walked over to the girls' side where the orientation class is. I see about twenty people hanging out waiting for the door to open. I'm standing by myself and I see Crazy Duke. He didn't look my way because, if he did, he would have seen that look I was ready to give him again.

The door opened up and everyone went inside, I'm the last one to enter so I got a seat in the back. I notice the crab is on the other side of the room. I feel like going over there and slapping his stupid ass. And I had given him a joint earlier, but I'll never let my guard down to another crab again in my life.

The counselor entered and said, "My name is Mr. Tam, and I will be with you for the three weeks you'll be in this class. Some of you will be leaving me in a few days, so let me tell the new people what to look for while you're here. You can get a good trade and you can get your high-school diploma so when you leave here you will be ready when you go to the streets. You will take four hours of school and four hours of work, and you can choose your hours. I see two new guys with us today. Please stand up and tell us where you're from and what kind of trade you want."

Crazy Duke stood and went first, I went after him. I said the same thing I said last night in group and, once again, someone said there is no openings in welding. I sat back down.

"We have good cooking and baking classes," Mr. Tam added, "or there are twenty-five other trades we offer. I'm sure you'll find one before you leave. There is fifteen hundred people up here and we even have a military if you want to join

JOB CORPS

a branch of the armed forces. So people, it's up to you to find that job you like and want in your future. We got five people leaving us this Friday and, once you're gone, you will get one hundred-fifteen dollars to buy some clothes. I'm sure you were told about this already. Also, you can get three-day passes to Salt Lake and Odgen city. But you are not able to leave the grounds until you have finished this class. Does everyone understand what I just said?" Everyone said yes.

I noticed this girl sitting to my left. She got long, silky, red hair, nice-sized tits and, when she got up to sharpen her pencil, she got a plump ass for a white girl. What is so sexy about her is her hazel-green eyes. I said to myself, "I got to have her."

When she sat down I walked over to her desk and asked her name. She said, "Lorna," with a bright smile.

With a big smile on my face I said, "You already heard, but, yeah, I'm Ru-al. So Lorna, when are you leaving orientation, this Friday?"

"Yes, I will be gone, this was a long three weeks."

"I'll see you later on, Lorna."

"Okay, Ru-al," she said with her sexy voice.

Later on in the day everybody is off work and out of school. I told G-Man about Lorna. He said, "Ru-al, what dorm do she live in?"

"Blood, I don't know. She got red hair and I got to have her, man."

10 TOEZ DOWN

"Oh, I know who you're talking about. That's B-Brown's girlfriend friend. I can see if I can get you hooked up. I did see her with this dude, so I'll see what's up for you."

"Blood, I don't care who she with or what you got to do, I got to have her," I let him know again.

Walking through the dorm I notice a blue rag on someone's bunk. I'm pretty sure it's one of them crab's rag. It had burned my eyes so bad I couldn't pass it up. So I grabbed it off the bed then took my lighter out my pocket and set it on fire. As it is burning I'm walking down the hall with the rag, black smoke is drifting everywhere.

Zack came walking quickly towards me and said in a loud voice, "What the fuck are you trying to do, Jones, burn down the dorm?" I threw what remained of the fiery rag to the floor and stomped it out. "I have to report you to Mr. James for this," Zack declared.

"I don't care, punk. Go ahead and tell on me."

An hour later it was group time. I walked in and everybody is looking knowingly at me. Zack began to speak, "Today we had an incident in the dorm and we need to talk about it. Whose blue rag was that that got burned?"

"It was mines, I had it on my bed," the crab said. He looked at me and I glared back at him. He was one of the guys in line when I got hit with a snowball earlier.

Mr. James said, "Mr. Jones, after group I want to see you in my office."

JOB CORPS

After group I found Mr. James behind his desk. With a quick glance at me he said, "Have a seat," in a soft voice. He continued, "What made you want to burn that rag in this dorm? You could have set the whole building on fire."

"I don't know why I burned it," I replied. I didn't want to tell him it was pure unadulterated hatred and rage.

"Since you don't have any town privileges to take away, and you don't start working until orientation is done, I can't suspend those privileges from you. But your actions cannot go unpunished. So for a week you will clean up all the bathroom stalls after night group, and you start tonight."

I cleaned up all the nasty, smelly stalls then took a hot shower. Then I went to the game room to shoot some pool. I was playing with this guy and when I stopped to talk to him, two Crips walked in. One Crip that's about my size said, "Cuzz, why did you burn my blue rag? You really disrespected me and my homeboy."

"First, let me say I'm not a cuzz. Second, I burned it because I don't like blue rags. So what the fuck you gonna do about it, blood?"

They both started walking towards me so I grasped tightly to the pool stick. I know for sure one of these crabs is about to get a serious beat down. The guy I was playing pool with stepped between us, and said, "Y'all be cool, it's not worth it. Somebody can get hurt and sent home. Nobody wants that." This white dude don't know this is very serious and we don't care about anything right now.

Somehow people heard the noise and began entering the game room to see what the commotion is all about. It got so loud that Mr. James came out of his office and told everyone to go to their cubes. I'm all pumped up, I don't want to leave, or go to bed. But I did leave and, as more time passed, I eventually fell into a restless sleep.

I got up this morning ready for some drama, but there was none. Sitting in my cube talking to one of my cube mates, I hear G-Man calling me. I looked out the cube and see him with five other homies, they all is smiling as I walk toward them.

"Ru-al, you're crazy, blood," B-Brown said. "We all heard that you burned a blue rag in your dorm."

"Hell, yeah, I did it!" I answered with some anger. "It was hanging on his bunk when I walked by, so I lit it on fire. Blood, I wouldn't have done it if they didn't hit me with that snowball earlier. They opened up this anger I got in me, so fuck'em!"

Leo said, "You know them crabs gonna try to do something for that."

"I don't care. They tried last night but the counselor broke it up. Blood, you know me, I get down where I get mad at. Next time I'm going to do more than burn they filthy mack nasty rag . . . ha-ha-ha!"

On our way to eat breakfast G-Man went to P-dorm and had this girl to get his and B-Brown girls. They eat every meal with them, I got to get me a girl to call out too. When their girls came out Lorna was with them.

"Say, G-Man, did you ask your girl to get at Lorna for me?" I was curious.

"No, I told Jessie to do it, she is closer to her. Say blood, what about that other girl that Janice hooked you up with?"

"Oh, shit! I forgot about her. Oh well, I'm after Lorna now. I'll tell the other girl that I'm into someone else."

When Lorna came walking out I could feel my heart beating faster. I got it bad for this redhead. She looked at me and smiled, and I smiled back. She then walked to this skinny white dude, walking away together.

"Damn, Ru-al, you got it bad for that girl," B-Brown recognized. "I seen the way you look at her."

"Yeah, I want her, blood, and I'll get her when we go to the T-dorm this Friday," I reassured him with confidence.

After breakfast Heroin said, "Let's AWOL tonight and get some beer."

"Where we gonna get some beer from?" I wanted to know.

"The store is a mile up the street and we are going to go behind the four houses on the road. We did it two weeks ago and got away with it. So is you down, Ru-al?"

"Hell, yeah, I'm down! I need to get drunk because the weed is not getting me high." G-Man, B-Brown, and Leo said they will go on the beer run, too.

10 TOEZ DOWN

After dinner we walked to the back of the grounds, it's cold as fuck, the snow is deep, and my shoes is already wet. The gate has this big-ass hole in it. We ran across the street and get to the first house. Running like crazy we jumped two fences and, at the third fence, dogs started barking wildly, but I don't see any of them. A porch light came on, we started running faster. I'm huffing and puffing, my heart is pounding like a jackhammer inside my chest, I'm losing my breath -- this thin air really got me winded. I'm waist deep in snow and I can't hardly run.

Out of nowhere I hear this loud voice, "HEY! What the fuck are you doing in my yard! I'm going to kill all you fuckers!" BOOM! BOOM! BOOM! Three shots pierced the silence of the still night that echoed like cannon blasts.

"G-Man, blood, we're getting shot at. Stop right here," I said, still trying to catch my breath.

Three minutes passed, the time click by at a snail's pace. I'm laying down in the snow freezing my balls off and getting shot at by some crazy-ass white man. Fuck this!

We heard the door close and see the porch light turn off. Back on the run, the best I could, we jumped two more fences and now we are only a hundred yards from the store. Heroin said, "Hold up here while I go get the beer."

Here we are, on the side of the road, it's pitch black out here. All I can think about is the Ole English back home. I'm going to drink and get a good buzz. Why is it taking him so long to get back? I suddenly wondered. I'm thinking he got caught but hoping otherwise.

B-Brown said, "Here he come!"

We got up and walked toward him. He got two cases of Budweiser, twenty-four cans in each case.

I said, "Blood, why the fuck did you get Budweiser? What happen to the Eight Ball?"

"Ru-al," G-Man said with a laugh, "they don't sell malt liquor in this state, so this is the next best thing."

We are walking on the road on the way back, I'm too wet to go back that way, plus that dude with that shotgun is waiting on us. We all grab some beers and started drinking them. I'm on my third one when this green and white K-10 truck passed by. Leo said, "Blood, wasn't that the security guards?"

I never seen the guards' trucks before. When we looked back they busted a quick U-turn. I grabbed two more beers and downed them before they made it back to us. G-Man wanted to run but realized how wet and slippery it was.

The truck pulled up next to us and the two guards jumped out. The short one said, "Okay, men, throw the beer in the back of the truck and get in, you're going back to J.C."

"How did y'all know that we had AWOL?" Heroin asked.

"That old man that shot at y'all, he called us, plus we heard the gunshots. Y'all is not the first that he shot at for being in his yard. And the lady at the store also called, so y'all was going to get caught no matter what," the guard said in an arrogant manner.

"So why did that man shoot at us knowing we are from Job Corps?" I asked.

"He got every right to protect his house and if he would had killed one of y'all, it would have been justified. Was y'all scared? All of y'all will be getting a write-up." We all admitted that we was scared, and I know Mr. James is gonna let me have it in the morning.

First thing the next day Mr. James wanted to see me. When I walked into his office he was doing some writing. When he looked up at me I could see anger in his face. "Have a seat, Mr. Jones. Do you really want to be here at Job Corps?" he asked with sincerity.

"Yeah, I want to be here," I responded seriously.

"It don't look like it because I'm looking at this write-up you and your buddies got for AWOL for buying beer. All you had to do is wait three weeks and you could have gone to town and got drunk as a skunk, but you had to AWOL. So this is what I'm going to do: Once you get out of orientation you will be on restriction for a month, and two more weeks of cleaning bathroom stalls," he finish with clear disappointment.

"Okay," I said and walked out of his office lucky I wasn't kicked out of the program and sent home.

On our way to eat breakfast G-Man said, "Damn, Ru-al, you only been here three days and you got two write-ups."

"Yeah, homie, and I don't want anymore. If I get kicked

out Moms and Pops will be very upset at me, so I got to be cool for a while. Plus Mr. James got me on restriction from town for a month," I wasn't proud to admit.

Back in my class I see that fine-ass redhead. I walked over to her desk and said, "What's up, Lorna? How are you doing today? I'm sure as fine as you look." I'm giving her my best mack.

"I'm doing fine," she replied. "I heard about you getting caught last night. Today is my last day here. I got four hours of school and four hours of work after this. I got into the painting trade. Now I get to go on weekend pass to my house in Ogden, so I'm happy about that. So have you thought about what kind of trade you want?"

"I think I'm going to try cooking. I like it, I did it in class all through high school. Maybe I can cook you a meal one day. I know you are glad to be leaving this boring-ass class."

"Yeah, I'm glad to get out of here. And yes, you can cook me a meal some day, I would like that. Are you going to T-dorm tonight?" she asked.

"Yeah, I'll be there," I answered with joy in my voice. "I hope I can get a dance with you, I know you got a boyfriend for now, but I'll see you later, Lorna." I looked into her eyes then walked back to my desk. I can feel her eyes on me.

I'm getting ready for the dance in T-dorm. I got on brown khakis, a black T-shirt, my black Vans tennis shoes, and my "P" hat. I got so caught up trying to get Lorna that I forgot I had plans with Kim tonight, too. She is not a bad looking girl, but Lorna got me on the hunt. I'll have to let Kim down easy if possible.

Everyone got together and went inside. The music is loud, people is on the dance floor, the lights is flashing and strobing in various colors. Yeah, this do have an Eve After Dark feeling.

We walked to the far side, it's a nice spot we can see everything. Janice grabbed G-Man by the hand and took him for a dance.

The excitement and energy was spreading. Kim said, "Ru-al, let's dance."

"Let's do this," I agreed, leading her out amongst the other undulating bodies. We are getting our dance on and she told me that she is from New York.

As she continued talking about herself, Lorna walked in. I noticed her immediately. She was wearing tight, white pants, a red blouse -- she is looking too damn good.

Kim and I stopped dancing and went back to our seats. I had to tell her how I really felt. "Kim, this is not working out for me, I got my eyes on this other girl. You're cool, but right now I'm not interested."

She looked utterly stunned, then said, "Are you for real?"

"Yeah," is all I could say. She got up and walked away without ever looking back.

Janice look at me all crazy and said, "Ru-al, what did you do to her?"

"I told her that it's not gonna work for us, that's all." Janice then got up and left too.

"Say, Leo," I said, "I'm gonna get her tonight, watch."

"Blood, you're crazy. Do you see her over there with her boyfriend?" Leo pointed out.

I did not hesitate. I walked over to their table and said, "Lorna, can I get this dance?"

She looked at me and her expression brightened. "Okay," she said. But first she introduced me to the dude sitting next to her. "This is my boyfriend, Troy."

I looked at dude and gave him a nod, then walked off with my girl. He didn't say nothing.

The next song that came on was by Roger "I Heard It Through the Grapevine." I grabbed Lorna by the hand and went to the middle of the floor. I watched her moving, that girl can dance. I smiled at her, and she smiled back at me. She is looking good in those white pants, they fit her firm ass perfectly.

The song ended and two seconds later a slow song came on by Earth, Wind and Fire called "Forever Mine." We was about to go back to your seats but then I said, "Lorna, I got to have this dance with you."

"Sure, why not?" she said. "But only one more dance then I got to go back to my boyfriend."

I put my hands right below her waist and can feel the curve of her beautiful ass. She put her hands around my neck. I pulled her in closer, I can feel her pert tits against my chest. Her hair smells like strawberries, she got my nose flared wide open. My dick started getting hard so I pulled her tighter against me so she can feel it swelling and throbbing through my pants. She didn't back away. "Girl, you got my ass horny as hell. You know I got to have you for my girl," I whispered softly in her ear.

She looked up at me and said, "You know I got a boyfriend."

"Not anymore, you're my girl. And I'm gonna tell him to beat it," I confidently declared to her.

After the dance I led Lorna to our table and her dude left. Leo looked at me and said, "Ru-al, you crazy. You said that you was going to get the girl, and you did." I looked at him and grinned knowingly. G-Man and the other homies laughed.

When all the girls went to the rest room, I said, "Blood, I need a smoke break."

"Let's hold up until the girls come back so they can hold our spot," K-9 advised. We all agreed to wait.

I see some Crips on the dance floor with their girls, some of them went outside and some stayed behind.

When the girls came back I gave Lorna a kiss and she returned the pleasure. We told them we would return in a few minutes.

Walking across the dance floor I notice Big "D" and that

tall crab stayed in their seats. We walked passed Sergio and his S.A. homies with their girls. I gave him a "what's up" nod.

As we approached the door it's packed, people are going in and out, and it's kind of dark. I'm walking behind Heroin and I see them crabs walking back in. Crazy Duke walked by me and, right as we got eye to eye, he threw up his set in my face, all I can see was this big-ass "C" he did with his fingers. Before he could put his hand down I socked him right on the chin with everything I had. That one punch knocked him to the floor. Then all hell broke loose. I seen his brother Darko so I hit him with a left and caught him in the nose. He backed up. We are swinging like crazy, he got in some good hits, but I'm making sure I get the most in. Everybody in the walkway is fighting now. I got my fists balled up so tight, I'm not going to open them until this is over. People is running everywhere, girls is screaming.

I got hit on the back of my head. I turned around to see Crazy Duke, he had got up and back into the mix. Now we are back at it. G-Man is right behind me fighting Darko. We fought all the way to the door. I can hear the guards yelling for everyone to stop. I see Mr. James at the door yelling commands to those in his vicinity. Finally the fighting stopped.

Mr. James grabbed my arm and said, "I'm not surprised to see you in the middle of all this mess."

We were all escorted to the guard's office where we waited. G-Man, Leo, K-9 and Heroin were beside me. I said, "Did you see me knock out Crazy Duke with one punch? That shit was fun, blood, but I lost my hat somewhere inside. I know I might get sent home, this will be my third write-up, and you seen what Mr. James' face look like when he seen me."

"I fucked up that tall crab, blood," Leo said. "That was crazy."

They got all the Crips in one office and we are sitting in another so we don't know what they are saying. We didn't say anything.

Mr. James came out the guard's office and said, "Go back to the dorm. I got to go home, but I will deal with you Monday. I should send your ass home right now, you're just too much to handle right now. Go to your cube and think about what you want to do with your life, because right now you're going nowhere."

Waking up this morning I'm sore all over my body, I got a knot on my forehead, and my back hurt. I know them crabs are in more pain because, once again, the Bloods won the battle.

I walked outside to get the homies for breakfast. B-Brown said, "Damn, blood, y'all shut the party down. By the time I got there it was over."

"Ru-al, you kicked that shit off," Leo spoke proud with excitement. "I know I didn't miss this one like I did in high school. Ru-al, what made you knockout that crab?"

"When we was walking out the door he threw up his set right in my face. You know I couldn't let that go without doing something."

We walked across the ramp to the girls' dorm. Jessie came out and then she went back in to get Janice. I see Troy, Lorna's ex-boyfriend. We was about to leave when Lorna come out wearing my "P" hat. That made me smile. She walked over to Troy and said something to him. Whatever it was he ended up walking away with his head down. She walked over to me and gave me a kiss, then said, "Here is your hat. I seen it on the ground and picked it up. Are you okay?" she asked, looking at my forehead.

"Yeah, I'm cool, I got a little bump on the head. You hold on to my hat, it looks good on you."

"Y'all know that three of them crabs went home last night," B-Brown mentioned. "It was Crazy Duke, Darko, and that tall crab. I don't know what they said to the guards, they never came back to their dorms. I did see some dudes carrying some suitcases."

"Damn, blood," I said, "I wanted to see their faces. After that ass-whipping I would have went home too... ha! ha! Well, we don't have to worry about them crabs no more."

"Ru-al, since you came here all kind of shit has happen, we been cool for months before you came," Heronin added.

"Blood, I can't help it, I just hate them crabs." Here I am, in another state, banging. I never thought I would be up here riding on crabs like this. I tried to come in peace, but since they want to bang, I'm down for that, and I got no

10 TOEZ DOWN

problem taking off on them that ask for it.

Mr. James called me into his office, the first words he said, "Mr. Jones, what the hell is wrong with you? And don't stand there and say nothing! You been here one week, you burned a rag in the dorm that could have set the whole place on fire. And you went AWOL for some beer. Then you were involved in a big-ass riot that shut down the whole Jobs Corps. Now tell me why I shouldn't send your ass home today because I got a ticket right here with your name on it."

I looked on his desk and there it was, a ticket with my name printed clearly on it. I know I got to come up with my best lines to stay here. "Well, Mr. James," I began, "that fight in T-dorm, I was just protecting myself when the dude got knocked out. As for the rag I burned, I just wasn't thinking. And the AWOL, I just wanted some beer. I know it look like I don't want to be here, but Mr. James, I really do."

He said, "If I get another write-up with your name on it you'll be packing up your suitcases and heading back to Compton. You will not leave these grounds for another two months, no weekend passes, no nothing for you. Do I make myself clear?"

"Yes, sir," I said, then thanked him before walking out of his office, very happy to be staying here.

Then I thought about what Mama said to me before I left, "Do the right thing and make something good out of this opportunity." I realized more than ever I come real close to fucking it off.

    This is my last day of orientation and I'm so happy. I got P.M. cooking and four hours of school in the morning. This weekend everybody is going to town. G-Man and Heroin is going to Salt Lake to Bloods brothers house. B-Brown is going to Ogden to Jessie's house, they are going to have three days of getting drunk and having fun. Of course I can't go. Lorna said she would stay with me until my time is up. So we found things to do to enjoy our time together. We went to the movies, went swimming, did some bowling, we really got to know each other over the weekend.

    Mr. James did let me go to the GAP so I could spend my one hundred-fifteen dollars in clothing vouchers that I got after orientation. We got in the van with about ten other people. Lorna said to me, "Let's get some clothes alike."

    "Okay." We ended up buying some brown khakis, and a red and white shirt that we had each other's names put on the backs. Then we bought matching burgundy Members Only jackets. Lorna was so happy.

    We went to Lovers Grass over by the gym. I laid a blanket on the ground, it's so dark you can't see nothing, and it's cold tonight. I kissed her soft lips, then took off her shirt and bra. Her nipples are standing erect, partly from being aroused and partly from the cold. I started fondling and sucking on them gently. She began moaning softly, then her sounds of ecstasy grew louder. My dick swelled and grew hard,

I wanted her so badly. We were both hot. I took off my pants while she eagerly took off hers. I laid her back and went between her silky thighs, plunging and flicking my tongue to taste her sweet pie. It was delicious. She moved her hips back and forth, faster and faster. She was about to climax so I got up and shoved the head of my hammer deep inside her. I felt her muscles grasp me tightly so I slid it all the way in. Damn, this pussy is tight. We were making love big-time until we both climaxed at the same time. I felt her body tremble and shake beneath me, then she wrapped her legs around to pull me deeper inside her, she wanted more. We continued pleasuring each other for hours. We really got to know one another intimately throughout the night.

I was sprung. After we got dressed we held each other tight, then I said, "I love you, Lorna."

"I love you too, Albert," she replied being both happy and satisfied.

This was my first time in love and it feels so good. We made this our special spot where we went at it like jackrabbits as often as we could. The only days we didn't do it were when she was on her period. Me and Lorna is the hot couple on the grounds. If you seen me, you seen her too, and I liked that.

We got on our matching outfits, chilling in the park, when Kim walked up and said, "So, this is the white bitch you chose over me?"

Before I had a chance to answer, Lorna responded harshly, "Yeah, this my man and you better keep your eyes off him. As for being your bitch, you got me mixed up with some other scary broad, because I'm no bitch."

I'm like, damn, this girl is down. She's not just a pretty face, she's down for hers.

Just as Kim started to walk away, she said, "Girl, I'm not gonna waste my time on you and that nigga." She stomped off.

We both looked at each other then Lorna said, "Who do she think I am? I'm no punk!"

"Calm down, baby, I know you're no punk. Now give me a kiss," I said as I leaned in closer for our lips to meet.

I finally had my first weekend pass. I took a hundred dollars out of the bank on the premises that I deposited when I first arrived here. We decided to stay at Lorna's house in Ogden. When I get there I'm nervous as hell because I'm about to meet her parents. We walked in and her two little brothers come running up, happy to see her. Her mother and her husband was sitting on the couch together watching TV. Lorna introduced everyone. "These are my two bad brothers, Jack and Jeff, my stepdad Jack and my mom, Jackie Lynch." We all said hi and exchanged pleasant greetings. Lorna's mom took my bags to the room that I will be sleeping in. They have a nice home with lots of land, and I seen all types of animals in their yard.

"Let's go across the street and see if Jessie and B-Brown is there," Lorna said, while leading me out the door.

She knocked and this tall, black man opened the door. He said, "Hey, Lorna. How are you doing? It's been a while since I last seen you."

"Mr. Johnson, this is my boyfriend, Albert. Is Jessie and Austin home?"

"No, they went to Salt Lake for the weekend," he answered.

We returned to her house and ate a good dinner with great conversation about our lives. Lorna's moms is cool, she gave me a beer and a glass of brandy to enjoy. She also let Lorna drink. I heard about the people that live in this state, not liking blacks. Lorna told me that her dad's mom would not come over if she knew I was there. They are real Mormons and hate blacks. I would like to meet her just to see the shocked look on her face when I reach out to shake her hand.

I woke up, took a shower, and got dressed. Today we are going to Salt Lake City to see the Mormon Tabernacle.

When we got there the first thing I wanted to see was the gold statue of the man blowing the horn perched at the top of the tabernacle's spire. When I looked up, there it was, a beautiful vision in gold brilliantly shiny and reflecting the rays of the sun. I walked around on the grass to go to the other side.

"You better get off the grass," Lorna warned. "You could go to jail. No blacks is allowed to walk on the grass or go inside the tabernacle. So you better get your black ass off the grass, ha-ha!"

JOB CORPS

    I got my ass off the grass and we kept walking around the grounds, viewing the magnificent and ornate structures.

    This blue pickup truck passed by slowly with five white guys inside. They started yelling obscenities and derogatory comments. One spoke louder than the others, saying, "Hey nigger! What the fuck are you doing in my town? Hey, you white nigger lover, fuck you too, bitch!" They drove away still spewing their brand of hatred and ignorance. I'm thinking these people are bat-shit crazy, but Lorna continued to hold my hand while walking as if nothing ever happened to us.

    We caught the last bus to Job Corps. We had a nice weekend at her house. On my way to my dorm I see G-Man and he look like he had been crying. "What's up, blood?" I asked.

    He spoke in a sad, broken voice, "Jerry got killed at Grump's house. He was smoking rock cocaine with Grump's Pops, Mr. Bennit, and something happened. Jerry tried to run and Mr. Bennit shot him in the back of the head." Tears were rolling down his face and I can see this look of disbelief in his eyes.

    I gave him a reassuring embrace, and said, "It's going to be okay, G-Man. Did you talk to B-Brown yet?"

    He was trying to focus enough to get his words together, but I've never seen him this emotional before. Finally he said, "Nope, I thought he would be on this bus since it's the last one. Blood is going to flip out when I tell him. I got us a three-week emergency leave, so we will be leaving in the morning. B-Brown got to get his ass here as soon as possible." G-Man stood impatiently and restlessly at the front gate waiting for him and Jessie to drive up. If you miss the bus you can get dropped off here.

After twenty minutes of waiting they pulled up. B-Brown came through the gate smiling big at us, but then he saw we weren't smiling back. He said, "What the fuck happened now?"

G-Man pulled him to the side to tell him the whole story. B-Brown started yelling and tears began flowing from his eyes. I can see all his anger and pain.

"I'm going to kill somebody! Not Jerry! No! My big brother is dead . . ." he trailed off abruptly.

We were able to calm him down, before G-Man informed him about some other bad news. "Moms also told me that G-Rab and Snoop is in jail. They was supposed to have robbed the casino on Rosencrans and Vermont, they are looking at a lot of time." When I heard that I thought I might have been with them, then G-Man spoke again, "Blood, it's crazy out there in the hood. Smoke Dog got killed last week over cocaine."

"Damn, the homie Smoke Dog is one of the J-Block's true original gangstas, now he's dead, too," I said in disbelief.

B-Brown, his eyes filled with tears, struggled to talk, "I'm gonna go inside, it's almost time anyway. Plus I got to pack my stuff for the ride home."

I gave them both a firm brotherly embrace, then said, "Blood, I'm sorry for our loss. Man, it's hard to believe

Jerry is dead. I'll get with y'all in the morning."

The next morning we walked them to the front office where the van is waiting to take them to the train station. We said our goodbyes and they left. They will be missed a lot. There was no talking while going back to the dorms, we had nothing to say in light of the tragedy.

Later on in the day, sitting in the park with Lorna and some of the other homies, I notice someone walking and struggling with these two suitcases. He stood five foot six and was about one hundred-ten pounds. I thought my eyes were deceiving me. "Reg? Reggie Taylor? Is that you, blood?"

The guy looked over and smiled, "Yeah, it's me, Ru-al, Lil' Bo-Slim."

When I walked over to him he dropped the suitcases. I gave him a hug and a hearty handshake, which he made sure I put the "P" in it. I said, "Bo-Slim, the last time I seen you was at the Ten in the riot. What the fuck is you doing here?"

"I had to get out the hood or end up going to jail. Blood, it's crazy out there. Everybody is selling or smoking rock cocaine, every hood is flooded with rocks and people is dying over it everyday, so I had to get on. I had heard how homies was coming up here, so here I am. So, what's up on the crabs?"

"Yeah, you missed out on the big fight we had with them crabs a few months ago, but they don't want any funk. But you know how they get down, can't be trusted. G-Man and B-Brown just went home this morning on a three-week pass to bury their brother Jerry. He got shot by Grump and Skinny's Pops over some cocaine. The homie Heroin went to town last month and never came back, he's in Salt Lake City living with his brother. We go kick it with him on our weekend passes. Let's go put your stuff up," I finished, changing the subject.

Four weeks has passed and the homies is back from laying Jerry to rest. They seem to be doing better than when they left. They talked about how the hood has changed in just ten months. G-Man said, "They still selling weed, but sherm and rocks is what everybody is selling now. I got some weed, let's go to the park and get high."

I got my three-week home pass coming up in a month, I'm going to tell Lorna that I'm going to stay."

Bo-Slim went on his first pass to town with B-Brown. I stayed here because me and Lorna both decided that I would go to her house for my three-week pass.

Sitting on the bench talking, it's dark and almost time to go inside. We see Bo-Slim is drunk, staggering to his dorm. He waved at us and kept going down the ramp.

Still sitting there, while kissing Lorna, I hear some noise on the ramp. I looked but don't see anything. The next thing I hear is, "Get off me, blood, you don't know me! I'm Lil' Bo-Slim from Westside Piru Hood, fool!"

I ran to the ramp to see him standing over this Asia guy, who was knocked out. To be so small he can fight, I know how down blood is. I seen the counselor grab him by his arm, Bo-Slim turned around and socked him in the eye. The counselor let him go. Two guards just happen to be walking on the ramp, they handcuffed him then took him to their little jail that they have on the grounds. They sent him right back to Compton. I told the homies what happened.

"Damn, blood wasn't here two months and now he's gone," G-Man said in disbelief. "His first time in town, he got drunk, and knocked out some dude. I can't wait until I go home and laugh at his crazy ass."

It's been nine months since our last encounter with the crabs. I got my utmost respect from them, they know that I don't like them, and it's good they are staying out of my way.

We're chillen in the park and the dudes from the east coast has been walking around all tense. K-9 said, "Yesterday the crabs had got into it with one of them dudes from New York, and all them dudes is in front of T-dorm as if they want some funk with them. Y'all know that they think we are going to ride with the crabs, so what's up, blood?"

"See, this is the shit I'm talking about," I replied with disgust. "I hate to say it but we got to roll with them crabs because it's a state thang. Let's get at Sergio and his S.A. homeboys. I know they are down to ride with us, it's L.A. against them, so let's get everything set up because it's on tonight. I don't trust them crabs, they might be up to some funny shit."

"If they do some funny shit we will deal with them," G-Man said.

"I'll go tell the crabs that it's on tonight and to meet us by T-dorm at nine o'clock, to bring their weapons, and I'll go get ours," Leo informed the guys. After he left we started setting up our move and who we were going to get first.

It's 8:45, we're at the end of the ramp talking to the S.A.'s. They are ready, we are ready. The crabs is at the other end of the ramp and the east coast dudes is over by T-dorm. We walked over to where they had been most of the night. This shit looked like a scene out of a warriors' movie where gangs is fighting other gangs. My heart is beating real fast. That's a good thing because I'm going to be alert and on my toes.

We walked up on them, and I said, "Rob, you had some words with a Crip yesterday?"

"Yeah, Ru-al, I did. What's it to you? He's not your homeboy," Rob responded in his deep-ass voice. Rob was from New York. He's six foot five and two hundred-thirty pounds with muscles everywhere.

"No, he's not my homeboy, but we're all from L.A. and we got to roll together." As I'm talking to him I reach into my pocket for my knife because I got to get his big ass first.

When I took my hand out of my pocket I looked over at the ramp and see the crabs is still there, they never intended to ride with us in the first place. I thought they was behind us when we first walked up on them. I told the homies not to trust them crabs. "Check this out, Rob. The Bloods don't have no beef with you or your homeboys anymore," I told him. "Our beef is with those crabs that's looking at us from that ramp with they scary ass."

We shook hands then Rob said, "Ru-al, I know you Bloods and S.A.'s are down, but them Crips, those are some foul brothers."

Leo spoke with a lot of anger in his voice. "Blood, look at them crabs laughing at us, they set us up!"

I went over to where they stood, I know the homies are behind me. I walked up to Big D's fat ass and slapped him like a bitch. He grabbed his jaw and looked at me in shocked amazement. I said, "You and your punkass homeboy tried to set us up. All y'all are cowards. Fuck all you crabs. I knew better to think we could trust you, Erickets. Y'all is on your own."

On our way to the park before we got off the ramp, Big D said, "We don't need y'all, cuzz."

Sitting in the park, we got the music going and smoking weed, I'm hugged up with my snowbunny, Lorna. G-Man is with his girl. B-Brown and Jessie and some of the S.A.'s got their girls. Sergio, said, "Damn, Ru-al, you slapped Big D like a bitch and he didn't even swing back."

"Ru-al, you're quick to take off on them crabs," K-9 added.

"I got to take off them first if I know it's going to be

a fight. Hell, I don't want to get knock the fuck out. Because it can happen and if it do, at least I can say I got in one punch. But I got to get the advantage, that's why I have not lost a fight to a crab."

I'm the new lead cook in charge of today's big cookout. This is my first luau. I heard about all the other ones and I seen photos, so this summer it's up to me to make it go well. This is going to be a big feast, we took out three whole pigs that were cooking in the ground. We got the park all ready to feed fifteen hundred people. I'm feeling good about myself, I am wearing my all-white cooking outfit, and all the tables are set up to feed everyone. I will be carving up one of those savory pigs. The live band is playing good music, everyone is in a good, cheerful mood. There is a long line of orientals waiting to be served a piece of pig. I don't see too many black or whites in line, they are missing out because these pigs are cooked perfectly. The orientals are asking for all the odd parts of the pigs; ears, nose, feet, tail. I'm like, "Wow, they are eating everything on these pigs, nothing is going to waste." Everyone is dancing and enjoying the delicious foods. All went better than expected. It's time to shut it down, clean the kitchen and the park. Now it's just a big-ass party!

On the way to my dorm to shower and changed into some clean clothes, Lorna walked up to me but didn't say anything. I'm happy to see her because she didn't attend the cookout, she stayed in her dorm because she wasn't feeling well. I was thinking about her though, I had sent her a big plate of food. I gave her a kiss, but I could see something was bothering her. "What's wrong, baby?" I asked with sudden concern.

She opened up her mouth and quietly mumbled, "Albert, I think I lost our baby. I went to the rest room and a lot of blood came out. But I have not had my period for a whole month, so I think I miscarried and lost our baby."

I hugged her reassuringly, then said, "It's going to be okay, sweetheart. Have you been to the doctor yet?" I feel so sad, and I know she is feeling miserable.

"No, I have not been to the hospital yet, I wanted to tell you first." She began to weep softly.

"Let's go and get you checked out, baby." The day had gone from joyous to one that was very depressing.

We see Jessie and B-Brown walking our way, I asked them to accompany us for moral support. We get there and the nurse wouldn't allow us inside because it's the weekend.

While standing outside I'm pacing nervously back and forth wondering and worrying about Lorna and her condition. Finally the young nurse came to the door and said, "Albert, the doctor is going to keep Lorna here overnight for observation. Just to let you know, she did have a miscarriage and she was six weeks pregnant."

My heart suddenly felt so broken and shattered. I felt even sadder for what Lorna was going through. I told the nurse, "Please let Lorna know I will be back in the morning, and that I love her."

"Okay," she replied then quickly disappeared back inside.

I picked up Lorna the next morning and everyone is with us. I'm holding her tight as we walk to her dorm. The doctor told her no work for three days and no sex for three to four weeks. I'm glad her health is going to be okay. We both are pretty upset for our loss. I was able to put a brief smile on her face when I told her, "Well, baby, we will have a lot of fun trying to make another one."

Today we are going to Salt Lake City to Heroin house to get high and drunk. We only got a day pass, everybody else are staying the whole weekend.

When we get there he got the weed setting on the table, beer in the refrigerator, and three bottles of Bacardi rum liquor. We're getting fucked up and having a good time, and the next thing we knew it's time for us to go. Damn. We should have got a pass for the whole weekend. We said our goodbyes and I took some weed with me on the way out. We got on the last bus back to Job Corps.

There is about an hour left until it's time to go in so me and Lorna is hanging out before I walked her to her dorm. As I'm walking down the ramp I see some crazy movement going on that don't look right. As I got closer I see five oriental dudes beating on this guy with some kind of rope or cord. The dude is trying to keep them off without much luck. Then he fell to the ground and now they are kicking and whipping him with that cord thing. When I got closer I see that they are beating the shit out of this black guy, he's all balled up on the ground.

I ran down the ramp and one of the oriental dudes turned and swung at me, but he missed. Then another one came flying at me with a kick, this dude think he's Bruce Lee. He ended up hitting my shoulder then landed on his feet in front of me. I put up my fists, clenching them tightly. The one guy that swung at me first, I hit him right on the chin and knocked him out. The other one came at me doing some karate shit with another kick. I blocked that one and hit him on the side of his temple -- he fell off the ramp headfirst. The black dude was up by now, fighting back as best he could. Now everyone is coming out of their dorms to see what was going on.

When I see who was on the ground it was that crab, Kal. The other three dudes ran off and so did I. I'm running through the crowd of people, trying to get to my dorm, passing up Leo on my way inside. I get in, took off my clothes, then jumped into bed. Leo came in and asked, "What the fuck happen, blood?"

"I seen them oriental dudes jumping on a black dude so I helped him. Leo, I think I killed one of them dudes because I knocked out two of them, but the one that fell over the ramp never moved again. I need you to go out there and see what's up. And make sure that crab don't tell on me, that's who I helped. Now go, blood, hurry up."

I'm laying on my bed nervous as fuck, my mind is racing, not sure what's going on. After fifteen minutes Leo returned and said, "Ru-al, whatever you did to that dude the ambulance came and got him, they said he didn't move still. The guards got Kal handcuffed in the back seat of their truck. Ru-al, what did you hit that dude with? Because it's blood everywhere."

"Blood, I just hit him with one punch and he fell off the ramp. If it wasn't a black dude I wouldn't got into it, but they was beating Kal's ass. Blood, you know I hate them crabs, I just couldn't watch them do that. It would have been wrong for me to watch another race beat up a black crab, I had to help. Now I just hope he don't drop a dime on me."

"I would have done the same thing," Leo admitted. "Ru-al, I don't think he will tell on you."

Two weeks after that fight Kal hadn't snitched me out and that other oriental didn't die either. I was glad to hear that!

Leo, G-Man, B-Brown, Jessie, Janice had all went home, I miss them. Me, Sergio, K-9 are the only ones left, until today. We got four homegirls from the Nickerson Garden Bounty Bloods out of Watts. I was glad to see them. I know Roz, Beep, Cookie and Nay-Nay are down because they are out of Watts. But Beep only lasted a week, she beat up this girl from New York with a broom. Roz got into the cooking trade with me. Cookie and K-9 are going together. They love Lorna, they got along real good, they never seen a white girl so down as her. A month later Nay-Nay was gone, she didn't like it up here. Two new crabs had also came, but they don't want any problems.

Walking the halls with Cookie, she said, "Ru-al, these two crabs is messing with me."

I said, "Take me to them and we going to handle it right now," I promised her.

We walked to their class and they are sitting at their desks next to each other. I walked up to the tall one and said, "Blood, is y'all fucking with my homegirl?"

The fat one spoke, "No, your homegirl started talking shit for no reason."

Cookie said, "One of y'all called me a bitch and I'm nobody's bitch."

I said, "Check this out, y'all have no reason to say anything to her. We are going to let this go."

"Okay, man," the tall crab said. Then we walked away.

"Damn, Ru-al, you got those crabs in check, they are scared of you."

"Well, over the past fifteen months I had to earn my reputation, and so did a lot of the other Bloods that was here. It has calmed down a lot since then."

After being here eighteen months, I got one more month to get my certification as a cook and I don't want to leave here until I get it. And I don't want to leave Lorna. Roz started going out with this dude from New York. K-9 and Cookie went home together. I got to talk to Lorna. "Baby, I'm ready to go home after I get my cooking certificate. So what do you think about that?" I asked, watching the expression on her face change.

"If you leave, I'm going to leave too," she replied. "But what about us? I don't want to do that long-distance relationship thing, it will be too hard to do. If you leave, I'm going too," she finished with tears welling up in her eyes.

I walked into the office. "Mr. James," I began. "I got one month to get my cooking certificate and after that I'm going home to try to find a good job in the cooking industry."

"Okay, I understand. You come a long way from your first month here, and I know you miss your family. You know you could easily get a job up here, they hire people who graduated from J.C. I wish you the best out there, I know you can do it. You became the lead cook and the dorm president, you will be a good leader, good luck. So, what about that pretty red-headed girlfriend of yours?" he asked.

"We talked about it, but have not come up with anything yet."

We have been making love for the whole month and it seems like we have fallen deeper in love with each other -- but it's time to say our goodbyes. I got my bags in the van, I leave in thirty minutes. I looked into her pretty hazel-green eyes and said, "Lorna, you're my first love and, no matter what, I'll always love you. You have been such a blessing to me in so many ways. We had our ups and downs, but most of them were ups. Baby, we can try the long-distance thing until it don't work anymore. My heart is hurting right now. The love making we did last night will always be with me. And baby, this is not the end."

She's looking at me with tears flowing down her cheeks. I kissed the moist trail streaming down her face, and she kissed the tears that began running from my eyes. She wanted to say something, but her words wouldn't come out, so I hugged her. I noticed she still had that sweet smell of strawberries she had when I first hugged her. She looked at me and wiped the tears from my cheeks, then said, "Albert, I love you. I never thought I would meet such a cool and handsome man up here until you ran off Troy in T-dorm. You're my heart, Albert, and I will never forget you. I never trusted anybody like I trust you. You made me a better woman and friend, and I thank you for that." She kissed me then gave me a firm, lasting hug.

I said, "Baby, we are leaving our mark in this place. We did it our way and we will be remembered as the "it" couple. I'll call you everyday, okay?"

We said our goodbyes, I got in the van and waved at her and the three other people that came to see me off and comfort Lorna. I looked out the back window and see her breaking down in sobbing tears. I felt more tears of my own coming so I just let them flow because they are for my redhead, Lorna.

Mama came to pick me up from the bus station. I was so happy to see her, I hugged her and didn't want to let her go. Once I got home I see that Paul and Katie had grown much bigger. Pops and I hugged for a long time also, I missed my daddy. It felt good to be home again. I called Lorna to let her know I made it back safely, we talked for a long time.

Nobody in the hood knew that I was coming home. I walked across the street to see Connie, she had her second daughter by now. Ludis came running into my arms, "Uncle Albert," she exclaimed with glee, "I missed you so much."

Connie husband, Doug, lit a joint and passed it to me. Ludis is right there to get her blow. But before I could do it, Connie said, "Albert! Don't blow that weed smoke in her face. Since you left, every time somebody lit a joint, she started acting crazy, so none for her."

I laughed, it sure feels good to breathe in the L.A. smog again.

I finally set it up for Lorna to come stay with me for two weeks. Moms and Pops was cool with that, they knew I was in love with her.

She came and stayed in Katie's room. I took her to one of Val's house parties and she had so much fun. Then a month later I went to stay with her for two weeks. Knowing they don't have any malt liquor I brought eight quarts of Ole English beer and some bomb weed from Nicki. Her moms and dad loved the beer. The two weeks went by so fast. Then we had to say our goodbyes again. It was hard.

Back in Compton I received a check in the mail for $2,100 from Job Corps. I put most of it up and used some to look for a job. I couldn't find one even though I checked so many restaurants, showing them my certificate. But no one would hire me. I felt sad because I worked hard getting this paperwork. Maybe I should have stayed and got a job there at Job Corps.

I called Lorna and we both agreed that the long-distance thing is not working. It was a very sad moment for us. Over the phone I said, "Baby, you know we had a good time and I will always love you. You will always be my redhead forever."

"I know," she said, through a broken voice. "And you will always be my Blood gangsta. And I will always be down with you no matter where we might be in this world. Goodbye, Mr. Ru-al. I love you."

* * *

CHAPTER EIGHT
(Curb Serving)

I've been home from Job Corps almost two months and I can't find a job. Pops asked me if I wanted to work for him, but I said nope, because of the many crabs I ran across in high school. I didn't want to work at any fast-food joint. All I need is for some dude I got into it with to pull up to the drive-thu and see me standing there.

I really tried to get a job at this high-class restaurant at the Executive Inn on El Segundo and Vermont, which is across the street from Hellen Keller Park. I know it would had been a no-no because it's in a Crip neighborhood. I tried some restaurants downtown L.A. by the airport, but none would hire me. My cooking certificate is not working for me, all that hard work getting it and I can't get a job. I'm getting very frustrated not being able to find any work. Mama has been letting me use her car, but I'm spending so much money on gas, I got to do something soon.

I finally gave up trying to find a job. And all this time I have not had any income because I was not selling no weed. Plus Carlton Street is not popping like it used to, the J-Block and dead end is the only spots that's making money. The alley is shut down since gangsta Mike went to prison. G-Man and the rest of the homies are still hanging out on

CURB SERVING

Carlton, only making one hundred dollars a day. The main reason I was still looking for a job was because I got a lot of applications out there, hoping that someone will call me soon before I get caught up in this street life again. But no one ever called.

So, I'm back on the curb serving. I used the last of my money to buy a quarter-pound from the Mexicans on Figueroa. They got some good weed, but not as good as the J-Block or the dead end, and Bo-Slim still got the bomb weed.

I'm hanging out with the homies and only made sixty dollars all day. I told G-Man I'll be back and he didn't asked me where I was going. I walked on the J-Block and sat on the brick wall for about forty-five minutes watching the homies down there making big money, life is good for them. Then I notice most of the cars was coming from the top of the hill by Val's house.

I walked up the J-Block to Val's and three cars pulled up to ask me for some weed. I pointed down the street. I sat there the rest of the day watching so many cars turn off 132nd Street on the J-Block. I want to be a part of them making all that money so bad. The time I have been sitting here I only seen the police once. I went to Val's house for the rest of the night.

It's Friday and everybody is talking about going to Eve's After Dark to party. I told them I didn't want to go, I need to make some money.

10 TOEZ DOWN

I took ten bags of weed to Val's and hid them in the bushes on the side of her house. I'm there three minutes when two cars pulled up. I told them to park on 132nd, and not the J-Block, because I didn't want them down there to see me short-shopping their customers. The first car wanted five bags and the second car wanted three. I made eighty dollars just that fast. I see how they got all them fancy cars and motorcycles. I let some cars go down the street so them guys don't notice me up here. G-Man and the other homies has been asking me where I been going and I would tell them I'm at Val's.

With the money I was making I bought me a fresh quarter-pound and I want to sell it in three days and on the J-Block is where I'm going to make my money. I took twenty bags with me and sold them in thirty minutes. I'm about to leave for the day when this car pulled up wanting six bags. I didn't have any on me so I told them to park and I would be right back. I ran home and got the bags. When I returned and handed them to the guy, he reached in his pocket as if to get the money, but then he hit the gas and burned off without paying for my bags. I tried to hold on to the car as best I could, but he punched me and I had to let go, or get my ass dragged down the street. Things was going too well for me today and now it had to end on a sour note. But at least I made some good money.

The next day, nobody still knows what I'm up to. I got twenty bags on my way to Val's to stash. I see the homie Baby Huey and said, "What's up, blood?"

CURB SERVING

"Not much, Ru-al What is you doing up here?" he asked.

"I'm just chilling. Say, blood, do you know anybody that's selling a gun? I need one."

"Yeah, I got a double-barrel sawed-off shotgun for hundred dollars."

"Yeah, I want it," I told him. "And if you got some extra shells, bring them too. Come through the back way so nobody can see you."

Fifteen minutes later Baby Huey called me to the back of Val's house. I gave him the money and he gave me the gun. It is sawed off to the size of a long-barreled .357 pistol. Somebody did a good job altering this gun. I put it in my pants and it stayed there, that was cool. "Okay, blood, I know this gun got some hot ones on it," I said. He smiled at me then just walked away.

I took the gun and hid it by Val's gate then I put the ten shells in a bush nearby. Now let somebody try to burn off with my weed again -- I'll blast their ass!

Standing on the corner by myself I don't see why the homies down there don't want to share, it's enough money for all four streets. I'm taking it upon myself to make some of this money.

Two cars pulled up, I told them to pull over to the curb while I go get my weed. The first car wanted five bags and, when I handed the second car the weed, Slim drove up, stopped, he had a surprised look on his face. I stared back at him until he drove off. Now I'm wondering what they are gonna do, because they feel that no one from the other streets can slang weed on the J-Block. Two more cars pulled up, I served them.

I looked down the hill and it's a lot of activity going on. A motorcycle come flying up the hill and it's Slim again. He warned, "Ru-al, you bet not sell another bag up here!"

"Fuck you, blood. This is my hood too and I'm going to sell my weed right here," I declared loudly.

He's staring at me and I'm staring back. Then he raised up his shirt so I can see a big-ass pistol tucked into his waistband. "It can get real ugly," he said before driving off.

My heart is beating fast. I'm up here by myself. I should go get G-Man and the other homies, but I thought not because if I'm going to open up the corner I got to be down. I never had a gun pulled on me, he's trying to intimidate me. G-Man should had shot his bumbass years ago.

A car pulled up and wanted four bags. I know they are looking at me, I'm in too deep to stop now. I told them to pull to the curb and I gave them their weed. I looked down the street to see Slim is coming back, and I know he got that big-ass gun. My heart is beating faster than ever.

I ran to the back of Val's house to get my gun and the shells. Slim is at the corner and I'm looking at him behind the fence. So many thoughts are going through my mind. Should I run out there and blow his head off? Or should I let him leave? If I do that without doing anything he will think

I'm gone for good. But I'm not going anywhere. But do I run every time he comes up here? No!

He turned to ride back down the street. I ran from behind the fence to the middle of J-Block and pulled the trigger just as he got to Timmy's house. The report was very loud and the gun had a big kick too. Then I pulled the trigger again. The second blast seemed to be much louder than the first. I ran to the back of Val's house to reload my gun and hide it, then jumped the fence into Val's backyard and walked inside the house breathing hard.

Val said, "Al, did you hear them gunshots? It sound so close."

I had hid my gun in her storage shed. I told her, "Yeah, I heard that, it was me. I shot at Slim down the street because he threatened me with a gun earlier today and told me not to sell any more weed. I said 'fuck you' and shot at him for that." My heart is pounding hard, I'm pacing back and forth in her living room.

"Al, you shot at him?" she asked as if not hearing me the first time.

"Hell yeah. I'm no punk and I'm not going to let him punk me, so I showed him. And I'm not going to stop slanging weed out there either."

"Al, you keep your crazy ass in this house and watch Fudd and Shanael until I get back," she said in a voice that sounded mad. When she returned a while later she said, "Al, you got them guys mad as hell at you. You didn't hit Slim, but you got buckshots in about three cars. You stay inside the rest of the night, you hear me?"

"Yeah, okay," I told her being relieved.

This morning I feel good. Val cooked a big breakfast and I rolled up two fat-ass joints. We're getting high and she's telling me how her relative, Angie, got two kids and she got married. I have not seen her since I've been back.

I still got thirteen bags of weed left, I told her, "I'm going outside to sell these bags, I'll be in the front."

"Al, do you think you should be out there after yesterday?"

"Val, them niggas is not going to scare me, this is my street too."

As soon as I got outside a car pulled up wanting eight bags. I went to my stash and got them. Five minutes later G-Man, B-Brown, Leo and a lot of other homeboys came to the top of the J-Block. Zell said to me, "Ru-al, you're crazy, blood, but you're down. We heard about what you did and we are here to back you up."

I told them the details of everything that happened, then I said, "Blood, this is our spot, now we let homies sell on Carlton Street. This is where I've been the past three weeks." I pulled out my wad of money and said, "This is what we been missing out on."

They seen that wad of money and G-Man said, "I got the next customer after Ru-al!"

CURB SERVING

Slim, Silk, and Bodien drove up the hill and stared at me out of everyone else that was there. So I glared back at them, giving them a nod as if to say "what's up?" They didn't say a word, then turned around and drove off.

I served the next three cars that pulled up, and informed my homeboys, "Do y'all have your weed? Because they are about to start rolling."

Months has passed and everybody is making money, at least two hundred dollars a day, all because I took a big chance with my life and now it's paying off for all of us. The homies down the hill is still making a lot of money. After dealing with them with gunplay, me and everybody stopped claiming the J-Block as our main set, we started claiming Athens Park Bloods. Athens had already been spreading across El Segundo and over to the Weak Side. Some homies stayed with the J-Block and some went to Miller Gangster Hood and Westside Piru Hood, but we are still down with each other. The J-Block will always be our street though.

Leo asked, "Ru-al, are you going to keep your name?"

"Hell yeah, blood. I might not claim the J-Block as my main set but I'm down with the street. Anyway, Athens Park was Piru territory in the early seventies, so it's all good in every way."

Me and a few other homies has been going to the park meeting the homeboys, they have been coming to the J-Block to hang out and merge. The love went well also on the Weak Side.

10 TOEZ DOWN

Today at the park I met Lisa. She is short and younger than me, got light-brown skin, a nice body, and a baby face, which is what they call her. I walked over to where she was and said, "Hi, I'm Ru-al."

"Hi, I'm Baby Face, but you can call me by my real name, Lisa. And I already know who you are."

"Say, Lisa, do you have a boyfriend? Because I don't want to step on any of the homeboys' toes, but I like you. So what's up?"

Before she could answer this dark-skinned girl walked up, so Lisa introduced her, "This is my relative, Pete. And no, I don't have a boyfriend. I did, at one time, go with your homeboy Pee-Wee on Cook Street."

"That's where I seen you before," I told her. "I still want to talk to you," I let her know.

One homie told me that Lisa and Pete had got kicked out of their school for fighting some crab bitches at Gompers Junior High School. She wanted to go back to school but no school in L.A. county would let them because they got kicked out of most schools for fighting Crips. I liked her even more for that!

"I could ask my mama if you could use our address then you can register to go to Vanguard," I offered her eagerly.

"You would do that for me?" she asked in disbelief. "Do you think your mama would say yes?"

"All I can do is ask, but my mama is cool, she'll say

yeah. I'm going to need all your information so we can get you checked in."

We been going together for two months now. Mama liked her, and Lisa has been going to school every day. I'm on the corner making money and Lisa sometimes comes to get money for her lunch or just hangs out. I give her some joints to sell so she is making her own money. I got me a down-ass girl.

The 1984 Olympic Games are in L.A. and the police has stepped up on cleaning the streets. We heard about all the raids they been doing in the hood and they have been driving up and down these streets taking homies to jail.

While I was getting my curb serving on, right when I hand this customer his three bags, the pigs hit the corner. I looked at them then took off running as fast as I could. One police leaped from his car and started chasing me. I jumped over the brick wall into the apartments and, surprisingly, he's right behind me. I'm thinking this is my hood, my spot, I know every little turn and hideout, plus this pig got on twenty pounds of gear, there's no way he's going to catch me. But he's still right behind me. These apartments is like a maze and I'm about to lose his ass. I went right and I can still hear his keys jingling and his boots pounding the pavement behind me. I jumped the fence at Wee-Wee house and laid silent. I hear the police run on by. Once I didn't hear him anymore I walked inside the house.

Wee-Wee and Mrs. White is sitting at the table. Wee-Wee

says, "Why are you coming through the back door?"

I was able to catch my breath and wipe the sweat off my forehead before I walked in. I said, "I just come from Lady Bug house so I just came through the back way."

"Al, I heard about you shooting a gun at somebody in front of Val's place," Mrs. White said disapprovingly.

"Oh, that wasn't nothing. I had to get an understanding with them, but everything is okay now." I ate lunch with them then walked back to Val's house about thirty minutes later.

When I walked inside, Val said, "Al, the police knew that was you that ran. They was on their loudspeaker calling out your name, saying 'Ru-al Jones, we know that was you that ran and we're going to catch you.'"

"Hell nah! They was on the loudspeaker like that?! I'll be back, I'm going home to change my clothes."

I walked in the back door and Mama was sitting there in her chair with a contemplating look on her face. She said, "Albert, why is the police looking for you? They came driving down the street calling out your name, saying they was going to get you. What in the hell did you do for them to be looking for you?"

Everybody seemed to know what was going on now since it was announced throughout the hood over loudspeakers. I told my moms, "I didn't do anything, Mama. They are mad because I ran and got away from them."

"Boy, if your ass go to jail I'm not gonna bail you out.

CURB SERVING

So you better get yourself together, find a job, and stop running them damn streets." She really wasn't happy with me.

"Mama, I'm not doing anything wrong," I said, listening to myself lying through my teeth to her. That's really bad.

I'm back on the J-Block getting my curb serve on. I know I got to watch my back now because the pigs are looking for me and they have been locking homies up.

I sold my first batch and, walking back up to the J-Block with my weed in my draws, I see the police rolling my way. I want to run into Carolyn yard and get away, or maybe they will just drive by.

No luck! Their car came to an abrupt stop, they jumped out, and one pig said, "Put your hands on the car." I did as he instructed me to do. He searched me roughly and grabbed my balls -- I knew he felt the weed. "Put your hands behind your back," he ordered. Then he spoke to his partner, saying, "Hey, look, we got something here, it's in his draws." Damnit.

The other officer is doing a check on my I.D. and said, "Well, look who we got here. We got the rabbit, Ru-al Jones. We've been looking for you. The guys at the station will be happy to see you," he said while grinning and giving his partner a high-five after securing me in the back seat of the cruiser.

We get to Carson substation and, as soon as we walked in, one pig said, "I told you, Mr. Jones, that we were going to get you." Everyone in the office was cheering for the arrest and laughing at me. I know Mama is not coming to get me this time, so there's no need to call her. I'm going to the county jail for the first time and I heard some of the scariest and sickest stories about what goes on in there -- and here I am, on my way.

Back on the streets after twenty days in jail, I survived. The Olympics are finished and the hood is not that hot anymore. Weed sales has went down and now everybody is buying rocks. A lot of homies are smoking premoes, which is rocks and weed mixed. The homies down the street has also changed, they are selling rocks and weed. Most of the customers are buying rocks and weed at the same time. No way I can compete with that by selling only weed.

I sent Val down the street to buy a twenty-dollar rock. This is our first time ever smoking a premoe. I rolled up one fat-ass premoe and when I hit it, I was high as a kite. It was the best high ever. What a rush! Now I want more, so I kept sending Val down there to buy it. Now I'm hooked on premoes. Everybody is now selling weed to get rocks. I even got Lisa smoking them with me, this went on for months. Soon I began smoking rocks out of a pipe and that first hit was even better than the first time I smoked a premoe. Wow! I didn't let Lisa smoke out of the pipe because of how addictive I heard it can be. I seen homeboys and homegirls hooked on this new high, they be up doing all-nighters, wearing the same clothes for three or four days at a time. I can't go out like that, so I made sure me and Lisa stayed fresh and clean, and smoked just enough for our enjoyment and pleasure.

Things has slowed way down, I was lucky to make fifty dollars a day. Eight months ago I was on top of the world curb serving, but now I can't make no real money and everybody has left the hill to find other ways to make some cash. I got to get off this corner and find some other way to make some money myself.

Sitting on the brick wall I thought about the homies I met in 3600 Blood module, how a lot of them are fighting murder cases. I learned a lot them twenty days in there, and I loved the B-Dog talk. I didn't know it was so many different Blood Hoods.

Not one car pulled up looking for weed, they all wanted rocks. My head dropped in disappointment and frustration.

I looked up to see this burgundy caddy roll up. The first person I see is Ted Baster, and Gangstablood in the driver's seat. He had been in prison for five years. "What's up Ted and Gangstablood?" I asked, surprised to see them. "I see you touched down, it's been a long time."

G-Blood said, "What's up, Ru-al? What is you doing sitting out here by yourself?"

"Trying to make some money, but it's slow," I answered.

"Come over to Ted's house in about three hours, I got some work for you," he offered without hesitation.

"Okay, blood," I replied with enthusiasm in my voice. One thing about G-Blood, he know how to make money. His

10 TOEZ DOWN

sister, Nicki, has not been selling anything either, if she was, I know I could make some money too.

I get to Ted's house, and asked, "Where is your moms?"

"She moved to Carson and gave me the house," he answered.

G-Blood came out the back room, he look the same. His hair went all the way to his waist and he got about sixteen-inch size arms. He said, "Ru-al, you want to make some money? Blood, I know you're smoking this shit, man. You're not going to make no money smoking it. Here is a thousand-dollars worth, go out there and let everybody know you got a spot open. And you tell them you only got twenty-fives and up. No fives! No tens! Because that will bring unwanted heat to the house."

I looked at all them rocks, my eyes got so big, I never seen so much dope in my life. I took two hundred dollars worth with me so they can sample it. I got on my old beach cruiser and hit the streets, I sold everything real fast. I came back and gave the money to Ted and went out again. Now the word is out that I got the bomb-ass rocks and customers are coming to our spot for them.

Ted had rolled up three fat-ass premoes, we smoked them, and I'm high as fuck. I called Lisa to come over and she is bringing Pete with her. When they get there Ted had hooked up with Pete. And we took shifts so somebody would always be at the door.

Two months passed and the spot is making a killing. I'm spending my money on clothes, but I'm smoking most of it.

CURB SERVING

G-Blood wants to open a new spot and I'm going to run it, it's the homie Black's house on 122nd. Just like the first spot, I had to go out and get customers then they started coming. I'm making fifteen hundred dollars a day, but I'm smoking up most of my profits. Ted had showed me how to shave the rocks and still sell them for the same price, so that gave me extra rocks to smoke. Me and Lisa is having a get-high party every night. I had told her to start staying home more, she understood and did as I asked.

It's late night and the doorbell rings. I opened it to see this light-skinned girl standing there with some sexy light-green eyes and these cute freckles on her face. "Hey, what can I do for you, beautiful?" I asked showing obvious interest in her appearance.

"Let me get a twenty," she responded with her **sexy-ass voice**.

"Baby, I only got twenty-fives. What's your name anyway?"

"Valentine," she replied, seducing me with every word she spoke. "But I only got twenty, so can you help me this time?"

"Come in. If you want to smoke it in here you can, I got two pipes and some weed if you want to stay."

We walked to the back room where she took off the jacket she had on. She was wearing a thin, white T-shirt that exposed her hard nipples pointing outwards perched on dime-sized areolas. It was 3 o'clock in the morning, I was able to fuck her and the pussy was real good. But it's time to get her out of here, the sun will be up in a couple of hours. I told her to come back later tonight, and she eagerly agreed.

I made all the money I was supposed to make, G-Blood picked up the cash and dropped off another batch of dope. I called Ted to see how he's doing because I have not seen him in weeks. "What's up, blood?"

"Oh, it's cool. I know you got it rolling over there," he seemed distracted.

"Man, this beats curb serving. Say, blood, what's that noise I hear in the background?" I asked, unable to recognize the odd sound.

"I got Toothless Mary over, Ru-al. She is giving me some head. Damn, blood, you can hear her?"

"Hell yeah, I can hear that. Say Ted, when you're done, send her over here."

"Okay, I got to go, Ru-al."

Toothless Mary, as her name implies, does not have any front teeth, and she gives bomb-ass head. I want some head tonight. Ted had this saying about girls that suck dicks: "You're my blow wienie queenie, my d-licker cum drinker, and you better check for leaks."

I hear a knock on the door. I open it to see Toothless Mary, she gave that smile with no teeth in front. She said, "Ted sent me, you know what to do."

I gave her the twenty-dollar rock, then dropped my pants and draws. I had taken all my money out my pockets beforehand so I don't get robbed. Dudes has been getting robbed by smokers, when they are sucking dicks they reach into your pockets and get you for everything you have in there.

I had to call Ted back. "Say blood, can you hear that?"

"I see Toothless Mary made it. Ru-al, I got to go, I got a customer at the door, I'll call you later. Enjoy!"

I hung up the phone while she continued sucking the shit out of my dick. I busted my nut, she swallowed, then left.

G-Blood came by this morning to pick up the money and drop off more dope. Things has been rolling. He said, "Come outside, Ru-al, I got something to show you." I walked outside and squinted, shielding my eyes. The sun hit me, it felt good, but I had not been outside for three days. He pointed at a vehicle and said, "Ru-al, I bought you a car."

It was a 1984 Fifth Avenue on wires with red interior. I said, "Yeah, that's good looking out, G-Blood." I was ecstatic. One thing about him, he took good care of me and Ted just like his sister Nicki did for me and G-Rab.

After G-Blood left I started shaving the rocks. They are still fat, I haven't had anyone complain.

Valentine came over and I sent her to the room to set up everything. I had some customer to take care of, then I was able to take a break. I walked to the room and Valentine is sitting there butt-ass necked, her small tits is standing up firm, she just took a big hit. Damn, this girl is too fine to be a smoker.

I dropped my pants and boxers. She already had my pipe loaded, she know how I like mines. I got a ten piece in the bowl and a ten piece on the screen. She handed me the lighter and I melted them down while she grabbed my dick and sucked it deep into her mouth. I took a big breath with that first hit. I'm holding it in as long as I can, and I can hear her slurping and moaning with my meat in her mouth. I want to cum because it feels too damn good. I exhaled fully, as my boy Ted would say, "I let out a London fog hit," because that was how much smoke that was coming out my mouth. I looked down at Valentine, she's still sucking and deep-throating the shit out of my dick, this head job is feeling fantastic, I'm about to bust my nut. I put my hand on the back of her head and started pushing it up and down, faster and faster. Then it happened, I cummed in her mouth and she took it all. She knows to check for leaks too. Valentine is a spitter so she went to the bathroom to spit my nut. Then she put some toothpaste on the tip of her finger and finger-brushed her teeth. She returned with a soapy towel to wash my dick and balls. "That was good, girl," I said, being completely satisfied with her performance.

"I know it was, I'm the best at what I do. Now let me go load up our pipes again," she said, licking her lips then getting busy loading the bowls.

I served a few customer. When I walked in the room Valentine got my pipe loaded. I like getting high with her, she don't talk much because she knows when I'm high on this shit I don't like to talk. I didn't have to worry about her robbing me because she know she can get high all day and night for free. Plus I told her that I know all the dope fiend moves and she know not to try anything scandalous on me. The rest of the night we got high and fucked repeatedly.

It's about 5:30 in the morning, almost time for her to leave, suddenly I hear a big-ass bang on the front door. I jumped up and put on my pants. That didn't sound like no customer knock to me. When I got my shoes on and walked to the front window I see about thirty police out there with guns in their hands. I ran to the room and said, "Get dressed, Valentine, it's a raid! There is pigs everywhere!" She got dressed and I put all the money and dope in the safe that we had built into the floor. I have been up for three days and I can't think straight, but I'm able to close the safe just in time. I hear a loud BOOM! BOOM! -- then the door came crashing down.

Valentine had flushed the broken pipes down the toilet, so we got everything out the way. When we both walked in the living room, the first pig issued orders to us. "Get on the floor and put your hands behind your back. If you move, I'll blow your fucking head off."

My heart is beating a hundred miles an hour. I can hear a dog barking and, then a pig said, "The house is clear. Pick them up and put them on the couch." Then he turned and spoke directly to me. "Okay, I know you're selling dope in this house, now tell me where it it."

"Ain't no dope in this house," I told him.

The phone suddenly rang. A cop picked it up and said, "Yeah, what do you want? It's too late, we're already here."

We were escorted outside and there are so many people I never seen before. Somehow Valentine's father was out there and the police allowed her to leave with him.

Here I am, back in Carson Substation, and just like last time, the police is mocking and laughing at me.

I'm in a cell with two other dudes when I hear a familiar voice. "Ted? Ted! Is that you over there?"

"Yeah, it's me, Ru-al. Blood, I tried to call to warn you, but when I heard a different voice on the phone I knew it was too late."

"Blood, that was you on the phone? The police did pick it up when it was ringing. Where did you call from?" I was anxious to know.

"I called from here to let you know they was on the way. They hit my spot, but they didn't find anything. Did they find anything at yours? Don't worry, G-Blood will get us out."

"No, they didn't find shit at my spot," I let him know.

"Jones! Jones!" the bailiff yelled. "Get up, you made bail." I was in a deep sleep. I needed the rest after all them days I had been up. When I walked out the cell I see Ted getting his property. I got mines and we walked out together.

CURB SERVING

Black was there to pick us up.

On the way home we stopped at Burger King for some food. I feel real good now. I asked Black, "How bad did they tear up the house?"

"Not as bad as they did Ted's place. Y'all got court dates in two weeks."

When we get back to the hood Black dropped Ted off at his house and took me to mines. Lisa is waiting on me, I was happy to see my girl. She said, "Mama Boe-Head put up the house and G-Blood put up the money."

We cleaned up the house and was back open for work. I got enough work for two days, I sold all that I had, we're making good money.

I told G-Blood I needed to go home for a few days to rest, wash all my clothes, and eat some good food. I told Lisa to come over, and she did. We kicked back at my house for those two days, got our love-making on, and caught up on some much needed sleep. Then I packed my bags with fresh clothes and went back to my spot, Lisa came with me.

I got a fresh batch of rocks. When G-Blood left, I rolled up some premoes for me and Lisa to smoke, we got high. Later that night she went home.

I'm here by myself getting high, I never kept count on what, or how much, I smoked. But when I did, I realized I was way short. Customers is coming and I'm telling them I'm out, knowing that I only have about three hundred dollars left, but

I smoked that up too. This shit got my mind tripping and I just fucked off all of Blood's dope and he's going to be mad as hell! I got to find a way to get all this money back.

I grabbed my gun then locked the door on my way out. I jumped into my car and drove to my childhood friend's house in Watts. This is the same place Humphery went when Mama kicked him out the house. I haven't seen them in a long time, but I know that I'm always welcome, they are like family. We grew up together in the early seventies, we lived on 117th and Gorman. We done everything together from playing tag to Hide-Go-Get-It. This is the only Crip street I showed respect to even though I didn't know anything about banging in the seventies.

I pulled up and see Don and Willie in the front yard. I get out the car. Don said, "Albert, what's up? It's been a while since we seen you."

"Yeah, big bro, it's been a while. So here I am for a few days."

They live on 112th right across the street from the Imperial Courts. I see a lot of crabs hanging out and I got on this red shirt. If they trip, I feel sorry for them because I got this gun in my pocket and they will be the first crabs that I shoot. But I hope it don't come to that because they's projects got hundreds of Crips in them.

Willie now calls himself "Blue." He got on some blue 501 jeans and he's sagging hard, and he got that walk that I hate. But I can't trip on my family, he's just getting his Crip on.

CURB SERVING

I said, "Blue, I need to make some money, I got the gun and the car."

"What do you have in mind because I need to make some money, too. I'll go get G.J. and see if he want to roll with us, but first you better go say hi to Me-Me."

I walked in the house and see her there, I gave her a hug and a kiss. Me-Me is like a second mother to me. When we stayed in Palmdale she would let me spend some nights there. I said hi to everyone, caught up, then went back to the garage.

G.J. came in, we had no idea what to do, so I said, "Let's go to Humphery house, I know he got something for us. He live in the peblose, so y'all can't wear all that blue, it's a Blood Hood.

We get to his house, these projects is almost bigger than the P.J.'s. When Humphery answered the door we went inside. "What's up, bro?" I said, getting straight down to business. "We need to make some and I know where we can do something. I got everything we need."

Before he could answer my niece Shameka and her mother Sonya come out the room, and the baby came running to her uncle. I gave her a big hug then they left. Humphery said, "Let's go, I got a few spots we can check out."

Driving through these factories I see three Mexicans walking along the street. I pulled up next to them and we all jumped out the car. Two of them ran with Blue and G.J. chasing right behind them. I got the other one with my gun out and said, "Put your hands up and give me everything in your pockets."

He looked at the gun then slowly pulled everything out his pockets. I see Humphery over by Blue making sure no one came out the factory on them. Once everything was over we jumped in the car and counted the money, we got about two hundred dollars.

We drive off and when I turn the corner the police is right behind us. I didn't slow down, I continued driving, but another police suddenly pulled in front of us with their lights flashing, cutting us off. I slammed on the brakes and stopped in the middle of the street. Over the bullhorn the pig said, "Driver, step out of the car with your hands up!"

I did as I was ordered. The rest of the guys got out the car the same cautious, careful way. All of us went straight to jail for three counts of robbery and possession of a firearm.

I know I'm on my way to prison. And I found out last week that Lisa is pregnant with my baby, but now I won't be around for the birth. This nightmare started with me curb serving then getting sprung on them rocks. If I had only listened to G-Blood I could be making thousands of dollars. But, instead, I wanted to do it my way and now I'm caught up. I lost my car and everything. I know G-Blood is going to be very upset at me, not for fucking off the dope, but because I didn't come to tell him that I fucked up. One thing about blood, he don't sweat the small shit, and what I did is small.

CURB SERVING

I'm now sitting in South Gate Substation thinking about how I curb served my ass right into prison. Hopefully when I touch down I'll do it right.

    *   *   *

CHAPTER NINE

(Touched Down)

Don't look back!" Grangsta Sam said loudly as I'm walking through the gates off the yard on my way to R&R (Receiving and Release). I did what anybody would do, I looked back -- and they all started laughing at me. The old prison saying is if you look back, you will come back. After three years in one place I had to see my homies one more time. I got the full Blood convict escort -- about fifteen Bloods, ten Northern brothas and eight brown brothers. They are sending me back to Compton as a smarter Blood and wiser man.

I got my two hundred dollars gate money in my pocket, I'm happy to be going home. The two guards took me and four other guys to the Greyhound bus station. It felt so good to get on a bus that don't have bars bolted over the windows and I'm not secured in handcuffs and ankle shackle restraints.

Three years ago I stepped off the Grey Goose to this prison, I weighed one hundred and twenty-five pounds, and fifteen of them pounds I gained the six months in the county jail, I was smoked out. Now after three years I'm two hundred and twenty pounds with nineteen-inch arms and a protruding muscular chest, I'm on swole. My Juri curl is long. I got two long braids in my beard with a red rubber band holding them together and, most importantly, I'm free. I'm coming home as

TOUCHED DOWN

fresh as anyone could. I even got a new dick from when I got circumcised. The new Ru-al is about to hit the streets. Not once did I send home any photos of me or did I get any visits. When I hit the scene people are going to be shocked at my new appearance.

I'm on the bus doing some real thinking on what I'm going to do when I touch down. Looking out the window people is doing their own thing as they was when I was on that other bus. Now I'm one of them, a free person. I'm missing the homies already, I'm leaving some down-ass Bloods, some will get out and some are there for life. I did learn a lot on how to carry myself as a B-Dog, and it all started in the 3600 Blood module. The O.G.'s in 4300 really spent some time to groom me on how to deal with the prison life and I took every word to heart. I earned my prison stripes but I got many more to earn. This nine-hour ride was long, but it gave me time to think.

The bus pulled up to the door and I got off. Relative Chantay "Tay" is to pick me up but I hope we don't pass each other, because she don't know what I look like and I don't know how much she changed. My sister Yvonne sent me my dress-out clothes: black khakis, gray sweatshirt and some Reebok shoes.

I walked up to the desk and this dark-skinned lady looked at me. I asked, "Can you tell me where is the front door?"

"You walk to those steps, turn to your left, and you will be in the front of the bus station," she said as she pointed in the direction I was to go.

"Bool," I replied.

"What did you say?" she asked being confused.

"I said bool." I laughed at myself, I knew she didn't understand what I said, I had just B-Dog talked to the woman. I got to watch my words. To B-Dog talk you change the letters in words to sound different, like I exchanged the "C" from the the word cool and used the letter "B". People are going to wonder what crazy language I'm speaking. I got to check myself when talking to free people who don't understand me.

I'm walking down the stairs with my sweatshirt off, I got on my tank top. So many eyes are looking at me, I'm loving it. I suddenly hear, "Albert! Albert!" I looked to my right and see my relative, she still look the same, dark-skinned about five-seven and one hundred twenty pounds. She came running up to me, we hugged then she said, "Damn, relative, you look good. Man, you got muscles everywhere!" A good-looking girl was with her and she finally realized she should introduce her. "Oh, shit! This is my friend Wanda, she live next door to me."

"Hi, Wanda," I said, liking what I'm seeing.

"Hey, Albert," she responded with a sexy smile.

This girl got on this miniskirt that is showing off her toned, thick legs, and she got a big-ass butt and a nice body.

Tay said, "Let's go, I got Joe parked in the front. Damn, relative, you're big, I can't believe how much you have changed. Boy, these girls are going to eat your ass up."

"Yes, we are," Wanda added being flirtatious. I smiled.

We got into Tay small car, me and Wanda is sitting in the back seat. Tay introduced me to her boyfriend Joe, we said our "What's ups?" Tay hands me this fat-ass joint. I hit it two times and started coughing, this is some good weed. I passed it to Wanda, she hit it and gave it to Tay. I'm feeling the weed and now it seem like Joe is driving too fast. I'm back-seat driving and they are laughing at me. I have not been in a car in 3-1/2 years, so everything is moving much faster than I'm accustomed to.

We pulled up in front of the house. I got out the car but I don't see nobody hanging out, no one knows I'm coming home. I said to myself, "I touched down." It's 11 p.m.

I walked in the house and see my family. I hugged Mama first, I didn't want to let her go, it felt so good to be in her loving embrace again. It seem surreal, just ten hours ago I was walking the prison yard, now here I am with family.

I gave everybody hugs, they are feeling on my muscles and saying, "Damn, you look good."

Tay said, "Relative, I got to go to work in the morning, I'll see you later." I gave her and Wanda hugs goodbye, and that hug from Wanda was saying something more.

Being high really made my arrival seem like a dream. I said, "I need to get some sleep because this all seem so unreal to me right now."

"Okay, son, we understand," Mama said, then hugged me before I left.

At 5 a.m. I wake up, my body is still in prison mode, and it will be like that for some time. I took a shower. I heard Paul and Katie wake up. While cooking breakfast I said, "Paul, I need you to take me to see my parole officer. I got to be there at eight o'clock, so let's leave early because we got to find it, it's in Gardena."

"Okay, and after that I'll take you to the swap meet to get some clothes," he offered.

K-Dae asked, "Have you notice that Daddy is not here? He left because he started messing with this other woman and Mama wasn't having that. So he been gone for a year now, but he is here three to four times a week as if he never left."

"Yeah, I noticed that last night," I said, "I just didn't say anything. Say, Paul, is you or K-Dae banging?"

K-Dae spoke first. "I go to Blood parties and picnics and I wear my red, but I'm not out there like some of the homegirls. I'm in college so I don't have too much time to run the streets."

"Same with me, I'm in school also," Paul said. "I see what happened to you, I was out there, then I got into school. But wait until you see Trevon, Derrel, and Gordon, they is out there banging hard."

"Good, I'm glad to hear that y'all is not out there like them or me because it is not a life for y'all."

TOUCHED DOWN

I'm back from seeing my p.o. and shopping. I put on my fresh gear, now it's time to go outside to let everyone see the new Ru-al after being gone for three and a half years.

It's a hot summer day and I'm walking down to G-Man house first. This four-door caddy pulls up and it's G-Blood, and following him behind is about ten low-riders. As they were passing by me they all gave me a nod, and I gave it back with a smile. These cars are clean, just like in the Low Rider Magazine, and they got the name of their car club in gold called "The Other Side." The caddy stopped.

"What's up, G-Blood?" I said, then stuck out my hand.

"Not much, Ru-al," he said while giving a firm handshake. "I see you touched down and you're bigger than a house. Say, Ru-al, I'm not tripping on what you did. Blood, you knew you could have came to me, you missed out on a lot of money, but I'm glad to see you out. Later on I got something for you."

"Okay, blood. So how many of these low-riders is yours?"

Before he could answer Cyclone pulls up in a silver Suzki on Datons. He is only one of five bellboys that live behind our house. He looked at me and I know he don't see me as that small guy that he beat up in the module. He drove on by. I noticed Tony Bell in one of the low-riders, but I didn't see the two younger ones. Their big brother Lonel is in the pen. Cyclone is one of the hardest Bloods I know and he got some size on him, some seventeen-inch arms. He don't smoke or get high, all he do is fight and ride on them crabs. Some see him as the neighborhood bully. I do remember that ass-kicking I got from him.

From all the music bumping out from all the cars everybody started coming outside. I see G-Man, Zell, B-Brown, Whoop, Dee-Dog, and a lot more people. Before I was able to greet the homeboys Cyclone walked up and swung at me. I ducked and caught him in the nose with a right punch, then on his face with a left. I can see it in his eyes that he is surprised at what's going on. He swung again and that one hit me in the jaw, but I brushed it off. He's bleeding real bad from his nose while trying to grab me. My heart is beating faster. He was able to get a hold of my shirt and pulled me closer to him. He tried to overpower me, but little did he know I just bench-pressed three hundred and fifty pounds. I easily pushed him off me, I felt the power surge from within me. He can't believe that he is losing and it's in front of everybody I know. I can't lose, it would look bad that I'm fresh out and he takes the reputation I worked so hard to get. He's still coming and taking all that I'm throwing at him. And I'm taking his best shots too. We are going back and forth at each other.

Now I'm starting to breathe hard, my chest is burning from the smog and the Camel cigarettes I've been smoking. We fought all the way back to my house, I'm losing my speed but he is still getting hit.

Mama came outside yelling, saying, "Y'all stop that damn fighting!"

TOUCHED DOWN

I can't stop, I don't want Blood to catch me and knock my ass out. So we kept punching at each other, he's not getting my stripes, Mama don't understand. She yelled again, this time we stopped. "Albert! You get your ass in the house, boy! You ain't been home eighteen hours and you're out here fighting like you don't have no damn sense. Michael, why is you out here fighting?"

"Mrs. Jones, me and Albert had something to settle."

I go inside the house and looked out the window because Mama is in the doorway so I don't go back out. Cyclone got blood on his shirt, I guess I won. He won one but I won the one that counted. Now he's out there fighting B-Brown and they are going towards his house. Cyclone just got to fight somebody no matter who it is. I got to say he's one hard-ass Blood.

Sitting in my backyard homeboys are coming over and Mama is sending them back to see me. She don't want me in the front talking about the fight and what everybody been doing while I was away. John Boy gave me a half-ounce of rocks. Gil gave me a pistol and said, "Blood, you're going to need this, you been gone, they are playing for keeps out here now."

"Good looking out, y'all," I told them graciously.

C-Man passed me the joint and said, "Damn Ru-al, your ass is on swole. You know the word is out that you got the best of Cyclone and blood don't like that, so watch your back. I don't think he would try anything, but he got an ego."

"Yeah, I hear you, C-Man. If we would had fought any longer he would have got me because I was getting tired."

B-Brown said, "You see blood turned to fight me after you. One thing about Cyclone, he will get you tired and T-Role your ass. Ha-ha!"

After everybody left Mama let me go on the front porch. Just as I sat down Lisa come walking into the yard. She said, "Hi, Albert. Glad to see you made it home."

I gave her a hug then a kiss on the cheek. We sat down, she still have that baby face that I fell in love with. I said, "So, how did you know I was out?"

"I heard about the fight that you and Cyclone had and I had to come see my ex-man. And I must say, you look damn good."

We talked about a lot of things, she has a boyfriend now, which was cool with me. I said, "I was so hurt that you lost our son. You see these teardrops? The one that's open is for our son so I will never forget what could have been. The other one is for the prison time I just done."

"It's nice seeing you, Albert. I got to get home to my boyfriend," she said reluctantly.

"Okay, Lisa, I'll see you around."

Today the family is throwing me a welcome home party, and everyone is coming. Both of Mama's sisters, Aunt Maple and Aunt Janice, and many more will be here. I'm ready to hug and kiss all my family. I've missed them.

TOUCHED DOWN

Tay pulled up with her brother Jerome and sister Teasa. She brought Wanda too, and I was happy to see her. She got on this body dress that hugged every part of her figure, and that got me really turned on. I've been home three days and have not got any pussy yet. Before I went to prison the girls I wanted to fuck wouldn't give me the time or day. Now they are lining up for a chance. So far I turned down five girls who wanted me to hit that pussy. I'm no fool, I watch a lot of TV and know that AIDS is out here and I'm not going to catch it, so I had to turn down strange pussy. But damn, one look at Wanda and I have to take that chance with her.

Tay said, "Let's get this party started." She lit a joint and the party was on. Some of the homeboys came by but left because they know it's a family thing.

Pops rolled up and I went over to hug him, it felt good to embrace him again. He gave me a Jones kiss. I missed them all so much.

The barbecue pit is going strong, it's food and drinks everywhere. We're taking flicks, laughing, drinking beer and just having a good time. Then it happened, I hear Pops say, "Boy, I'm going to kill you."

I looked to see he was talking to Anthony. Then Anthony said, "Do it, man. Fuck all the talking."

I just knew it was going to happen every time we have a get-together. Somebody got to shut it down. Pops went to his truck where he got out his big-ass pistol. He got that look in his eyes, he's mad as hell. Me and K-Dae stopped him from going back in the yard. Paul kept Anthony in the backyard.

Pops finally calmed down and said, "I'm cool. Everything is cool."

K-Dae left and just me and Pops is sitting in the truck. I said, "Pops, you see that girl in that tight dress? She look good, I think I'm going to ask her out."

"Yeah, I seen her and she do have a big butt," he joked unexpectedly. We both laughed openly then went back in, it's getting late.

We ate and drank everything that was there and now people are starting to leave. This turned out to be a lovely Jones cookout. If there wasn't a fight or a big fuss it wouldn't have been a typical Jones' party. I'm truly back home.

Standing in the kitchen with Mama, K-Dae, Connie and Yvonne, I said, "Yeah, this was a good Jones' party with all the drama. I set up a date with Wanda."

"No you didn't!" Yvonne voiced her opinion. "You don't know where she been. I think she been messing around with other guys. I think you can do better than that."

"Big sis, I know you're looking out for me, but I've been home three days and have not yet got me any, and I want some."

"Make sure you wear a raincoat," Connie offered her advice. Mama agreed with her. I'm saying to myself, "Yeah, right. I got this new dick, I want to feel it and test-drive Pecker. No raincoat here!"

TOUCHED DOWN

Mama kept me inside for three days, I have not yet seen Val. When I finally did she jumped up and hugged me, then she socked me in the arm. "I heard you had a fight with Cyclone and you won. Al, it's not like it used to be out here, people is getting killed and the youngsters are a hundred times as crazy as you was, so be careful."

"Okay, Val. Now where is Fudd, Nell, and Will?"

"They are at Mama house and Will don't live here anymore, he moved in with this lady on the other side of the apartments. But everybody is doing just fine."

I spent about two hours with her and it felt good to be there again.

G-Man came and got me from Val's and we went down the street where everybody is. The J-Block is the hangout spot. Everyone is selling rocks and weed. The spot that the O.G.'s wouldn't let us sell before now we're in front of their main house. Dekum and Belly got it going on. A lot of youngsters is hanging out as well and they all got gang names, calling themselves Young Gangster Bloods (Y.G.B.), and they are all killers. These are the same kids that went to church and stayed in the house, now they are a killing machine. I'm glad that they are on my side. Frog and Luna-Tick are brothers. Val wasn't lying, they are doing it harder than I ever was. I'm glad Paul and K-Dae is in school away from all this shit.

I said, "Frog, what's up, blood? I see that the Y.G.'s is putting in work on them crabs."

"Yeah, we got this. You get your slang on and make your money, big homie. The Y.G.B.'s are in every hood and we are laying them down in a real way. But you got to know that they are doing the same to us, it's a war out here. If you get caught slipping, you're on the ground with your head dripping."

Sike added, "We don't do that drive-by shit like them crabs. They started doing that shit on homies, but that's a coward way to get down. We are putting the yellow tape up."

The homie Tone said, "Let's go get some drinks, Ru-al."

"Okay, let's go, I need some smokes too." I got in the back seat and one of the Y.G.'s got in the front, he wanted to go to this other store because they had the Ziploc bags he wanted. The store is in crab hood.

We got some Thunderbird and red Bool-Aid, some gin and socko, and the Ziplocs. We got back in the car and, as we was about to leave, the Y.G. said, "Hold up, blood, I see something."

Y.G. stopped the car in the middle of the street and jumped out, running toward this person. It was dark, I couldn't see shit even with the streetlights on. Tone stopped running and started walking, then he stopped. His hand came out quickly from his pocket and then I hear BANG! BANG! BANG! I could see the muzzle flash from the gun after each shot. His hand dropped lower and lower until the last two shots were fired. I know whoever that was is xed out the game or shot up real bad. I notice Blood had his hand on his hip as he was putting slugs into whoever that was. The Y.G. had some style with what he was doing.

He came running back and jumped into the car. "Okay, blood, take off! Let's go get drunk!" he said with excitement.

"Blood, was that a crab?" I asked.

"Yeah. Did you see that nasty rag on his face?"

"Nope," I admitted. "Say, blood, did you have your hand on your hip?"

He was happy and laughing with so much excitement. He said, "I walked up on him and when he seen me, his eyes got big. When he seen that cannon come out he knew it was lights out for him. I lit his ass up! The yellow tape will be put up tonight. I didn't kill him, I shot him in the arms and legs. I just want him to live in pain the rest of his life, he might not walk again. That's how we get down, Ru-al."

We are back on the J-Block getting high and drinking like nothing ever happened. Val wasn't lying, these Y.G.'s are brazy. I said, "Blood, take me home. I been out five days and have not had any pussy, so I'm on a serious mission. Get my black ass home, I got a date tomorrow and I'm staying inside until that time come. Y'all can laugh, but I'm getting some pussy before I fuck mines off."

Six days out and it's that time, Tay let me use her car. I did everything, got a room, drinks, and weed were all ready before I picked Wanda up. We are in the Edge Of Town Motel in the hood. We walked in the room, I rolled some joints, and filled our cups with gin and socko. She slowly got undressed and sat on the bed naked, smoking on a joint. I wasted no time taking off my clothes. The drink and weed is starting to hit me, Pecker is standing straight up and he's ready. I jumped into bed and she started laughing at the way I did it. But she stopped laughing immediately when I opened her smooth legs wide, looking at her shaved pussy. It was just the way I like it. I had to eat the pussy first. In prison I thought about eating some pussy from all the fuck books I used to look at. I'm just going to dive in head first. I got my face deep between her silky thighs and she is moaning with a great amount of pleasure. I'm putting major work in on this pussy, licking and sucking and maneuvering my tongue in spots that drive her crazy. Now she's trying to squirm away but I got these big arms wrapped tightly around her legs and she can't get loose. Finally I felt her quiver and climax. I stood up and she automatically grabbed my dick and gently slid it into her hot, eager mouth. When her lips touched my throbbing head, after never having a girl touch me there before it very sensitive, within a minute I exploded down her throat. She savored all my creamy cum and continued to suck me while I stayed rock-hard. Then she turned and got on all fours and I hit that pussy hard from behind. Looking at her cheeks shake back and forth as I rammed in and out of her, I grabbed two hands full of her big, firm ass. We busted our nuts again, and I keep fucking her, I'm making up for lost time. We got a good sweat going, this pussy is gripping and massaging my dick. I busted another powerful, explosive nut. Now it was time to lay back and light a smoke.

"That was good," I finally said, breaking the calm silence. "And the best part about it is, we are just getting started."

"Boy, that was the best sex I ever had. I hope it's not the last."

We smoked on another joint, got another drink, then turned on the TV. I paid ten extra dollars for some sex video. While watching the porno we went at it again and again. We went all through the night. We can sleep later on, but, for now, I want to fuck her all night, and so did she. We took a shower together and got our fuck on again.

It was time to go so we went to McDonald's to eat breakfast. Then I pulled up in her driveway, walked her in her house and we said our goodbyes. Teasa is sitting on the back porch watching.

I went to talk to my favorite Aunt Janice, I see Tay and she is smiling at me. I said, "Relative, I rocked her world."

Aunt Janice started laughing. Tay took me home and I went to sleep, I was exhausted.

So many things are happening so fast for me it feel like I'm on a moped in the fast lane of a freeway and I don't want to get ran over, or come up missing in action. Since I've been out all I hear is helicopters, police sirens, and gunshots. That's just too much to handle for me right now. After me being in a very controlled and restrictive environment for three and a half years to now be in all this wild shit is too crazy for me.

I'll call Kathleen to see if I can stay with her for a while to get out of this chaos. She stay in a small hicktown in Riverside called Parris. Mama understood me when I told her my reasons. I talked to my p.o. who gave me the okay to go and he gave me the address to my new p.o. office. I'm leaving this coming Monday so I made my rounds to let everyone know and said my goodbyes. I did some shopping and now I'm ready to go.

Wayne, who stood six foot three and weighed two hundred and fifty pound, is going to take me, he's a cool big brother. I got a few joints for us to smoke on the way. When he arrived he said, "Albert, are you ready? Put your stuff in the car." I put my bags in the back and off we go, I'm on my way to Kat's house.

We pulled into her driveway and I look around. There was no streetlights or sidewalks, the roads were all dirt. She live in this small trailer.

We walked in and hugged her and my two nieces, Tee and Cristal. I greeted her husband Prentes. They only have two bedrooms so I got to sleep on the couch or the floor, which either one is cool with me.

Wayne took me next door to meet the Timmons who are the people that own this land that her trailer sets on. Come to find out, they are kin to Jean.

I walked back to Kat's house to put all my stuff up. We sat and talked about old times. Kat was a bad girl who always took some crazy chances. If she was to gang-bang she would claim Mona Park Crips, that was her hangout growing up. But she never got into the gang life.

It's nine o'clock and Wayne came to say goodbye. "Thanks for the ride," I told him graciously.

"No problem. And if you need anything, give me a call, okay?"

"Alright," I said, then watched him drive away.

While sitting in the living room talking to Kat this heavyset girl walked in. She said, "Hi, Albert, I'm Rochael. You just came from my father house, I was in the bathroom when you came over. So I hear you're staying with Kat. Do you smoke weed? I got some in my trailer in the back. We can't smoke up here, my dad would get upset, so let's go to the back."

"Yeah, I smoke weed," I told her. "First, let me tell Kat I'm leaving, she's in her room."

Walking to Rochael trailer it's pitch black, I had to hold her hand so she can lead me through the dark.

She got a nice looking trailer. When we walked in she reached under her bed and came out with a brown box. Inside it had a bag of weed and some joints already rolled up. She hands me one, I lit it, and it tasted pretty good. She turned on some music and said, "I'll be right back."

I'm starting to feel the weed.

She came back to the room wearing a green see-thru nightgown, I can see her big-ass tits and her hairy muff. I'm like, "Damn, what's up with this?" Whatever it was my dick is getting hard. I'm fresh out and I only had sex one time two days ago.

She laid on the bed and said, "Take your clothes off." She didn't have to ask twice. I hit the joint once more and by the time I let out the smoke, I was butt-necked.

My dick is standing tall so I straddled right over her giant tits. She grabbed my meat at the base and started sucking it like a pro. In thirty seconds I busted a nut, filling her mouth. She's a spitter, but she made me cum six times from just giving me head. She was good. I climbed down. This is a big country girl but I'm going to handle her properly. She opened up her legs and I see all that hair. I put Pecker in and gave her a good fucking. I cummed three more times in thirty minutes. She said, "Damn, Albert, you cummed nine times already. I never seen a man cum so many times nonstop. Damn, it was good."

"Yeah, I see all them oysters and vitamins I was taken has my ass real potent and ready to go. I was gone for three and a half years so I'm overdue."

She smiled at me, she was happy and satisfied. We got dressed and left to go back to Kat's house. "Rochael, don't forget I got to see my parole officer in the morning," I reminded her.

"Okay, Albert. I'll be ready to take you," she said.

I got a good night sleep, took me a hot shower, and was surprised to see Kat up. "What's up, sis?"

"Nothing much. Do you want some breakfast?"

"Yeah. Do you have any oyster?"

"Yeah, I got one can left," she answered, thinking it was an odd question for me to ask. "What are you going to do with them?"

"Make an oyster omelet, something I said I was going to do when I got out."

As I'm cooking, Tee come in the kitchen and said, "Uncle Albert, what is you cooking?"

"Uncle Albert's oyster ala king. You want to taste some?"

"Yes," she said, then took a small bite from the folk I offered her. Her eyes lit up with excitement. "Mmmm, it taste good, uncle." She turned to see Kat staring at her, so she said, "Mama, you should taste it."

"Nah, I'm cool."

Rochael came in smiling with some bounce in her step. She said, "Albert, are you ready to go see you p.o.? After that we can go hit the town and see if we can find you a girl."

"Yeah, let's go." I was curious to check out the town and meet new people.

When I walked outside it had to be at least one hundred and twenty-five degrees, and it's mid-July. Don't know how long I can put up with this sweltering heat.

I seen my p.o., he seem to be cool, I only have to report to him once a month, so that was all right with me.

We went to this complex named The Jarvis Apartments. I was like, "Damn, they got a J-Block out here too." I'm wearing some burgundy pants, a white slingshot T-shirt, and white tie-up Vans.

As we're walking across the grass people started coming outside. Rochael seem to know everyone, she's waving and saying hi to them. I see some dudes wearing all blue, this is a crab hood.

We go inside this lady house, she didn't look too hot to me. She got three kids running around the house all wild, throwing shit everywhere. I gave Rochael a look that said, "Let's get the fuck out of here." So we left.

"You didn't like her?" Rochael asked, wondering what's wrong.

"Hell, nah! You seen all them bad-ass kids, hell nah. That was a turnoff for me."

As we walked back to the car I see more crabs had came outside and a lot of girls who was looking at me. I see some nice looking girls, but I'm not going to get at them because I would have to come in here to see her and I know these crabs is not going for that.

I'm in the living room watching TV with my two nieces when someone knocked on the door. Kat is in the backyard so I see who it was. When I open the door there stood a fine-ass girl. "Hi. How can I help you? I'm Kat's brother, Albert."

"Hi, I'm Judy. Is Kat home?" she asked, mesmerizing me with every word she spoke.

Kat came walking in, and said, "Judy, you met my brother?"

"Yeah, we met."

At this point I don't know what they are talking about because I was looking at how beautiful she is. She stood five foot six with cocoa-brown skin, a very pretty face, and some full, luscious lips that I wanted to kiss. And she got a killer body going on. I'm not hearing a thing, she got me all stuck with her fine ass. I got to have her, I hope she don't have a boyfriend.

Her and Kat finished whatever they were talking about and said their goodbyes. When she walked out the house I was right behind her. She looked at me and smiled warmly. I asked, "Can I talk to you for a minute?"

"Yeah, you can talk."

"First, let me say that I mean no disrespect, but do you have a boyfriend?"

Her face was radiant and her eyes twinkled bright. "No, I don't," she replied. "But I do have a five-year-old son name Vance who is the only man in my life right now."

"Can I walk you to your house, if that's okay with you?"

"Sure, why not."

As we are walking I was staring at her ass and she caught

me looking. "What is you looking at?" she asked, but she knew.

I didn't say anything, I just smiled sheepishly at her, knowing she busted me. She seem to like the attention I'm giving her.

When we walked into her yard it's a bunch of people sitting under this big tree watching TV and drinking Budweiser. Judy introduce me to her family. "Those are my brothers Rob, Charles, Melvin, and David. This is my baby sister Lola, and my mom, Mrs. Johnson. Everybody, this is Kat's brother Albert. He is living with her now."

I said hi to everyone and they warmly greeted me back.

Three kids come running out the house, Judy, said, "The short one is my son Vance. The boy is Alon and the girl is Nona, they're Melvin's kids."

I chilled for two hours and her family is cool. Her dad is at work, he's a trashman like my Pops.

When it was time to go I made my rounds saying goodbye to everyone, and Judy walked me to the front of her yard. I said, "Judy, could you put some ponytails in my hair tomorrow?"

"Yeah, I can do that for you," she was eager to accept.

I'm walking down the dirt road thinking that I got to have her as my girl, she got that Plain Jane look about herself that I am really attracted to.

Roe came over and I told her that I found the girl I want. She asked, "Who is she?"

Kat spoke before I could say anything, "He like Judy."

"That's cool, Judy is a good girl. Y'all will make a

nice couple," Roe said with some sincerity.

I couldn't wait to see Judy the next day. I walked over to her house and went in, "Are you ready to hook me up?" I got my own rubber bands and comb."

"Sit right here," she said and she quickly began.

I sat between her shapely legs and my mind started to drift. I liked that she was done in thirty minutes. We went outside to talk. She's telling me how her son father got killed and that she has not been with a man in eighteen months. She talked about her church, which is down the street. While looking at her talk she got these lips that made her words sound so sexy, I wanted to kiss them. I told her about myself, I spoke of my gang life, and that seem to turn her on. I let her know what she was getting into if we got together. We are two opposite people and that made me want her even more. She is too perfect. She don't smoke, drink or get high. She went to church three times a week. I never met a girl like this before and I can see myself falling in love with her.

Coming from the store with Kat I see Wayne's car in her driveway. I walked in the house and see him and Roe hugged up on the couch watching TV. I said, "Hey, big bro. What you doing here?"

"I come to kick it with my girl."

I went to the kitchen and asked Kat, "Wayne and Roe is going together?"

"Yeah, they been together for two years now."

I'm thinking, "Damn, I fucked my brother girlfriend. I don't know why Roe didn't tell me. I can't tell him and mess up his thing with her, plus he's a big dude and I don't want to fight my brother. So he been hitting Roe and he got a wife at home. Damn.

I gave Roe a nod to meet me in the kitchen. When she came in I said, "Why you didn't tell me that you're my brother's girl? If I had knew that I wouldn't had sex with you, that's not cool."

"I didn't tell you because I wanted to fuck you before any of these bitches did, and it was good too. So are you gonna tell Wayne because I'm not."

I spoke in a low voice, "Don't you tell Judy because I really like her and I don't want it to end before it even get started."

Roe leaned over to whisper in my ear, "This will be our little secret, squirt."

I looked at her and said, "Okay." I don't like this but I want Judy and I don't want my big brother mad at me. And why did she call me squirt?

Me and Kat are the only ones in the house, sitting on the couch, I asked, "Sis, what is the history of the Timmons and the Johnsones?"

"They don't get along. Back in the days Roe and Judy had a fight and Judy won. Things has never been cool with their families. Oh, they speak to each other, but they got deep hate for each other over the fight. They even go to the same church."

"Good looking out, sis," I said. Now I really can't tell Judy that I fucked her enemy or she wouldn't give me the time or day. I hate I got to start this relationship holding this secret. And Roe likes that she got this on Judy. I got to keep this under my hat because I want Judy bad.

I can't find no job and my p.o. has not helped me. I've been doing some work around the house with Mr. Timmons in his junkyard, but I need to make some money. I called Wayne to come get me so I can kick it at home over the weekend.

I hung out at home, went to see Val and a few other people. What I really came home for is to get some rocks to take back with me and get my slang on out there in Parris. I got three hundred dollars worth, I'm thinking I should bring my gun that Gil gave me, but then I thought I better not.

Wayne took me back to Kat's. It felt crazy riding in the same car with him knowing that I fuck his girl. I know if he knew, he wouldn't drive me nowhere. I was happy to see and spend time with Mama. I told her about Judy and she was happy for me.

I'm selling rocks and got some money in my pockets. Judy's brother Melvin smokes rocks and he has been helping me. I sold all I had and I won't be going back home for two weeks. Kat's friend Gwen is having a house party tonight and asked me if I wanted to go. I told her yeah. Kat said, "You better get ready because we are leaving in thirty minutes. Call Judy to see if she want to come." I called Judy but she didn't want to go, but she told me to have a good time.

We get to Gwen house and she got her backyard hooked up and the music is playing. Kat is introducing me to a lot of her friends. Just like the rest, Mead Valley is a hicktown that has no streetlights, but that was cool. I found my dance partner, Gwen's youngest daughter Keyma, and this girl can dance. I danced with her all night and nothing else. I didn't want word getting back to Judy that I was all over another girl.

The song "Wild Wild West" came on and the party came alive, everybody is dancing and having fun. The energy and excitement reminded me of one of Val's parties. I said, "Gwen, this was a good party. Let me know when you have another one, okay?"

"Okay, Albert, I will. We will be having more."

I had Wayne take me home one more time and I brought back some more rocks. It went on for one week. But then Mr. Timmons told Kat that people has been walking through her backyard going to her house at all hours of the night, so Kat said, "Albert, I heard that you have been selling dope out my house. I already called and told Mama. And Wayne is coming to get you in two days, so don't sell anything else out my house."

"Okay," I said, "I'll get my stuff ready."

I was disappointed. I walked down to Judy's house and said, "Baby, I got kicked out of Kat's house and my brother is coming to pick me up in two days." We been together two months but we have not yet had any sex. It's been times when I could have laid her on the ground and did her, but I want to make love to her in a real way.

She got tears in her eyes. Her heart is breaking slowly. She said, "Albert, when are you coming back?"

"Real soon, baby," I told her knowing it was a lie. But I said that so I don't lose her love. When I looked in her eyes I could tell that she is not going anywhere, she'll wait for me. We hugged and kissed and spent the last two days together, building a strong bond. Then it was time to go.

Wayne parked in the driveway, I took my bags out his car and put them in me and Paul's room. I walked outside and looked around, then said to myself, "I'm back in the hood, I have re-touched down."

I called G-Man to tell him that I was back home at Mom's house. He came down and said, "Yeah, Moms told me that Kat kicked your ass out her place."

"Kat was tripping, blood. Let's go on the J-Block, I need to make some money."

We get there and it's a lot of homies there who are happy to see me. I got in line to get my turn. I made some good money.

I went home and asked Mama if I could use her car. She said yeah. I went to Wanda's house to get some pussy, I had called to let her know that I was coming over. I pulled up in her driveway and see Tay and Joe sitting on the porch. I said, "What's up, relative?"

"Not much. I heard about you getting kicked out of Kat's house. What! You come to get some from Wanda?" Tay asked.

"Yeah, I got put out," tired of hearing that the whole hood already knew about it. "And yeah, I come to sex up Wanda."

I walked inside and Wanda was wearing a nightgown. Her daughter Nyea is occupied watching something on TV. "What's up? What have you been up to?" I asked.

"Well, I'm two months pregnant and it's yours." She saw the expression on my face change. "I heard you come home two other times but you left before I could tell you. So Mr. Jones, you're going to be a daddy."

I looked at her not quite sure what to say, but I could tell she was dead serious. "For real? I'm going to have a baby? Wanda, that's cool," I reassured her, but I really didn't want to tell her what I was about to say next. "I got something to tell you that I know you're not going to like. I'm in love with this girl name Judy. She live by my sister house and we been together for two months now, I'm sorry." I see the hurt and dejected look on her face. "But I'm going to take care of my baby." Her eyes remained sad.

"Wow, Albert, I wasn't expecting to hear that," she finally said with a lot of effort. "But I got to respect that we only had a one-night stand. All I ask of you is be here for your baby."

"I will, Wanda. I'm at my Mama house so if you need me,

call, okay? Now I got to go, I want to tell everybody that I got a baby on the way."

I walked over to Aunt Janice and when I went inside they all started saying, "Hey, Daddy Albert!" laughing and cheering. Tay said, "Damn, boy, one shot and you got her pregnant."

I get back home, walked in, and told them I got a baby on the way. Yvonne said, "I told you that she was no good. How do we know it's yours?" she asked, with frustration.

"Girl, leave that boy alone, we will see when the child is born," Mama said, trying to keep the conversation tranquil.

Back on the J-Block I see this 1976 silver caddy with a black fathom and a sunroof. It has a For Sale sign on the side window. I said, "Blood, who car is this?"

Ant said, "It's mines, why? You want to buy it? If so, I want fifteen hundred dollars for it."

"I want to buy it, blood, give me five days to make the money."

"Okay, Ru-al, I'll take the sign out the window. You got five days to get it because I know you just touched down."

I'm selling day and night, John Boy is showing me love on his half-ounces. I'm getting up at six o'clock in the morning, me and Avrey Dog did this for five days straight. On the fifth day I gave Ant the money and he gave me the pink slip.

I pulled up in the front yard where Mama is watering her flowers. She looked up in surprise, then said, "Albert, where did you get that car from?"

"Cutting grass," is all I managed to say. I know she don't believe that, but I can't say I'm selling dope.

I got the hood up on the car looking at the motor to see how much work needed to be done. Freddy Lay walked up and said, "Ru-al, you need some work done on this engine."

"Okay, do what you got to do. If you need any parts come on the J-Block and I'll give you the money for it." Two days of engine work and Freddy got her purring like a cat. Now I can take her to the paint shop, then get some new tires. I called Robin to take me and she said okay, she's on her way.

I told Mama that I was getting my car painted and she said, "Don't get that car painted red."

"I'm not, Mama."

Robin came, we went to the paint shop, I gave the painter nine hundred dollars, and he told me to come pick it up in four days.

I got dropped off on the J-Block to get my curb server on. I got to make some money for the tires and, once that's done, I'll get more so I can get me some new sounds and tint for the windows.

Four days later I called Robin to take me to get my car. When we get there I see the car, I'm in love. The burgundy paint with silver flakes and black pinstripes got this thing looking different and better than when blood had it. Robin followed me to Good Year Tire Store and they put on some new rubber on the Cadillac A-wires. I drove her off the lot and

TOUCHED DOWN

Robin followed me.

We went to my house first. Mama is in the front yard, she looked up and said, "Boy, didn't I tell you not to paint that car red?"

"Mama, it's not red, it's burgundy."

"It look nice, Albert," she admitted.

I bought the sound system and the new tint, and put them in the trunk so homeboy Avrey can hook them up in the morning. When I pulled up everybody was like, "Damn, Ru-al, you hooked that car up proper!"

I'm on the 91 Freeway on my way to Judy's. I got a fresh Jeri curl done in Swan Hood, Mr. Akins hooked me up. I got on fresh gear, the sunroof is open, and I'm smoking on this fat-ass joint. I can't wait to see Kat's face when I drive up. I've been gone for three weeks and I got a new caddy and a pocket full of money.

I pulled up in her driveway with the sounds bumping loud. I can see Kat looking out her window. I had drove in real slow so I don't kick up dirt on my fresh paint. Everybody came running out the house. I went in my pocket to pull out my big wad of money and gave my nieces twenty dollars each. Kat said, "Where is mines? And who car did you steal?"

"This is my car and here is a hundred dollars for kicking me out. Because if you didn't put me out I wouldn't have this."

Roe came out the house and said, "Nice car, squirt. And you look good too." I found out why she called me squirt was because of all the times I busted a nut inside her. I stayed for a few minutes then I left.

I drove to Judy's and everybody is sitting under the tree. When they noticed me the kids came running to the car. I got out and Vance gave me a hug, this was our first little bonding moment. He said, "Albert, I like this car, is it yours?"

"Yeah, it's mines. Where is your mama?"

Rob answered, "She's in the house cleaning up. Albert, you only been gone for three weeks and you got this car."

"Yeah, man, I had to get a car so I can see my Judy."

I go inside and see her, she look so good in that gown, I said, "When will you be done because I got to talk to you."

"I'm almost done, I got to shower too. Is that your car out there?" she asked while glancing out the window.

"Yeah, that's my ride," I let her know. I sure missed them soft lips of hers. I can't wait to kiss her again.

I went outside and asked Rob and Charles if they wanted to smoke some weed. They both said yeah, they know I always have the bomb-ass stuff.

Charles is a Mead Valley Crip, but he's not out there banging hard. I seen a lot of crabs at their store where they hang out, but I'm not going to trip on them, this spot is where I can get away from the crazy shit in Compton.

Judy came out the house and she look so good. Her mama gave me the okay to spend a night, I'll be sleeping in David's room. We get in the car and I look at her in the eyes, then I said, "Baby, I got some news to tell you and I hope it don't mess up our relationship. When I got out of prison I had sex with this girl name Wanda. When I went home this last time she called and told me that she was having my baby. I was happy to hear that but I did tell her that I was in love with you and I can't be with her. That hurt her because she thought I would be with her because she's having my baby. Like I said, we had sex before I came out here. So what do you think or feel about that?"

I can see in her eyes that she is a bit hurt by this news. In a soft voice she finally said, "Well, Albert, you did that before we met, there's nothing I can do or say, it's done. I want to be with you and I trust that was the last time you have sex with her."

"Yeah," is all I could say, happy to still have a chance.

She leaned over the center console and gave me a long, passionate kiss. I was happy she chose to stay with me. Then she said, "I hear that Roe is having a baby too, and it might be your brother's."

"Oh, yeah," is all I said again, knowing that I fucked Roe and that baby could be mines too. I'm not going to say shit because I know Judy would leave me for sure if she found out.

Judy got on this sun dress and some white sandals, she is looking beautiful. I want to sex her up right now, but I got to wait until tonight.

"Okay, everyone," I said, "let's go to the store." The kids got in the back and we took off down the street.

We get to the store and it's about six crabs hanging out in the front. They are looking at my car and when I stepped out, all eyes are on me. I got on brown Khakis, a brown tank top, a red belt, some red tie-up Vans, and footies with the red ball on the back on them. I got my .380 pistol in my pocket just in case one of these crabs act stupid.

Judy said hi to some of them who know her and the others just looked at me like "What the fuck is you doing here?" Being with her and that she know some of them meant everything was cool.

We get back home without any troubles and everyone is happy. I can't wait for tonight.

On our way to a motel I don't know where I'm going, I want to find one where there are lots of lights. I see one that looked okay. I paid thirty dollars for the night for a room upstairs.

We get to the door and I said, "Hold up, baby." I pulled out my gun and stuck the key in the door then turned the knob real slow. I pushed the door open with my shoulder and pointed my gun in every direction.

Judy started laughing out loud and said, "Man, what the hell was that?"

"I always wanted to do like the Miami Vice dudes, ha-ha!"

We ate dinner at home and, since she don't get high, I

started making myself a drink and rolled up two joints. I put everything on the table while Judy took a look around the room. She got undressed and slid under the covers. I got necked and finished my drink and joint. Standing in front of her Pecker is up and ready for action. I'm going to be real gentle, I'm going to make love to her like never before, no rough riding tonight.

I slowly pulled back the covers exposing her naked intimate parts. She got a shape and body that is out of this world. Her breasts are firm and her nipples are hard. She's looking at me looking over her body. I left the light on and got into the bed. I kissed her from her head to her pretty soft feet. We made love all night long and she is very satisfied. Me too. We took a short nap. When we woke up we took a soothing shower together while making love beneath the steamy water. I said, "Damn, baby, that was the best love making I ever had. I love you, Judy."

"Yeah, you wasn't bad either, ha-ha!" she laughed jokingly.

We got dressed and now I'm looking around for the door key. Judy said, "Did you take it out the door last night?" She walked over and pulled on the knob, and there it was, still in the keyhole. Damn, somebody could have came in here and killed the both of us. The gun laid closer to the door than the bed. Judy gave me a disapproving look and said, "Boy, you was trippin'. Miami Vice my ass." We both laughed.

We ate breakfast at McDonald's then went home. When we

walked in the door Mrs. Johnson went off on us. I knew Judy never been to a motel before, and we never told her moms or anybody that we was staying overnight. Moms is talking loud, I feel so bad. After the verbal grilling she asked us if we want to eat breakfast. We both said no. We walked in her room then started laughing. I was wondering why her moms tripped out like that. Judy is twenty-nine years old and I'm twenty-five, we both grown adults. I said, "Baby, we got to get our own place. Since you got a son it should be easy for you to get on Section Eight."

"Okay," she replied, "I'll try to sign up in the morning."

Judy took me to her church for the first time, the United Church of the Living God. We walked in and everybody is looking at us. Here I am with two long braids in my beard and muscles everywhere, I'm very nervous.

Judy introduced me to the couple approaching us. "Albert, this is our pastor Bishop Reynolds and Mother Reynolds."

"Hi," I said politely and shook their hands. I can see the bishop didn't like me having their Judy. She been going to this church all her life and now this thug has her. She is the sunday school teacher and an usher, so I got me a good girl. I soon became a member of the church.

Months has passed and Judy got our first place around the corner from her mother, a one-bedroom nice little house. Vance had been staying at Judy's mom's so we got the house to ourself most of the time and we are having fun. She got a job at Starcrest Factory. They wouldn't hire me so I have been going home for weeks at a time to make my money. Since Judy don't know how to drive her Pops has been taking her to work while I'm gone.

Kicking it on the J-Block, everybody is out today. G-Man said, "Two days ago some crabs rode through and shot up dumb Darryl car, he was right there on 130th and the J-Block. They got out and tried to kill him with a AK-47. They shot about twenty times and not one bullet hit blood."

"Damn! He got very lucky," I told him.

Luna-Tick spoke, "Ru-al, the crabs has changed their tactics. They started wearing their hair like Kid In Play, and wearing cross color clothes looking like dancers or a rapper. They have been putting in work on B-Dog hoods with their new look."

Sike said, "Blood, them crabs that shot at my brother, all of them had mauie heads. They are not wearing khakis and Chuck Taylors anymore, and Bloods are getting caught slipping and we got to stop them."

I'm listening to these Y.G.'s talk and they are serious. I beat up crabs but never shot one. But the way they are talking I will because they know what's on these streets, I got my strap unlocked and loaded.

Frog passed me the joint and said, "Homie, all them mauie heads is gonna get lit up banging or not, they don't get no pass ever again. If you see them you better dump on them because they are going to dump on you. We seen how they rolled up on dumb Darryl looking like they ain't banging."

I have been taking K-Dae to school to Compton College driving through crab hoods. I dropped her off and got all the windows down, it's a crisp morning. I like cool mornings like this, it keeps me awake and I got the sounds bumping loud while smoking a joint. There aren't too many cars on the roads this morning.

Rolling down Santa Fe I get to a stoplight and this bucket pulled up next to me. It's four dudes inside and I'm sure they are crabs. One said, "What's up, cuzz? This is Compton Crip."

I drove away, turned the music off, and rolled up my windows. I left my sunroof open so I can hear them still wolfing shit, and I notice at the light that two of them got mauie heads. I hear one say, "Fuck you slob, get out of our hood." They giving up their hoods showing gang signs I never seen before. The slob word never made me mad because, at the last Blood picnic I went to, the homie Hot Dog from West Piru had it spelled out on the back of his red sweatshirt: S.L.O.B. was for "Super Loked Out Blood" -- and I liked that definition of that word. But if they said it in my face I'll have to take off of them. However, this is a different situation.

Both cars drove to the next light and they are still talking shit. I pulled my .44 caliber bulldog out of its stash. I remember what the Y.G. said about "Don't give no mauie heads a pass." The light turned green and they are still following me. I stopped and they pulled up next to me. So I put my car in park, stood up on my seat and popped out the sunroof, then I lit they ass up. The first bullet hit the driver in the shoulder and he is now screaming like a bitch. The one in the back seat ducked, but I seen the fear in his eyes as I hit him in his back. One dude jumped out the car and ran, I shot at him but I missed. I shot one more time and the bullet hit their front window towards the passenger. I kept one in the chamber just in case I need it because I didn't bring any extra shells. I know I didn't kill any of them crabs because there was no head shots, but I know they are in some pain that's going to last the rest of their lives.

I sat back down on my seat and slowly drove off like nothing ever happened. I know them mauie heads won't be fucking with nobody else this early in the morning.

When I got back to the other homies I didn't tell no one exactly what I did. But I did say, "Blood, y'all better be on watch. I put in some work this morning, I shot my first crabs and it felt good. I believe if I didn't get them they might had got me. Too bad for them the yellow tape got put up on them."

When K-Dae came home I said, "K-Dae, this morning I got into it with some crabs and I can't take you to school in my car anymore. We got to use Mama car, okay?"

"I don't want to know what you did, but okay," she said.

10 TOEZ DOWN

    I didn't tell no one the details of my encounter because there's so many homeboys in prison because they told what they done, then somebody went back and told on them. So if I'm by myself all I got to say is "Watch out."

    Since I've touched down my life went from the slow lane to the fast lane. I had adjusted to the streets and these streets are more dangerous than I ever thought they would be. Now it's up to me to keep my ass alive because, if I don't, I'll be ten toes up in a casket taking my dirt nap.

    *   *   *

CHAPTER TEN

(My Seed)

I'm in 4300 Blood module waiting to catch the chain to the pen to do a parole violation. For the past two days my stomach has been hurting. It's not one of them cold or flu bug sicknesses, but a pain deep inside my gut. The homie Luke said, "Ru-al, do you have a baby on the way? Because that seem like the same pain I had when my wife was having my first child."

I'm laying in the fetal position on my bunk and said, "Yeah, blood, I got a baby on the way, and she should be born any day now."

I've had no way to check, the phone in the dayroom has been broken for weeks and we haven't been able to go to the roof for exercise time for three days either. It's now been five days since I last had that excruciating stomach pain, so I'm wondering if Wanda had my baby yet.

Today we finally get roof time and I was able to call. Mama confirmed my suspicions, "Congratulations, Albert, you have a baby girl. She was born March 7th, weighing eight pounds and nine ounces, and she's twenty-inches long. Wanda called and told me four days ago. Your daughter's name is Albanisha Shunice Jones. Both are healthy and at home doing well."

"Wow, I'm a daddy," I exclaimed proudly. "Mama, I have been sick in my stomach and it was more than four days ago."

"Well, most men get that pain when they are having a child. Some say the mother is thinking about you and the thoughts and pain carry on to the father, it could be good or bad. But if you still feel sick you might have more on the way. Are you still having pain?"

"Yeah, I was sick last night."

"Well, you got another one on the way. Okay, now get off the damn phone running up my bill," she said jokingly.

"I love you, Mama, goodbye."

When I hung up I told the homies that I got a baby girl named after me. "Blood, your baby is name Ru-al," one homie asked in disbelief.

"Hell no, blood. My name is Albert and her name is Albanisha, close to mines." The homies started laughing at my name.

Back in the cell my stomach is hurting again, this time I'm throwing up. I'm thinking, Who could be having a baby by me? Then it hit me, "Oh shit! Roe is having a baby."

The phones are fixed in the dayroom so I called Judy to let her know the news. "Hey, my love, I got a baby girl."

She said, "I heard that, Kat told me. I'm happy for you, Albert. Rocheal had a baby girl seven days after you had yours. She named her Jewel Parker."

"That's cool for her."

MY SEED

"We have a boy and a girl. Now you got to get a job when you come home and stop running them streets," Judy said sternly.

"You're right, baby, I'm going to look for a job as soon as I get out of here. I got to go now, somebody else want to use the phone. I should be catching the chain any day now, I'll let you know when I get there, okay? I love you."

"I love you too, stupid face, and be careful," she said.

My first week in the pen I got my baby name tattooed on my chest and Judy's name on my wrist, now I got both my girls' names on me. Dude wanted to go over my "Ru-al" tattoo on my knuckles but I told him, "No, I got that done in Job Corps and it's my power fist. When I knockout them crabs I leave 'Ru-al' on that chin."

As soon as I touched down I went to Wanda's to see my baby. I walked in and gave Wanda and her daughter Nyea a hug. Wanda said, "Your baby is sleeping, let me go get her for you." She came back into the living room with this bundle and handed it to me, then said, "Here you go, Daddy, your firstborn child."

I got her in my arms and she is a big baby, now ten months old. She look so beautiful, I kissed her on her lips and she open up her eyes and gave me a smile that made me want to cry. We're looking into each other's eyes, and I said, "Hi, Albanisha, I'm your daddy. How are you doing today?" She gave me another cute smile.

I had to give her a check-up to make sure she got all the

Jones' traits. She got the big forehead, check. The thumbs don't bend backwards, check. The toes, nope, those are your mother's feet. She's looking at me while I'm admiring her. She reached her tiny fingers up to my face and I nibble gently on them. She gave me another radiant smile. I said, "Yeah, this is a Jones' baby."

"Wanda, go get me her bottle," I said, "she look like she need a drink."

"First check and see if she need her diaper changed."

Yeah, she needed changed. As I'm doing it Wanda is hovering over me, watching every move I make. But I know how to change diapers, I did it to Ludis when she was a baby.

It feel so good to hold my child. Then all of a sudden out of nowhere the ground started shaking. Nyea said, "We're having an earthquake!"

I got up and walked to the doorway holding my baby close to my chest. "I got you, baby. Daddy will protect you." The ground stopped trembling and we all relaxed. That felt crazy but everyone is okay and doing fine.

I got her with me for her first weekend and she didn't want to leave her mama and sister. I strapped her into her car seat and we took off, but she's still crying like crazy. I'm telling her "Shhhhh," but she got louder. I said, "Okay, baby, everything is going to be okay." She got tears running down her angelic face. I turned on some music and she stopped crying. "Oh, so you like Naughty By Nature 'O.P.P.,' huh?

MY SEED

Look at you bobbing your little head up and down -- now you're a happy baby." I drove around the corner from her house to show her that I was born right around the corner from her.

Her first birthday is going to be a big one. At Mama house I got Ludis and Nasha to hook up all the decorations and the games for the kids and the grab bags full of candy for when they leave. I got a big Roger Rabbit piñata filled with all kinds of candies and other treats. I picked up Joanna's son Lawrance, Cassandra and her daughter is here, and Jamala got her daughter here also. My Y.G. Froggy got his son here as well, his son is a few days older than Albanisha. K-Dae daughter Mitchshalae is in her walker chasing all the kids, she is having a lot of fun.

It's time to hit the piñata and Albanisha is up first. I put her in front of the giant rabbit, but she started crying hysterically. Wanda said, "Albert, she's really scared of that thing."

I picked her up into my arms then gave her the stick to swing. She hit it twice and seemed okay doing that from the comfort and safety of my arms. There was no real force in her swings so I let the other kids take turns until it busted open. Paul put his son right into the pile of kids scrambling for the sweet treats. Everyone is having a lot of fun.

Now it's time to cut the two cakes that Mama made, and my girl loved this part of her party. Wanda helped her hold the knife while sitting on her lap, she cut herself a big piece, then she ate it all with no problem.

The day came to an end and everything went better than expected. She had the best first birthday ever. "Happy birthday, my child."

I got her for a week now, it's time she meets Judy. It went well, she like Nona and Alon. When it was time to take her to our house she started crying for Nona and Alon. So I let them keep her for the first night. When she came to our home I let her play with the neighbor's daughter Tori. Tori came inside and said, "Albert, Alanisha is saying a cuss word."

I called my daughter into the house and asked, "Baby, did you say a cuss word? Because it's not good to say bad words."

"No, daddy, I didn't say a bad word," she replied with her puppy dog eyes. I sent them back outside to play.

After fifteen minutes they both came back inside. Tori said, "She said that cuss word again."

"No, I didn't. Daddy, she is lying on me. She got mad because I didn't let her play with my toy."

"Okay," I said, "play time is over. Tori, you go home, y'all can play tomorrow, okay? Albanisha, you go in the bedroom and I'll be in there in a minute."

"Look at you getting your daddy on. So what are you going to do?" she inquired.

"I'm going to spank that ass."

I walked in the room and closed the door. She's laying on the bed looking the same way I did when I got into trouble.

MY SEED

I got my not-so-happy daddy look. I said, "Now, baby, tell me, did you say that cuss word that Tori said you said?"

"No, daddy, I didn't say any bad words."

"Okay, baby, I believe you, but it's not good to say cuss words. You take a nap and I'll wake you up for dinner later."

I walked out and Judy is standing there grinning at me. "I didn't hear any crying or butt getting hit," she said. "I knew you couldn't do it. Al, that girl got you wrapped around her little finger. She's going to run circles around you when she get older."

"I put her to sleep. Yeah, she showed me them puppy dog eyes and I gave in. Hey, that's my baby, I can't be the bad guy," I told her while grinning back to her.

I enjoyed my seed but I couldn't stay out of prison or off them streets. I got my priorities all fucked up. I have a beautiful baby and she loves her daddy, I just can't shake these bad habits. Not finding a job when I looked for one really made things hard on my ego and masculinity. And not being patient, that's one thing I didn't have. But I'm not making any excuse. I'm the father, you're my seed. I got to stay out these prisons so I can watch you blossom into a beautiful flower. Know this, Daddy loves you very much, my seed.

*   *   *

CHAPTER ELEVEN

(Ru-al Girls)

Over this period in my life I'm in and out of prisons, and every time I got out I would meet a new girl. I got some fine-looking girls; pretty ones and down ones, and I'm fucking them all. Most people would call them hood rats. Me and my Y.G.'s gave them a new name: Eba heads. I like them all, they had their own special way with me, but not one could come close to Judy. They all tried to get me away from her but Judy just had too much class. But I couldn't just be with one girl. At one time I had six girls at the same time. All the homegirls gave me the nickname "Shredded Wheat." I would tell them how I would fuck them girls, and I knew it turned them on, but they couldn't get none from me. This is the story of Ru-al girls.

I met Robin at the dairy. I had been back from Job Corps almost two months and I was turned on by her sexy smile. When she got out of her car I seen that she is a big girl with ass for days, I had to have her. She's five-eight, weighed one hundred and forty pounds, and was wearing these tight jeans that fit her really good. She live on the Weakside and I wonder why I never seen her before. I got her phone number and called her the next day -- she said it was cool for me to come over. When I walked over to her house I met her brother,

Ru-al Girls

sister, and mother. She got this poodle name Packer, she loved that dog. I took her to Val's and she liked her. Robin didn't smoke or get high, but we got real close. We had our first sex encounter, I ate her pussy and it drove her crazy. Over the four months we were seeing each other I never fucked her, she never asked me to fuck her. At this time I was fucking Lisa. But there was something about Robin that I always just wanted to eat that pussy. And if she called, I would be right over there. We broke up because of Lisa. But when I got out of prison I would go over to her house just to eat her pussy. I don't know what it was, but that's all I wanted to do, and that's all she wanted done to her. She never sucked my dick, I never asked her to do it. If I did, I'm sure she would have. I didn't ask about her boyfriend, frankly I didn't care. She didn't ask me about my girlfriends either. I just love eating her pussy, and she wanted me to do it, so that was our relationship. We are cool with this arrangement.

Hanging out on the J-Block is where I met most of these girls, and where some homies met their wives.

I'm getting my curb server when this car pulls up with two fine girls inside. The homie Antony B knew the driver and I walked to the passenger side to introduce myself. Her name is Joanna, and I asked her to step out of the car. She did. I liked what I seen. She's very short, about five-five, and weighed hundred and twenty pounds. She got long, brown hair that went down to her ass. She told me that she is Italian and that turned me on because she started talking that language to show me she could. It sounded very sexy. She gave me her phone number and I gave her mines, but I never called.

Two weeks later I'm chillin' up at Val's house when Joanna drove up. We talked and set up a date at her house. She live in Cudahy Huntington Park area in a trailer park. I thought that was cool, now I got a place to go when the hood gets too hot -- as long as she don't live in a crab hood -- which she don't. I called and told her I'm on the way. She asked me to get her some E&J brandy. I was glad that she get high so we both can have some fun.

I found her spot not far, about thirty minutes from the hood. I knocked on the door. She glanced out the window before opening it. She's wearing a pink see-thru gown. I rolled up two joints and she made the drinks. She got a son name Lawrance that she sent to her mom's house so we could have privacy. She got a nice little place, candles are lit everywhere and slow music is playing. I took off my pants and shirt, sitting in my red boxers. We're talking while she is smoking on her joint and drinking on the E&J. I can see she is getting a bit tippsy. She got up and grabbed my hand to lead me to her room. As we are walking I'm looking at her ass, and it's fat. I'm going to fuck the shit out of her.

She got colorful, scented candles going in here too. She took off her gown and laid on the bed. She put her long hair over her titties and that look turned me on more. When I took

Ru-al Girls

off my boxers my dick was hard as a rock. She opened up her legs and I could see her shaved pussy. I got on top of her, her head was raised up resting on a pillow, so she grabbed Pecker and pulled him up to her face. With very small hands she got him at the base and started sucking. While my meat slid in and out of her mouth I was finger-fucking her wet pussy and she is cumming like crazy. She's still sucking me but I really want to fuck her now. I finally got her to let him go, which she was holding gently with her teeth. I already know this pussy is going to be good. She turned over and got on all fours so I could stick the head in her wet, tight pussy. Once I pushed it all the way in she started rocking her hips back and forth, I liked her big, fat ass. It's been a while since she had sex and this pussy is ready. I'm hitting it and talking to her and she's talking back, telling me, "Fuck that pussy, shaboinken." She's slanging her long hair all over the place while I got two hands full of ass banging that pussy. I busted my nut and laid down, with her laying on my chest, and she's telling me how good it was. I told her it's more where that came from. We fucked the rest of the night and in the morning we took a shower and she cooked a big breakfast.

While we were eating I had to ask her, "What did shaboinken mean?"

"It means big dick in Italian," she said with a smile.

We did a lot of things together for two years. When I

went to prison she sent me packages. Every time I got out she knew that the sex was coming. I never fell in love with her but she was in love with me. It ended because she wanted me for herself but I didn't want that. So we stopped seeing each other, but there's no doubt we had a lot of fun with each other.

Cassandra was tall and slim, light-skinned, five-ten, and weighed about one hundred and fifteen pounds. This girl is just too damn pretty. She came on the J-Block with her sister to see Whoop. I never seen her before and it's about fifteen homeboys hanging out. I had to see if she had a boyfriend, and she didn't. I introduced myself, but she had already heard about me. She told me that she got an older daughter, and she got baby by the homeboy but they are not together anymore. I didn't care anyway, it's the summertime and I'm a cockhound. I'm looking at her ass wearing these tight jeans, a white shirt, and open-toe shoes. Her toenails are painted bright red and that turns me on. She got her hair in French braids, she look more white than black. She gave me her phone number and I gave her mines, the next day I called and went to her house. She stayed on Figueroa in the hood, so that was cool. We set it up to go out later. We got a room for the night at the Edge O Motel, which is still in the hood. I got weed and my drinks, she got her wine coolers.

While sitting at the table talking, she got up and casually undressed, I stared in lust, I never had a slim girl like her before. But this girl got some meat on her body, some long-ass

Ru-al Girls

legs, some mouth-size tits with dime-size areolas, and her nipples are pointed out. I got necked in a rush. When she laid down on the bed I noticed she got her pussy shaved with this diamond-shaped patch of hair right above it. I never seen something like that before, I thought it look very sexy. I'm standing there with Pecker hard and ready to go to work. She open them long legs and spread her pussy lips open. My mouth got watery, I'm going to eat that pussy up. As if I was on a diving board, I dove in headfirst. I'm eating away and she can't stop cumming. This girl got the prettiest pussy I ever seen, and it taste really good too. When I was done I laid on my back and watched her suck my dick. This girl has it all, she's deep-throating all my meat and shaking her head from side to side as if she was trying to scratch her tonsils with the head of my dick. She stopped, walked to the table, put two ice cubes in her mouth, chewed on them, then came back to suck on my dick some more. I'm like, "Oh shit! She is putting in serious work! Damn, this girl is good!" Now the head of my dick is numb from the ice. She got on top and started riding me wildly while digging her fingernails into my chest. This girl is a freak. I'm watching her little tits bounce up and down while I busted a nut, and she's still riding hard. We fucked all night long, she put it on me real proper. We had two years of this kind of fucking. She was in love with me but I wasn't in love with her. When I had got out of the pen she was messing with this baller dude. I wasn't mad because she knew that I had other girls. I had asked her to let me jack his ass, but she said no. She wanted me for herself and when she seen that wasn't going to happen, we broke up. But before we said our goodbyes she told me she had two abortions. I was hot at her, this Eba head killed two of my babies. I I should have let Jamala beat her ass, but we did have a lot of good sex for two years.

Melisa, now this girl is fine, half-black and half-Mexican, she got a smooth brown complexion and silky black hair that went to the middle of her back. At five-seven and one hundred and fifty pounds, she's thick and carried it all in the right places.

As always, on the J-Block, Froggy brought her over with his Eba head and I got at her first being the cockhound that I am. We kicked it all day on the block. She told me that she lived in Carson, in a crab hood, and she got a one-month-old child. I know I won't be going to her house, ever. Too many homeboys got caught slippin' at a girl's house in crab hood. Nobody got it bad as G-Baby at his girl house, some B-Dogs lit his ass up and smoked some crabs that was hanging out. He got lucky and lived.

Melisa called me after two days and wanted to hook up. I was cool with that. I asked her if she wanted to go to a picnic and she said yeah.

Earlier in the day I ran into the homie H.B. (Hard Blood) from Miller Gangster, he told me about 62 Brim Hood is throwing their yearly picnic, all kinds of Blood Hoods is going to be there. I told him, "Hell, yeah!" because I try to go to all the hood parties and picnics.

H.B. is driving his '76 Brougham caddy, it's burgundy with a black top just like mines. I told him to meet me at Mom's house, but none of the other homies wanted to go.

Melisa drove up, she's happy to be going to this picnic. She got on red short pants, red tennis shoes, and a white top. This girl is looking good. I got on a red tank top, black khakis, a red belt with three belt buckles with the letters "A.P.B.", and I got on some red slip-on Vans. I got my red flag hanging out my right back pocket, and my ponytails hooked up with red rubber bands. We are flamed up and ready to go.

We get to Harvard Park and it's B-Dogs everywhere, everybody got on some kind of red. I got my girl, H.B. got his girl, and we are meeting so many Bloods, a lot of homies I met in the Blood modules. H.B. is doing what he do best, saying Blood like no one else, "What's up blooooooood?" When we hear that we know that it's him.

Melisa is having fun, she don't smoke weed but she is drinking on her wine cooler. The homies is looking at her, I know I got a bad Eba head with me.

We are all having a good time when I hear somebody say, "Where is my gun?" I get over there and it's two Y.G.'s from the hood about to fight the Y.G.'s from 135 Piru. The homie had loan them some straps and they never gave them back. Me and H.B. calmed everything down and the homeboys from the fives said that they would give the straps back when we get home.

Right after that incident everyone started to leave. The ghetto bird is hovering over the park and announcing on their loudspeaker for us to disperse and leave the area. I got my gat in my pocket and I didn't want to get caught with it. I told H.B. that I was leaving, but he stayed behind. I get to the house and Melisa told me she had a good time despite the copter breaking us up. We hooked up a date for a room tomorrow.

I got the room at the Edge O Motel, the drinks and weed were already set up. While we are getting undressed I had been thinking about hitting that pussy all day. She laid back on the bed and I'm looking at her big-ass titties. I got this thing where I like to look at naked women laying down before I get into bed with them. I'm standing over her necked body, my dick is hard and ready to go to work. I look at her shaved pussy and then at her shapely, contoured hips. But when I looked down at her feet they are busted up, she got corns on every toe and the bottom of her feet got this crust on them. Pecker instantly went limp. I'm so turned off there's no way I'm gonna be able to get Pecker up to perform the way I want to. How can a girl who look so damn fine not take care of her feet? I'm very disappointed, and repulsed. Now I'm thinking of a way I can get out of this.

Suddenly my beeper goes off -- thank God! -- it's 611, a

customer that will spend over two hundred dollars a call. I really want to make this money since I'm not able to get Pecker hard. I told her the call was my mama and she really needed to see me as soon as possible. We got dressed and left. I had the room for only three hours, that's enough time to bust three nuts and get on. I told her that we would have to do this another day. After she left I went to call back that customer and made that money.

I really wanted to kick it with Melisa, this girl is fine, but her feet just turned me off. We hung out for two more weeks, off and on. She wanted to get a room but I always found some reason not to, then Jamala ran her off. This girl never had a fight in her life and Jamala was all that. Melisa was a good piece of eye candy with her fine ass, as long as you didn't look at her feet. I know she was hurt because she wanted me to hit that pussy but nothing ever worked out. We did a lot of kissing, fondling; she felt up on Pecker and wanted him, but never got him.

I've been out the pen for three weeks. After my second joke I'm at Mama house to make some money. I needed to get my caddy washed before I go to the J-Block, so I went across the street to Leo house to get his brother Fellow. I'm going to give him a twenty-dollar rock to wash my car. Last year the homie from Denver Lanes got shot up while washing his car in his front yard. Fellow came over and I'm sitting on the porch, with my gun at the ready, to make sure if someone come through

I'll be prepared to bust back.

This car pulled up in front of Leo house, his sister Rosebud and this red bone I never seen before got out. I walked over and said, "What's up, Rosebud?"

She responded, "Hey, Albert, this is Jamala, she live on Cook Street. Jamala, this is Albert." We both said hi to each other.

I'm looking at this true red bone, she got on this multicolored sun dress, no bra, some white sandals, and she got her toes painted pink. She got her hair hooked up and she got this sexy-ass smile, I'm liking what I'm seeing. I asked them what's up for the day, they both said nothing much, just hanging out at home. I said, "Rosebud, you know I'm fresh out and I want to find something to get into. Say Jamala, why I never seen you before?" I asked her.

"I've been living in the jungles. That's where my baby daddy stay at and, before you ask, no, I'm not with him," she answered.

"So, can we kick it later on tonight?"

"Yeah, we can do that."

I went back home and Fellow is done with my car. I paid him then I went to the J-Block.

Jamala live at Gary Mae House where blood hookup low-riders and he's her uncle. She came out the house and got in the car. To my surprise she gave me a kiss, quite unexpected. We drove to the Liquorama to get some drinks. I parked the car on the hill of the J-Block and opened the sunroof, it's a warm night. I let her roll up the weed. We kicked back and got to know each other. I told her about Judy and she was cool with that. I let her know I would be coming down just about every weekend. We are really liking our vibe with each other. I'm not going to tell her about the other four girls I got on the side because I want to hit this pussy. But I had to leave, I said, "I'll see you next weekend, okay?"

"I can't wait," she replied in her sexy voice. She leaned into the car and gave me a deep, passionate kiss.

The days went by very fast and I have been thinking about her all week long. But I made sure Judy was always happy before I left.

I picked Jamala up at her house and we went to the store to buy some sodas; it's too damn hot to drink liquor. We got a room at the Satellite Motel on Fig. and 120th that G-Man told me about, it's still in the hood. When we got in the room the first thing I did was turned on the air conditioner, but it didn't work. Jamala walked in the bathroom while I'm rolling up the weed. A minute later she came out necked. I looked at her and said, "Damn, girl, you look good and I see you're ready." She smiled then sat down and lit a joint. I didn't wait to hit the weed, I got necked too, because I'm going to sex her ass up. After smoking the weed she got on the bed. I'm standing over her looking at her beautiful body. She's a big girl and her body is tight. Her pussy was not shaved but the hair she did have is very thin, I can see her pussy lips beneath it. She opened up her legs and I went in, putting in work. I ate her pussy and she just went crazy, this girl is a screamer. After she got off a few times she grabbed Pecker and started sucking him. It felt good, she can get down. She got this look in her eyes that is telling me she's very happy to have him in her mouth.

I wanted to fuck her now. I put Pecker in and this pussy is wet and tight. I got both of her legs pushed up to her chest and I'm slamming away. I looked at her and see that she is loving it. I busted my nut and kept going, Pecker is loving this pussy. We both got a good sweat going. After my third nut we took a break.

She's sitting in the middle of the bed and said, "Albert, that was too damn good. Man, you got me hooked now."

"We got the room for six hours and you just got a taste of what I'm about to do to you."

She gave me that sexy smile and lit another joint. I can see she is up for another round. I know she never made love like this before. These dudes is just fucking, they don't know how to get a girl sprung, but I do and it's working on her and my other Eba heads. Plus I got this new dick and I'm trying to make up for lost time. We got our fuck on the whole six hours with only a few breaks. It was time to go and Jamala asked, "When am I going to see you gain? Because I got to have this again."

Ru-al Girls

"I'll be down on weekends and we can kick it then."

Months has passed and I've been coming to the hood every weekend. I'm fucking Cassandra, Joanna, Jamala, and eating Robin's pussy, then I'm going home to make love to Judy. For months I'm fucking two girls in the same day. I would get three nuts off in one girl and spend the rest of the night with another one. I'm putting in work. I see why the homegirls is calling me "Shredded Wheat" -- I'm the only one fucking them and they are not thinking about no one else but me, I'm the only one in their lives.

Judy knew I was up to no good and told me, "Don't bring home no other babies or S.T.D.'s."

"I'm not doing anything out there," I told her, lying through my teeth. If Judy had told me to leave all my Eba heads to save our relationship, I would. But since she never said anything, I kept on doing it with them.

For two and a half years I had been having fun with these girls. It was only sex with them, but they all had fallen in love with me. I had got strong feeling for Jamala, I let my emotional guard down with her. Judy is the only one that had my heart though. But there was something about Jamala that opened a piece of my heart to her.

Jamala came to visit me in county jail. I was already being visited by Cassandra when I seen Jamala turned the corner and knew she would act a fool. And she did. She got into this big argument in the visiting room and I know that

Cassandra is a girlie girl who never had a fight. But Jamala, on the other hand, is a fighter and that's what I loved about her, she is down for hers. So Cassandra ended up going home and then she started messing with this baller dude. Jamala had ran off Melisa who she didn't put up a fight, which I didn't care because she had turned me off sexually. Joanna had left because she wanted me to live only with her and I couldn't do that, so we broke up. Now it's just me and Judy and Jamala, but Jamala know not to fuck with my Judy because she would fight her ass back.

Jamala was down for whatever. She sold dope and made her own money. She did get pregnant but lost our baby, that really hurt the both of us.

I went back to the pen, to Corcoran prison, for some dope on her street. Once off the level four yard she found a way to call my dorm. The homies was clowning me, she got the number off her phone bill and every day at three o'clock the phone would ring. This went on for two months until the guards had the ringer cut off. When I got out Jamala asked me if she can have a dude since I got Judy. So I said yeah, but when I come to Mama house we were to be together and she was cool with that.

One day I called Jamala and told her that I'm at Mama house. She said, "Okay, Albert, I'll be over later on."

I went on the J-Block and the night had passed, but no Jamala. I called the next day, she said the same thing, that she would be here. She couldn't leave last night so I didn't trip.

It's Sunday night and I got to go back home because Judy got to be at work in the morning. I know this dude that Jamala is with stay in crab hood but he don't bang. All he do is work and give the money to Jamala and she spend it on us, so I wasn't tripping on her hustle. But I still don't know why she ain't coming to see me. I'm so hot I can kill something. I go in K-Dae room and said, "Let me use your gun, I left mines at home." I had gave her a .380 pistol a few months ago. She went under her mattress and handed it to me. She didn't ask me what I needed it for.

I got in Mama car and drove down the 110 Freeway. I parked two houses from his, got out the car, and walked to the door. I saw some crabs hanging out down the street but me being in Mama blue car they didn't trip on me. I took the safety off the gun and knocked on the door three times. Someone on the other side said, "Who is it?"

I cleared my throat and said, "It's Don, cuzz." I don't know if it's dude or someone else so I had to say a name I wouldn't forget. The door open and it's this tall dark-skinned man who said, "How can I help you, son?"

"Is Everrett home?" I asked.

"Yeah, let me go get him. Come in so I can close the door," he told me politely.

I looked around and see this other guy watching football

in the den. I watched the dark-skinned guy walk down the hallway and turn into a room. He came back and said, "He will be out in a moment."

My heart is beating so fast and my hands are sweaty. The man went back into the den and sit down, I can hear the announcer on ESPN say that Miami is playing the Jets.

I went straight to the room the man had just came from. I kicked open the door with gun in hand, and there was Jamala sitting there with her baby in a chair. Her eyes got so big they could have popped out of their sockets. She yelled, "Albert! What is you doing here?"

I see dude look at me with fear in his eyes. He made a move for the closet but I said, "Blood, stop right there or I'm going to smoke you."

He stopped in his tracks and looked at Jamala. She said, "Okay, Albert, I'm coming out. Put the gun up."

Dude is looking scared to death, he never seen me before. I grabbed Jamala by her arm and walked out the room back the way I came in. She got her baby by the hand and the baby said, "Hi, Albert. You come to get me and Mama?"

I looked at her and gave her a little smile, I couldn't say anything to her because I'm in a zone. She never seen me like this. But I got to handle this because, if the wrong person make the wrong movement, it's going to get real ugly in here. I'll smoke everybody in here except the baby, who I'll take home to her grandmama.

Ru-al Girls

Now dude's Pops and his friend come running out the den, they heard all the noise and screaming that Jamala is doing. Pops said, "Man, what the fuck is you doing with that gun in my house? And why did you kick in my door? Everrett, what's going on here?"

"I don't mean no disrespect to you or your home, I just want my bitch and I'll be gone," I let him know.

Pops said, "Man, you didn't have to come in my house like this."

"Man, it's a love thang and all I want is my bitch."

He's looking at me with kill in his eyes, but I'm the one with the gun. His friend reached for the phone but I pointed my gat up to his face and said, "Come on, man, put the phone down, I don't want to shoot you."

He cradled the receiver and stepped back. I can see it in his face that he want to beat my ass, but he knew I wasn't joking about blasting him. Everrett then said, "Man, you can have her. Just get out of my house."

I'm still holding Jamala by her arm, she is not getting away. We walked outside, I'm so fucking mad I tightened my grip around her arm so forcibly I know it will leave an ugly bruise mark soon. As she's writhing in pain I got the gun gripped firmly in my hand, and she said, "Albert, I'm sorry."

"Oh, it's too late for all that. You knew to have your ass at Mama house and when I called, you lied. So get your ass in the car and drive us home."

10 TOEZ DOWN

She's driving on the freeway, I'm so pissed off I screamed like a madman in her face the car jumped into the other lane. "You bet not wreck Mama car," I warned her. "You brought this shit on yourself."

Now the baby is crying, Jamala is crying, and I'm yelling like a mad man. I told her to go to the park so we can talk. She stopped a block from the park on this dark street. I said, "I should blow your fuckin' head off. If you had did what you supposed to do, none of this shit would have happen. But you want to play games. You know if you was having any problems with dude I would have come got you, like the last time you was having problems with him. But you know I come down on the weekend to be with you."

"I know, Albert, and I'm sorry. I love you and I hope you can forgive me. It won't happen again," she pleaded. She gave me a kiss and I kissed her back. Her baby had fallen asleep in the back seat, I guess this was too much for her.

We get back to Mama house. As soon as we walked in the door, she said, "I just got off the phone with your mama, Jamala, and she told me what happen. Albert, you're wrong for going in that man house like that."

"Give me my gun," K-Dae wasted no time saying. "If I had known you was going to do something crazy like that I wouldn't have let you used it."

I handed her the gun and she took it back to her room, Jamala and the baby went with her. They are real close and I know Jamala is telling her everything that happen. When they came out I said, "Come on, Jamala, let's go. I know your mama got some word for us. Plus I got to take Judy to work in the morning. Mama, I'm going to use your car, I'll bring it back in the morning."

"You better bring it back in the morning," Mama said.

We went to Zell Pops house first. I know that G-Man is over there. We pulled up in front of the house and Jamala mama pulled up behind us. The first words she said were, "Put my grandbaby in my car!" She sounded very angry. "And what is your problem, Albert, going in that man house like that? People could have got killed with you over there acting like a damn fool. I told you Jamala about being with this thug, he is no good. You get your ass to the house, I want to talk to the both of y'all when I get there."

When I walked in the house G-Man is sacking up some weed and watching football. He looked at me and knew something was wrong. He said, "What happen now, Ru-al? I can see it all over your face that you done something."

"I kicked in Jamala dude's door and I pulled a gun on everybody in the house until I got Jamala out. Blood, you know I only come down to be with her over the weekend, but she was playing a game with me. So I went and got her."

"Where is Jamala now?"

"Oh, she's outside talking to her mama, she'll be in soon." I grabbed the bottle of gin and socko that was setting on the table and took a big swig.

G-Man said, "Blood, you're brazy. You and her are made for each other."

Jamala walked in and G-Man saw that she was crying. He looked at me and shook his head.

"I'm about to take her home," I said. "Her mama got some words for me. So I'm going to keep the bottle, and give me a bag of this weed."

He gave the weed and told me to take the bottle, then said, "You take care of yourself, Ru-al. If you need me you got the number."

We get to her mama house, which is thirty minutes from Mama house and thirty minutes closer to my house. Her moms has not arrived yet. We're drinking the gin and socko then we stepped outside to smoke the weed. We went to the patio where I asked her, "Jamala, why you didn't tell me the first day that I called that dude was making you stay in the house? You remember the last time that happen I sent Bay-Bay, Queenie and Tonya to go get your crazy ass. So what makes you think I wouldn't come get you? You know I love you and all I asked is that you give me them three days."

"I know you would had came and got me, but he really wanted me to stay home with him. Now I don't know where he stand after you kicked his door in. Man, that shit was crazy. I love you, Albert, and I'm sorry for not letting you know what was up. It won't happen again."

Ru-al Girls

By the time we walked inside her mama had put Antonisha to bed and she came in the living room and sat across from us. She said, "Albert, I don't know what made you do what you did but I'm very disappointed in you and Jamala the way y'all did that man house. He called and told me what happen so I called your mama. Albert, I think you and Jamala need to stay away from each other for a while. If you're spending the night, you're not staying in the same room. That's all I have to say." She got up and disappeared into the kitchen.

Me and Jamala smiled because we went straight to her room and got our fuck on. This make-up sex was very intense, we made love and fucked hard all through the night.

I got up early to take Judy to work. I took a shower and changed my clothes. I picked up Jamala on my way back to the hood. The word had spread on what I did, the homie Kal-Koat even heard about it way in the jungles. Everybody is telling me how crazy I was for doing that. Kal-Koat said, "Both of y'all are brazy."

"Homie, you know I had to get my bitch out that dude house. Koat, you know I don't play when it comes down to Jamala. Say, have you seen my boy Fat-Rat?" I asked.

"No, I have not seen blood in a few days. Ru-al, you and Jamala is sprung and tripping."

I had fun with all these Eba heads. Each one had their own special way with me. I just couldn't help myself. I'm fresh out and I had a lot of catching up to do, and I couldn't get it from just one woman. I was looking for that one dream girl. If I could take parts off each girl she still wouldn't measure up to Judy, she just have too much class, and I was in love with her. No matter how these girls tried to get me to leave her, I wouldn't. Judy put up with my crazy ass because she is in love with me and she see there is some good in me if I could only leave these streets alone. But that was something I just couldn't do.

If I had to put together my dream girl from parts of these other girls she would have Robin's tits, smile and one hundred forty pound body; Melisa's silky black hair; Joanna's sexy voice and the length of her hair; Cassandra's pussy and the way she fuck; Jamala's pretty feet, legs, face, her brown eyes, skin complexion, how down she is, the way she walk, the love making and fucking she do. She almost had everything I wanted in one girl. And the way I was doing my thing with all them Eba heads for me to fall in love with her, I think she beat me at my own game. Because I had all them girls to myself and they didn't want no other man. I was their everything, or was it me fresh out and they had to have me like I had to have them? No matter what, I had fun. I couldn't find that dream girl so I'll go home to my perfect girl. And why she keep putting up with my crazy ass I will never know. But I know this, she love her some stupid face, and she will always be my Judy. As for all my Eba heads, thanks for the ride. And y'all will always be labeled as "Ru-al Girls."

*   *   *

CHAPTER TWELVE

(The Drive-by)

It has been a very hot summer here in Mead Valley, the Fourth of July is a day away. This will be my first Fourth of July on the streets since the mid-eighties, all the other ones has been in prison. I have been out four months and doing well. I can't find no job but I'm doing the house-husband thang and Judy is cool with that, and I like it too. I get the weekends in the hood and she get me for the five days during the week. I'm so excited about this whole weekend, I'll spend the Fourth with Judy's family and the rest of the weekend in Compton at Mama's. It's a four-day holiday so it's going to be people out and about everywhere.

K-Dae had called earlier this week saying that she was coming over, that's cool because Judy's family is having a BBQ and Judy want to see her baby Mitchshalae (Lil China). I'm looking forward to their visit tomorrow.

I woke up at seven o'clock and Judy is already out the bed. I thought she would still be sleep after last night's love making, I did put it on her real good. I smell some food and it smells good. I turned the shower and radio on. The man on the radio said, "It's going to be one hundred and ten degrees in the shade today."

I get out the shower. My clothes are laid out on the

bed; my red short-pants outfit and my red tie-up Vans. Judy hooked up my ponytails last night. After I got dressed I walked into the kitchen.

Judy is standing over the stove in her robe. I walked up behind her and said, "What is you doing up first after I put it on you like I did, girl? I had you calling out my name." As I walked away I gave her a playful slap on her butt.

"Hey, stupid face. As for last night, you know I put it on you, so don't go there, Mr. Jones. I need a smoke break." She took a few minutes then set the table for us.

Breakfast was good. I lit a Camel and rolled up five joints to smoke at the BBQ. While Judy is in the shower I did some cleaning. I washed the caddy yesterday, I'm glad I got that out the way before this scorching hot day today.

I'm smoking on this Endoe joint, damn it taste good. I said, "Judy, you know we got to go to the store to get some beer and food for the BBQ. K-Dae won't get here until one, she know that we will be at your mama house."

"Wow, it's hard to believe that her baby is fourteen-months old already. Time is flying by so fast," she said in awe.

Judy came out the bedroom looking good, this girl got a banging body. She got on this red, white and black sun dress, and she's wearing some white sandals that show off her pretty little feet. She got her hair in a bob style. If we wasn't about to leave I'd sex her up right this minute. One thing I like about her style, she's old school; no perm, no makeup, she

The Drive-by

would put a hot comb on her hair and roll it up and still look fine as hell. I'm looking at her with lust in my eyes when she glanced over her shoulder and said, "Boy, what is you looking at? You're not getting none, so put your eyes back into your head. Ha-ha-ha! Now, is you ready to go?"

"Yeah, let's go, baby," I said, dashing my hopes of some early morning sex.

We pulled up in front of the house and all the kids came running to the car. I gave them the bags to take inside. I see Rob at the grill, he's the cook and he can get down. Just about everybody is sitting under the big tree drinking beer. I said my hellos to everyone. Judy's Pops is inside, he don't drink, he is a pastor at their church. The music is playing, kids is running everywhere, this is going to be a nice Fourth of July.

Rob said, "Albert, you want to smoke a joint?"

"Yeah, let's go to the backyard."

He pulled out his joint and lit it. When I hit it, it is some Plain Jane stuff. I said, "Put that up. I got some bomb-ass weed, we call this E.T. and it will have you trippin'."

"What's E.T., Albert?" he asked with curiosity.

"It's Endoe weed mixed up with some Thai bud. So let's get high, put some fire on that fatty." Rob hit the joint and started coughing, he's coughing so hard he got tears coming out his eyes. He passed it to Charles who started coughing too. After we smoked the joint we walked back to the front and Rob went back to the grill.

I'm chillin' under the tree talking to Mrs. Johnson, she's cool with me now. We got off to a rocky start but now I call her my mother-in-law. I'm high as fuck, the weed just hit me. I looked at Rob and he looked back at me, he shook his head. I know he's high as a kite.

I'm feeling good now, I said, "Is y'all ready to get your butt whipped in some spades? Because the Jones' gang is here to kick some ass."

Mrs. Johnson spoke. "The Jones' gang, oh, no you didn't. Judy is still a Johnson and yes, me and Nona is ready. Did you bring that damn spade trophy with you? Because it's staying at the Johnson's house after today."

"Judy, are you ready to kick some Johnson botty?" I asked her. "Because I am."

She looked at me and said, "Stupid face, why do you always start a war with Mama?"

"You just be ready because today is our day, like all the other days we played. So let them see the trophy because we know who it's going home with."

"It's three Johnsons at the table, you can't win," Nona said. "Now shut up and deal the cards."

I fixed us a glass of gin and socko and got Mrs. Johnson a Budweiser to go with her drink. I don't like to drink in the daytime but this is a different story, I got to talk some trash. I said, "Mrs. Johnson, we need seven books and y'all

The Drive-by

need six, let's get them off the table so we can beat up on Alon and Lola." I'm talking big-time shit and Mrs. Johnson is talking it back to me. I can tell that the drinks had hit her and I'm feeling it too. I'm dealing the cards, this is the last deal. I only shuffle them once and Nona had cut them. If I done it right we should get all the right cards.

I dealt them out on the table. When I looked at my hand I knew Judy had her half. I said, "What's your bid, mother-in-law? Because this game is over with. Judy, you just sit there, look pretty, and let me do all the shit-talking."

"We're going board," Nona offered without any resistance.

"Judy, have you ever been to Manhattan? If not, put on your prettiest dress because we're going in style. The Joneses are going to send the Johnsons out in the blaze of glory. We're going to Manhattan."

"Albert, what's a Manhattan?" Nona wanted to know.

"We are going to get all thirteen books and y'all gets none, Nona girl."

Judy is sitting there just shaking her head as I win each hand that is played. I keep talking big-time shit too.

"Boy, you better shut your mouth, ha-ha!" Mrs. Johnson said, but laughed less and less the more hands I scooped up.

We ended up winning the last two games and the Jones' house get to keep the spade trophy.

After two hours of playing cards K-Dae pulled up. I walked to her car and grabbed Lil China out of her car seat.

10 TOEZ DOWN

She is happy to see her Uncle Albert, she started pinching my nose. I see K-Dae haven't cut her fingernails yet because she already scratched me. I introduce them to everyone and they all said hi. We sat down and talked.

Rob said that the food is done. I must say he can get his cook on. Judy's sister Betty made her famous potato salad. I filled up my plate with hot links, chicken, ribs, greens and had a tall glass of grape soda to wash it all down with.

It's getting dark so I went to my trunk to get the fireworks I bought from the hood. I wished I could had Albanisha with me but she is with her mama family. I let the kids do the fireworks and they is having a good time watching the colorful flashes, exploding burst of brilliant lights, and whistling spinner that disappeared into the darkness. I'm hugged up with Judy enjoying watching them leap around and frolic with excitement.

It's time for K-Dae to leave. I told her to tell Jamala that I would be there in the morning. K-Dae said her goodbyes.

I'm still chillin' with the family and Judy's brother Melven came up to me and said, "Albert, you got that ready for me?" I had told him that I would give him something earlier. I didn't want to give it to him while everybody was enjoying the day. When he gets high on this shit he gets his tweak on. I gave him a twenty-dollar rock and he went off to do his thang.

Me, Rob, and Charles went to the backyard to smoke my last two joints. I'm really high now and I want to be with my

248

The Drive-by

Judy. I see her over there talking to Betty. Damn, she look good. Judy caught me looking at her and she smiled. I did a head nod for her to come over to me, and she did. I said, "It's eleven o'clock. Are you ready to go home? Because I am, and I want to sex you up."

"Shut up with your horny ass and let's say our goodbyes," she said in her playful manner.

We get home and Judy went right to the shower. I turned on the TV to watch some ESPN. I'm chillin' on the couch and Judy come out the bathroom wearing her sexy pajamas. I got my shower out the way then we went to bed. I said, "Baby, we had a good day. The food was good, we beat the Johnsones in spades and K-Dae came down with Lil China, and we done some nice fireworks. I liked today."

"Yeah, we had a very fun day. So what time is you going to leave in the morning? Because I want to go over to Mama's."

"Whatever time you want to be there, I'll take you."

When we make love, I love me some Judy. She like to play while making love. She's just the perfect girl for me. But I just got to have more.

I dropped Judy off at her mama house. I see Mr. Johnson working on his truck. He's a very quiet man, that's where Judy gets her values. I opened the sunroof, turned up my music, and hit the 91 Freeway to the hood.

When I get to the house K-Dae and Paul was gone. I said "Hey" to Mama and went to the backyard to dig up my dope. I need to make some money. I called Jamala to let her know that I'll be on the J-Block.

When we met up there I said, "What did you do last night? I had a good time."

"I took Antonisha to the jungles to be with her daddy Boo and they watched the fireworks. I chilled with my sister Dundiva. K-Dae told us she went out to your house. I'm happy to hear you had a good Fourth."

The weekend went by so fast, now it's time to go back home. I took Jamala to the jungles, we got our sex on and made up for lost time. I must say this was a good weekend, but all good things must come to an end.

Yesterday I had asked K-Dae to let me use her car for two weeks so I can look for a job. With her car being small I can save on gas and she is going to keep my car to use. I'm about to leave when G-Man rode up with about ten other people. He said, "Ru-al, the smoker got a gas card and we are going to fill up. If you need some gas, you better come on."

"Okay. Paul, go get Mama keys and K-Dae your car need gas too." We jumped in line with all the other cars. The gas station is in crab hood so I got my gun in my stash. I took it out once we got there just in case. I always got to be ready. Once everybody got their gas we rode back to the hood.

I parked the caddy in the driveway and K-Dae parked in front because I'm about to leave once she get all her stuff out the trunk. I got on some brown khakis, a red belt, white

The Drive-by

Chuck Taylors, and a white T-shirt. K-Dae is setting her things on the curb, and I got all my things out of my car, except my pistol. I'll wait until I'm about to go because I don't want the one-time to roll up and catch me with it then I go to jail. I grabbed Lil China out her car seat and gave her a kiss, then put her over the fence to run to where Paul was sitting on the porch.

As I'm taking the baby seat out I hear some music bumping real loud. I look up and see this car, but didn't think nothing about it, it's just someone enjoying the summer. Two seconds later -- POP! POP! POP! POP! I felt a sting in my shoulder then everything went black.

Some days later I woke up in the hospital. I open my eyes but I don't see anybody. I hear some familiar voices though. I look to the side and see my homegirls Rosebud, Tonya, and Queenie. I got this banging-ass headache too. I said, "What the fuck happen?"

Rosebud responded, "You got shot and you been in a coma for three days."

I notice a cast on my arm and I got a bandage wrapped around my head too.

Tayna had called the doctor. "Doctor! Doctor! Albert is awake." He came in the room and told everyone to leave.

"How do you feel, Mr. Jones?" he asked with careful observation. "You're a very luck man. I don't see many people live through what happened to you. Let me tell you how you survived your potentially fatal injuries. The first shot hit your shoulder. That bullet went in and broke your arm, that's why you have a cast on it. You were also shot in the ear. This is where you got lucky. When you were shot in the shoulder your body turned and the second shot glanced your head and came out the back of your ear, ricocheting off the hard part of your skull. If you had gotten shot anywhere else in your body, other than your shoulder, the bullet that hit your ear would have hit you right in the head instead, and you would be dead. So Mr. Jones, the first shot saved your life from the full impact of the second bullet. When I looked at your brain scan I see some swelling that came from the trauma of you falling to the ground. We knew you would come out of this mild coma, I guessed it would be three to five days, that's why you have that serious headache right now. I will prescribe you some medication that should reduce the swelling and help the headache go away. Do you have any questions?"

"Yeah, when can I go home?"

"Well, if the swelling decreases more overnight you can probably leave tomorrow. As for your shoulder, the bullet went right through the bone and that will heal on its on. I will prescribe some pain meds, and pills to reduce the swelling. But first and foremost, you need to get some rest, okay?"

The doctor left the room and the homegirls came back in. Rosebud said, "I called your mama and Yvonne is on her way up here."

The Drive-by

"Cool, because I want to go home. We got caught slippin' when that car came from the J-Block direction. They must had seen too many homeboys, them cowards did a drive-by. They is not getting away with this."

Tonya said, "We got to go, Yvonne is here. We took some pictures while you was in your coma. We'll be waiting on you to come home, Ru-al."

Yvonne come walking in, she got a half-smile on her face. I gave her one in return. She gently kissed me on the cheek and said, "How are you feeling? We thought you was going to die, but the next day the doctor told us you would come out of your coma."

"Yeah, I got real lucky I didn't get killed. I got this crazy headache and my shoulder is hurting bad, but I want to go home."

"The doctor told me to come back tomorrow night at six, he will know if all the swelling went down enough for you to leave. I can't stay because he want you to get some rest. I'll see you tomorrow, okay?"

"Okay, Yvonne."

After she left I started wondering how did I not see them bangers and why I didn't have my gun in hand? I hope everyone else is okay. No one told me if anyone else got hurt. This reminds me of high school, not having our gun when we know that it should be in my pocket. But this is not high school and them crabs is going to pay. I'm sure the homies is out there putting in work. I wonder how's Paul, K-Dae, and Lil China doing? They must be okay since no one said otherwise.

The doctor wheeled me out early this morning to do more brain scans. Afterwards, while laying in bed, waiting for the doctor to tell me I can go home, I hear a knock on the door. It opened and my mouth dropped open too. It was Joanna. "Hey, stranger," I said in disbelief. "It's been a while since I last seen you. What brings you my way?"

"Hey to you," she answered back. "I called your mama to see how she been doing and she told me what happen, so I had to come see my ex-man. So how are you feeling?"

"I'm blessed to be alive. I got a bad headache and, as you can see, I got this cast on. Other than that I'm cool."

We kicked it for two hours then she had to leave. "Thank you, Joanna, for coming to see me."

"I had to come check in on shaboiken. You give me a call when you get home, okay." She walked out the door. Her visit really lifted up my spirits and put a smile on my pained face.

The doctor finally returned. "Well, Mr. Jones, I see your latest brain scan looks pretty good, so you can go home today. I had your sister called to come get you. I'm going to put you on this medicine that will keep the swelling down, and something for your pain and headaches. Do not drive while taking this medication because it will make you drowsy. I don't want to see you back in here after a car wreck. You will have some problems hearing out of that ear, but it should

The Drive-by

get better in time. I was able to extract some of the bullet fragments but there are some still close to your eardrum. I will refer you with a consult to the ENT specialist and they will work on getting the rest out. That's about it. If you have any problems come back and we will fix you up. You should recover just fine. Mr. Jones, you need to count your blessings and thank God because you should be dead, but you're not. Before you leave pick up your medications. I made an appointment to see you in ten days, okay?"

"Thank you, doctor. I do feel grateful to be alive."

Yvonne walked in, I was happy to see her. "Are you ready to go home?" she asked, although she already knew the answer.

"Hell yeah! I'm hungry as a dog." I took a second to look around the room then asked, "Yvonne, what hospital is this?"

"Damn, Albert, no one told you where you're at? This is U.C.L.A. Harbor General. You don't know what happened, do you?"

"Yeah, I was about to go home, we just gassed up, I put Mitchshalae over the fence, and the next thing I knew bullets rang out. Then I woke up in here three days later."

"So nobody told you what happened to Paul, Katie, and her baby?"

"No," I said, feeling dread creeping into my soul from what I'm about to hear.

Yvonne pushed me out the hospital in a wheelchair. The

sun has a weird hue but it feels good to breathe the fresh air. I looked around and everybody is looking up at the sky holding pieces of x-ray film or some kind of black paper. This odd activity distracted me from my previous thoughts and questions. I asked a lady standing nearby, "What is everybody looking at?"

She told me, "It's a solar eclipse. See look." She handed me her piece of x-ray film and I looked to the sky through it. True enough, it is a solar eclipse. It looked crazy because everything around me began to turn hazy and dark as the seconds ticked by. I'm very amazed by this gift that God has given us to see. This is my first time ever experiencing a solar eclipse. Yvonne had been looking up at it too. I'll never forget this date: July 7, 1991.

Once we got in the car I asked, "How is the rest of the family? Because I know I heard more than just three shots."

Yvonne paused at first, making sure she was ready to explain the details of that bloody day. Then she said, "Katie said this car drove by and started shooting. You were hit first. Then Paul got shot trying to get Mitchshalae out the way. But she got shot in the face and died. Katie got shot too. Mama came running outside and seen everybody laid out on the ground and she had a massive heart attack."

"Damn, everybody got shot. Was mines the worst?" I asked, comlpetely shocked by the news, not realizing what I had already been told.

"No, Albert. Mitchshalae was killed. She was shot in

The Drive-by

the face, the bullet went into her brain, and she died in Paul's arms. He couldn't get to her in time to protect her."

Tears are slowly rolling down my face. As I'm looking out the window my heart is breaking into a million jagged pieces. I can't hear nothing, my mind went blank, and I'm just sitting here looking at the black space in front of me. I started feeling this rage building up inside me, something I never felt before. In a whispered, strained voice, I said, "She was only fourteen months old. Why it wasn't me? I know K-Dae is devastated, she lost her only child. I didn't even see the dudes, I didn't bother to look twice and they shot us up. We was seconds away from leaving and then that happened." I grew silent and wiped the tears from my eyes. It didn't help.

"Paul is still in the hospital, he got all kinds of pins in his leg. They got it in some kind of sling because the bullet broke his leg in four different places. They say he got to be there for ten to fifteen days before he can come home. Katie was shot and the bullet went right through her thigh, she came home the same day. They had to keep Mama overnight because her heart wasn't acting right. They all went to Killer King Hospital. But because you got shot in the head you went to U.C.L.A. Harbor. Even Lady the dog was shook up, she was under the car trembling when all that chaos happened. Katie said she wouldn't eat for two days. The whole family is in pain and brokenhearted, Albert."

We both went silent, my mind is racing like crazy. Them

buster-ass cowards did a drive-by and killed a baby and shot up my family. I know there is no rules or referees in this game, and I know things like this happens, but to kill a baby, oh, they are going to pay -- and pay hard. I'm sure the homies already put in some work. Them crabs started that drive-by shit because they are too coward to get out the car and put in some real face-to-face gangsta work. Doing them drive-bys, bullets are just flying everywhere, anybody can get hit, no matter how innocent they might be. They could had got their proper stripes if they would had got out and just smoked me. I'm the one that been letting their homeboys have it. But that's how them cowards are. That's why I got to lay them fools down ten toes up in their caskets as soon as I get on my feet. The yellow tape is going up in all enemies' hoods, that's on blood.

  We pulled up on Carlton and I don't see no one hanging out. We parked in front of the house and the first thing I notice was the piece of yellow tape still tied to the street sign, the wind is blowing it back and forth. I felt bad from what all it represented -- the chaos, the pain, the death, the vengeance -- I had to walk over and take it down. Them crabs had put the yellow tape up on my block. What's going to happen and who's going to die next?

  I see my caddy still in the driveway as I got in the yard. I hear someone say, "Hey, Ru-al." I look across the street and it's G-Baby and Mrs. Timmons standing on the porch.

The Drive-by

I said hi to them then Leo, G-Man, and some other homies came out the house to greet me, it was a very emotional moment, there was lots of hugs and tears. They left because they knew it was a family thang, they understood. The Mexicans that live next door came out to say hi to me too. I'm feeling the hood love. Now it's time to feel that family love.

I walked inside and the first person I see is K-Dae. I went over to hug her tightly. I felt so hurt and I know she was hurting more than I could possibly fathom.

I went to Mama to get one of those hugs that speak louder than words. It felt so good to be in her arms, I feel so protected and I don't want her to let go. I went back to K-Dae and gave her another hug because I know her heart is broken.

Jamala is here too, she gave me a hug and kiss. I can see that she been crying a lot. We went to my bedroom, sat on the bed, then we broke down into tears together. I said, "They made this real personal. I'm going to hurt them and make them suffer as much as I can. I know the Y.G. has been doing their thang, but this is very, very personal for me now."

In came K-Dae. I said, "We got caught slippin' and I was just about to get my gun out the car. When I seen the car I'm thinking that they is just bumping their music and that was it. Then I heard the three shots and that was it for me."

"Yeah, I felt the same way about that car, it's just passing by, then you got shot," K-Dae reflected sadly. "By the time I bent down to get you I was hit in the leg. The bullet went through the trunk and it came inches away from the gas tank. If that bullet had hit that tank it would had blew us all up. When I did get you in my arms I seen all that blood coming from your head and your shoulder, I just knew you was dead because you wouldn't move anymore. But then you started saying the Lord's Prayer, you said the whole thing and after you finished, you stopped talking. I started shaking you but you wouldn't move or say anything more. I thought you had died in my arms.

"Then I looked in the front yard and seen Paul holding Lil China in his arms. I seen blood on her face and Paul is crying, saying 'No! No! No! Not the baby!' That's when Mama came running out the house and seen everyone laid out, she had a heart attack right there on the grass. The ambulance came and took Lil China first, seconds later three more ambulances came. We went to Killer King Hospital and they took you to U.C.L.A. Habor because of the shot to your head. Man, you was out."

The room went silent after K-Dae's account of the incident. We both have the look of deep loss on our faces and tears are filling our eyes. Our dog Lady even gave a little bark as if she wanted to tell her part of the nightmare too. It made us all laugh. She knew that we was hurting and her bark broke the solemn mood, if only temporarily.

"The funeral will be in four days," K-Dae let me know. "Paul is not going to make it because of his leg."

The Drive-by

"Damn, this seem so unreal to me," I said still unable to process everything that happened to everyone that day.

K-Dae and Jamala is sitting across from me, they have been together since this happened. I feel so sad for my baby sista. It look like she has been holding up okay, but I know she have her own way that she will grieve privately. But she is a Jones and we are a very strong breed.

"K-Dae, we are going to be okay," I reassured her. "We have a very special angel in heaven who is looking over us." She gave me that special smile that she do, and I gave her one back. We hugged and she walked back into the living room.

Me and Jamala is still talking, she said, "You know Froggy, Luna-Tick, Clone, Sike and other Y.G.'s from other hoods had been putting in work for what happen. After y'all got shot the hood has been hot, the one-time has been rolling through every ten minutes. Let me see your gunshot wounds because I'm going to be the one to change your bandages and get you well."

Mrs. Ezell, Leo moms, came over to see me. Mrs. Marie, G-Man's moms, also came over with a fruit basket and some much needed hugs. So many homies has been coming over, I got so much weed. I tried to smoke a joint but I couldn't get high because of the medication I was taking. But Jamala was happy that she get to smoke all the weed that I can't. A lot of homeboys is coming to show their love and everyone said that they put in some kind of work for me and my family. I felt all that Blood love. I told them not to trip because this is personal. But I know I can't stop them from doing what I would do for them.

I said, "Jamala, Judy is coming down for two days. I'm gonna need you to give her all the space she need to be with me and do her part, okay?"

"Okay, Albert, I won't start any drama. This is too serious to start any crazy shit. But you know I will be staying in K-Dae room and I'm not leaving her. It's time for you to take your medication."

"Make sure you wake me up at six o'clock so I can eat dinner, okay, baby?"

Wanda brought Albanisha over to see me and I took her to the bedroom to talk, just her and me. "How is you doing?" I began. "Let me tell you what happen to Daddy. This bad guy shot me, Uncle Paul, and Auntie Katie. And your relative Mitchshalae got killed. She is in heaven right now so you have a angel that will always be by your side, okay?"

"Daddy, I'm happy you're not dead. I do believe in angels and I know Lil China is mines. Daddy, do it hurt where you got shot?"

"Yeah, it hurt but I'm going to be okay. Daddy need you to say a prayer for your family every night, okay?"

"I always say a prayer for you Daddy because you run the streets, and I will start saying one for our whole family now." I'm looking at her and see a very smart kid. I know her mama told her that I run the streets. I hugged and kissed her then

The Drive-by

we just laid back on the bed being comforted by our closeness. She fell asleep on my chest. "I love you, my child," I softly whispered in her tiny ear.

Judy came and I was so happy to see her. I gave her a big hug and a deep kiss. When I did that Jamala walked into her room. I can tell she don't like that but she know not to trip on my Judy. Judy is looking good too. She said, "Hey, Albert, how are you feeling? I'm sorry for you and your family's loss. Mama and the rest of the family send their love and say hello."

I'm holding her by her hand when K-Dae and Jamala came out her room, Judy said, "Hi Katie. Me and our family send our love to you and sorry for your loss."

"Thank you, Judy," K-Dae replied.

I introduced Judy to Jamala, they both said hi. Judy don't know that Jamala is my lover and that is the best right now because Jamala is not going anywhere if she can help it.

Mama walked in the living room and Judy said, "Hello, Mrs. Jones. How are you doing today? My mama and family send their utmost love to you and your family. Also our church has your family in their prayers and they send their regards and condolences. My mama is so hurt right now because she just held Mitchshalae some days ago, so she is feeling a part of your loss too."

"I'm feeling better, Judy. And thank you, the family and the church for the kind words. Yes, it has been hard on us but we will make it. Now come over here and give me a hug. Albert told me that you're down here for two days. Thank you for coming," Mama finished.

Me and Judy went into my room to talk. I told her everything that happen that day. She's looking around the room I grew up in. Mama has always said that I got a room in the house and when I come down I sleep here. Judy is changing my bandages and looking at the hole in my arm and my ear. I can see the sadness in her eyes. I'm glad that she is here.

It's a very gloomy day for the funeral. There are going to be a lot of tears today. All the homies and the kids will stay home. This is the second funeral I ever been to. The last one was G-Man's relative, Green, he died of cancer. We knew that he was about to die. When me, Judy, and G-Man went to go see him at the hospital he knew that he was going to die and that was a very sad time for us. His funeral was a gloomy day like it is today, but the sun did come out after it was over. During the ceremony I couldn't control my emotions, I cried like a baby. I also was one of his pallbearers, this is something no one can be prepared for.

The limousines has pulled up in front of the house, everybody is slowly getting into them. Judy is with me. Daddy drove his truck, he has been really shook up by what happen to us. When I got in a limo the first time I was going to my niece funeral. That's no good. Sitting in this car I realized I might have put other people families in the same position

The Drive-by

that I find myself now. But it's my turn to feel the life-long pain and, so far, it's not a good feeling. I'm also thinking once I get well more families will be hurt because I just can't let this go without some get back.

While going to the mortuary we passed Robin's house and she had just walked inside. She knew I got shot. Passing by her house brought back some good memories.

When we get to the mortuary our family sat on one side, I'm in the front row, and the father Mitchell and his family sat on the other side.

As the ceremony commenced me and K-Dae is both crying while looking at Lil China's small casket. It's tearing my heart apart. In a loud, anguished voice I said, "Lord, no! No, Lord! Not Mitchshalae, she's just a babe. Lord, no!"

The pastor stopped his speech to allow me that personal, painful moment. I was very loud and I had a lot of pain and anger wanting to escape from me. When the pastor resumed his eulogy I'm so shook up I can't walk to her casket because I didn't want to say goodbye to her like this. Judy and Daddy walked me outside, then everybody else began coming out to get into the limousines to follow in the procession to the Compton Cemetery to lay Lil China to rest.

I said, "K-Dae, I can't handle this, I need to go home."

"Okay, Albert. Don't worry, she will be fine and she know that you love her. I'll see you when we get back."

Daddy took me and Judy back home but, before we get

there, he stopped at the liquor store so we could get some gin and Miller Draft beers.

We got home and the kids is playing, people is cooking food, I need a drink. I made one then rolled up a fat-ass joint and went to the backyard to get high. The sun did finally come out and the gloomy day was gone, my angel is shining her light down on her grieving uncle.

I called Albanisha to the backyard, she came running to her daddy. I looked into her brown eyes and hugged her tightly and she hugged me back just as vigorously. Judy got her a nice hug too. I told her that her relative is in a better place now.

"She's in heaven, Daddy," she said automatically.

"Yes, she is, baby. Yes, she is. Now go play with your family," I told her lovingly.

Everyone is back from the cemetery with smiles on their previously grieved faces. That was a good sight to see. I walked up to K-Dae and gave her a big hug. She looked at me and smiled. I said, "I'm sorry for my outburst earlier and not going to the cemetery. It was just too hard for me."

"It's okay, I understand. You cried enough for everyone." I thought to myself, just like on TV when black folks act a fool at a funeral, I did just that. But this definitely was not scripted in any way, it was real.

Everybody is getting their eat on and having a good time. This is what Lil China would want her family to do, enjoy life

The Drive-by

and celebrate hers.

The house is packed with people, the streets is full of cars, and the Y.G.'s is on patrol to make sure no crabs come through. There is homies with our hoods carrying two CK-47's, three mack tens, and lots of handguns. The homies made sure everything went will for my family and that was good looking out to protect our special moment together.

The evening is coming to an end and everyone gave hugs. On their way out they straightened up and cleaned up as they left. The homies are last to leave. Mama enjoyed all the homeboys, half of them she didn't know but she knew that they was here for our loss. They said goodbyes and condolences, but I know they will be driving up and down these streets for the next few hours. I told K-Dae and Mama to stay away for a few days because crabs like to come back and do some more damage. They both agreed and in the morning Judy will be going back home because she got to work.

K-Dae packed up some clothes and went to stay with Connie on the Weakside. Connie got her a house over there, that was cool. Mama didn't want to leave so we talked her into staying with Frances right across the street, so she was cool with that.

It's time to say my goodbye to Judy. "Thank you for being here for me and my family. I love you so much. I'll be home once I get my doctor appointments changed to Riverside Hospital in about three weeks, okay, baby?"

"Albert, you be careful out here, I almost lost my stupid face. Don't get yourself into trouble. I know you want to pay somebody back for this but, Albert, it's not going to bring her back, so don't do anything crazy."

"I hear you, sweetheart. I love you and I'll be home soon. I got to call my parole officer in the morning and I hope she don't violate me for this. But I'll let you know what she say. Bye-bye, my Judy."

K-Dae is at Connie house and Mama is across the street. She would come home in the daytime and leave at night. Paul will be getting out the hospital today and he is going to live with his homeboy for three days. It's me and Jamala and some other homies at the house. We got guns everywhere. G-Baby is sitting on his porch with his guns at the ready. On the day of the shooting he had just walked inside his house or it could have been him, or he could have shot back at them crabs. We got this street under tight guard now. For three days nothing happen so K-Dae and Mama came back home, and so did Paul.

This is our first time seeing him. His leg was broken and he still got pins everywhere, they are sticking out the flesh of his leg. We cried with him, he felt sad because he wasn't able to go to the funeral. We talked about that day, how we got caught slippin', I can hear anger building in his voice and see it burning in his eyes. He's not out there banging like I am so I told him that I would be handling all that, all he got to do is get well and go to work. I didn't want

The Drive-by

to see him fuck his off.

I'm laying in the bed with Jamala and hear a knock on the door. "Come in," I said. I was very surprised to see Dr. Gibbs step in. "What's up, blood?" I have not seen you in years. Where have you been, homie?"

"I heard about you and your family getting shot and I had to come see you. First, let me tell you that I'm now Pastor Eric at a church, I'm not Dr. Gibbs anymore. I changed my lifestyle six years ago and I tell you the Lord has been good to me. I come to say a prayer with you, is that okay?"

"Yeah, that would be cool. I need all the prayers I can get." We held hands and he said a nice prayer. Even Jamala prayed with us.

"I see you got shot just about the same place I did," Eric noticed.

"Yeah, I thought of you but the bullet didn't hit the nerves like what happen to you. But I'm truly blessed to be alive."

Eric spoke with his humble voice, "Yes, you are blessed. Well, I'm gonna take off, I just come to see you and your family. Albert, you take care of yourself and always know that God is with you and you are in His loving, protective hands."

"Okay, Eric. Nice seeing you."

I'm sitting on the front porch by myself and ten minutes later Jamala come outside to sit with me. I got my gun next to me and ready to go if I got to use it. I let Lady the dog come outside to use the rest room and get her run on, we been in the house all day. It is nice, clear and warm tonight. Jamala lit a joint and two minutes after that we hear: POP! POP! POP! POP! I said, "Baby, do you hear that somebody is getting off? It sound like it came from the J-Block."

"Yeah, I heard that. I hope it's just someone shooting off some rounds."

But we suddenly hear police sirens and now the ghetto bird has just arrived over the J-Block with their big-ass spotlight searching the darkness. G-Baby come flying around the corner in his car and stopped. I said, "Blood, what happen?"

"Homie, some crabs did a drive-by and killed Mel's brother and shot Silk relative in the neck and he might not live."

Mrs. Timmons, Glen and Junior came outside to make sure that G-Baby is okay. I got my gun in my hand now. Mama came out, but went back in. I sent Lady in with her. In the last three weeks the quietude of our hood has been shattered with these punk-ass drive-bys.

"Let's go see what happen," Jamala said. "I want to check on my family too."

We got in Mama car and drove to Cook Street. They got it all blocked off with yellow tape. When I see yellow tape I know it's bad. Jamala went to her house and learned everyone was safe. We walked down the street and stood in front of Ron G

The Drive-by

house and his niece Tree Tree is standing there. She is one of many homegirls that's a true crab rider. She said, "Blood, them crabs shot them and they don't even bang. They was on their way to the store and them bitch-ass crabs did a drive-by. They passed right by us and shot them. I'm sick and tired of these cowards."

Everyone has come out their house to look. Tree Tree uncle, Tear Rock, said, "Blood, these crabs are doing these drive-bys and hitting the wrong people. That's okay, we will keep laying them down in a gangsta way."

Lee Lee drove up, this is another homegirl that is a crab rider, this girl put in more work than most dudes. Mel live right next door to her so I know she's hot. She said, "These crabs want to kill people that don't bang, they have took banging to a whole new coward level. One thing about B-Dogs, we don't do this shit. This is a buster move and they will pay for this ten toes down."

A month has passed and I still have not got my doctor appointments moved to Riverside. Yvonne has been taking me to see the ENT doctor. They have been successful in removing big pieces of lead from the bullet fragments out of my ear and a lot of congealed blood. My hearing has been coming back too.

Paul still got all them pins in his leg. K-Dae is walking around just fine, and her spirit is up so that's good to see.

Today I got a doctor's appointment for my shoulder and Jamala is driving me there. I got on my big red U.N.L.V. shirt, black khakis and my red Vans. After all that has been happening with us Jamala got the .380 pistol stored secretly in her purse.

We get to the hospital thirty minutes before my appointment. While we're walking down the hall I see this dude who is doing his job sweeping the floor. I'm not thinking twice about him. When we got closer to him, he said, "What's up, cuzz?"

"What's up, blood?" I replied.

He looked directly at me and said, "Cuzz, I should beat your ass with this broom."

I stared back at him and said, "Man, I got a cast on my arm and you want to hit me with a broom? You're a bitch-ass coward, you crab."

When I called him a crab I can see he was mad. He said, "Fuck you, you slob."

I looked at Jamala and said, "Give me the heat. I'm about to smoke this crab right here in this hallway."

Jamala went into her purse to pull it out and handed it to me.

The crab seen that we wasn't joking, his eyes got real big, and he know that he came up on the wrong Blood. He took off running down the hall and I chased after his ass. I'm going to give him a headshot when I catch up to him. He kept running then turned left through this doorway. I ran in through the same door close behind. I'm not going to just shoot at him, I want to get up on him to let him see my face so I can dirt nap

The Drive-by

his crab ass.

Jamala is running close behind me. I can't catch this crab, he know where he's going and I don't. As long as I can keep him in my sight I'm going to keep chasing him. We're passing people and I got this gun in full view. Somehow he ran in this room and disappeared.

I stopped and Jamala strode up beside me. She said, "Albert, give me the gun and let's get the fuck out of here. I'm sure the one-time is looking for us by now. Let's leave this way, we can get to the parking lot from here. I'll just make you another appointment, but we got to get on."

We get out the hospital okay and made it to the car. Today was that crab lucky day because I was going to put the yellow tape up in that hallway. We went to Steven's Burgers in the hood to eat lunch.

That felt good to chase that crab. I'm feeling about 55% okay with my balance, the headaches is not as bad now either. Jamala had made another appointment for me for next week. One thing I love so much about her, she is one down girl that I can trust. This girl got game and she's not skinny scary, that's why I can't let her go. To be so damn fine and good in bed, hell yeah, I'll kick in another door for my red bone. But I got to stay with my soft girlie-girl Judy, I'm in love with her. But there is no way Judy would have done what Jamala just did.

I got up early this morning and went into the kitchen to cook some breakfast, but we are out of sausages and eggs. So

I'll just do some shopping at the dairy first. I called Lady to roll with me, she jumped into the caddy and put her head out the window. I went the long way. I got my gun in the stash. It's 7:10 in the morning and nobody is out. I don't even see any smokers.

I parked in front of the dairy and Lady jumped out and followed close behind me. I said hi to Popa and Mama Sun who was standing behind the counter, they said good morning in return. Lady broke off, running around getting her sniff on. I bought eggs, sausages, milk, bread and a vitamin power pack. I got a small orange juice and took one egg out the carton and busted it in the orange juice and dranked it down right there. This was my thang to keep my strength up after I had sex with my girls so I can last the whole day. I paid for the food then left. Lady followed right behind.

I'm rolling down San Pedro to 130th going through the hood to see if I can catch some early morning customers, I need to make some money. I happen to look in my rearview mirror and notice this burgundy Regal, or Cutlass, driving on the Weakside. I'm thinking that a homie got a new car because I don't recognize it. After so many drive-bys our hood has been hit with we look at every car that roll through. Passing Cook Street I thought about going to Jamala, but I'll let her sleep after last night love making. She need her rest and it's still early.

When I get to the corner of 130th and Jarvis Street I

The Drive-by

stopped to change the tape in stereo. I want to listen to some Ghetto Boys "I Got A Mind Like A Luna Tick." The tape slipped from my fingers and fell on the floor so I reached down to pick it up. When I raised back up I'm staring at this big-ass cannon, it got to be a .44 magnum or a Tramp Five Seven (.357 magnum) pointed right at my head. I can even see the hollow-point bullets in that big-ass barrel. I said, "Aaah, blood," then hit the gas peddle. I heard a big-ass "BOOM!"

I took off towards Dereck's house, my heart is beating real fast. I raised up my head and looked in my rearview mirror, it was that burgundy Regal, they went up towards Val's house. I stopped my car and got my strap out. Lady is huddle down on the floor with panic in her eyes. If they go the way I think, I can meet them on Main Street. They is not going to get away this time.

I punched the caddy to El Segundo and then down to Main Street. Just my luck they went toward San Pedro, so I can't catch them. I'm glad that I had Benzo put in that Posi-track rear end in my caddy so both tires grabbed traction at the same time. If not, that big-ass hole they left in my side panel could had been my head instead.

I'm glad that it's summertime because if it wasn't them crabs would have a had a field day shooting up the homies that was walking to school. Once again they tried to smoke me. If they wasn't such cowards he could had got out his car and done me good, but as always they did another drive-by. When I shot up them crabs at lease I put my car in park and raised out the sunroof. They had me at the same corner that the Y.G. Dumb Derrel got his car shot up at. I guess it's a lucky corner because neither one of us got killed.

I went home and, as soon as I opened the door, Lady ran to the backyard. All this gunplay keeps her shook up and makes her very anxious. I walked in the back and put the food in the kitchen then left. Everybody is still asleep. I looked at the big-ass hole in my car and said, "Damn, that could had been lights out for sure. If they would had done it right, it's bool. Now I'll just go show them how it's done gangsta style."

I took my car back on the J-Block so Bodine can get that big-ass hole closed up because I don't want Mama to see this or hear about what happen. She's been through enough. I still got my cast on my arm and I drove like it wasn't even there. Adrenaline is amazing and useful that way.

I pulled up and the homies is already out there, they heard the shots and knew it was me. Bodine said, "Ru-al, them crabs is trying to kill you. You got some kind of angel looking over you because you should have been dead."

"Yeah, I got an angel looking over me. But them crabs is getting real close. Blood, close up that hole for me." I brought some rocks with me so I can get my curb serve on.

Today the homie Big Evil from Eight Nine Family Swan is throwing a welcome home party for his brother Sinister at

The Drive-by

Magic Johnson Park by Eugima Village Hood. I had told Yvonne and K-Dae about it and they wanted to go. Yvonne never been to a hood party. The last time I been to this park I brought Lil China, Nasha, Tiff, Ludis, Rinsha, Relly, Albanisha, Peanut, Jamala, Antonisha -- all packed in the caddy for the carnival. It brought back some good memories.

It's about two hundred Bloods here. We are getting a lot of love because they knew about the loss to our Lil China and they all said that they put in work for us. We felt their love. Yvonne is taking photos and enjoying the music. Evil is doing this for his brother because he just got out of L.A. county jail, he beat two murder raps. He look different from when I seen him in the Blood module.

The Doo Doo Brown dance contest is about to start and everybody is trying to get the best spot to see these Eba heads. There is five girls about to shake that ass for two-hundred dollars, the crowd is going crazy. The first girl got up to dance, she got a big ass, but her dance wasn't any good, so she got booed off the stage. The others went and did their thang. Now it's time for Evil to make the announcement, he said, "The winner is contestant number three!" Everybody agreed with loud claps, cheers and whistles. She did have the nastiest dance and the biggest booty so she deserved it.

The picnic is going well. Lots of fun until my Y.G. Clone got into it with a homie from the Millers over a gun. They had loaned him a gat and he never gave it back and they had not seen blood, so when Clone seen him, he said, "Blood, where is the tech nine? We don't mind letting any hood use our straps to put in work, but you got to return them. You had the strap too long, so what's up?"

"Blood, let's go get it. I got it at the house." They took off to get it. Everybody is back enjoying the party.

It's getting dark now and Yvonne is ready to go, so we said our goodbyes. She told me, "This was fun but I don't think I'll go to another one."

Today was a good day. There wasn't any Bloods fighting and no shooting, and the one-time didn't shut down the party.

I'm feeling much better, and stronger now, so it's time for me to put in some work on these crabs. They had me dead to right a few times but never was able to finish the job. I'll be going by myself because I don't want anyone to get weak on me just in case things go bad. I like to do this on my own then I only have my back to watch when the bullets start flying. But I will let the homies know to be on watch, they know what that means.

I'm at my home. It took longer than I thought to get my doctor's appointments moved to Riverside Hospital. Now Judy can take care of me. They got me on some medication that put my ass to sleep for hours and give me some crazy nightmares too. I'm still in a lot of pain but I can move if I have to. Mama let me use her car for three weeks. I said goodbye and got on the freeway.

The Drive-by

This has been a very sad and chaotic summer in so many ways. I'm blessed to be alive. Them crabs has taken gang-banging to a true coward level. They will pay for all those drive-bys.

               *   *   *

CHAPTER THIRTEEN

(Dressed In Blue)

It sure feel good to be home with Judy, she is happy that I'm here with her. The drive took a lot out of me, I'm very tired. I said, "Judy, I got a doctor appointment this Friday. I need to change my Medicare card and pick up my prescription, they got me on some very strong medication. I have been having dizzy spells that last for hours, so when I'm on these meds you got to get your Pops to take you to work."

"Okay," she said, "now come over here so I can change your bandages, I can see some blood coming from the one on your ear." Judy is getting her nurse on taking care of her man, and her touch feels so good. I soon fell asleep but I awoke in pain, I must had went to sleep on my arm.

Later in the day we went to my mother-in-law house. Everyone is happy to see me, I got lots of hugs and they showed a lot of love for me and the family. Vance want to see the gunshot wounds so I showed him. Billy and his kids is here wanting to see the wounds too, so I obliged. It felt good to be around them again. It's been a little over a month since I last seen them and I feel right at home.

Mrs. Johnson said, "Is you ready to play some spades? Judy can deal the cards for you. I know that you got that little trophy in the car so go get it and come get your butt whipped."

"Okay," I said. We played two games and the Johnsons won them both, they are talking trash. It sure feel good to be around them and not the craziness in Compton because I was buck wild out there.

I didn't smoke any weed or drink any beer because me and Judy is going to Bible studies tonight. I drove into the parking lot and the lights in the church is on, everybody is already there. When we walked inside everyone looked at me and got up, gave me a hug and kiss, and they said how sad they was for my loss and that they had been praying for my family. I'm happy to see everyone and it's nice to be welcomed and comforted so warmly by them.

After Bible studies it's time for prayer. Everybody is standing in a circle and I was asked to get in the middle. I did as I was asked. I knew what is about to happen and I'm nervous but I calmed down and let the Lord do His thang. They all said a prayer for me and my family, and I thanked them. I felt the holy spirit touch my soul. These are some good people and they love me very much. I know it didn't start off like this because I had their Judy and not everyone was so accepting of our relationship. But it's all good now.

Back home Judy ran my bath water then I got into the tub. She washed my body making sure that she don't get any soap in the hole in my arm. When she was finished I got out and she carefully dried me off. This isn't so bad, I can get used to this everyday. Since we ate dinner at her Mama house we went to bed.

Laying there together Judy is hugging me from behind as I'm facing the wall. Out of nowhere I started crying and didn't want her to hear me. But she felt my body trembling, she knew. She said, "Albert, it's going to be okay. I know you're hurting right now. But you know you got to change your way of living, you could have got killed. The Lord is trying to tell you something, you better start listening to Him. You know I got your back but you got to want to change before it's too late."

I just laid there quietly for a moment then said, "I know that you got my back, and I do got to make a change in my life. I'll try, Judy, but it's going to be real hard for me. I have a second chance to make that change. I love you, Judy."

"I love you too, stupid face. Now try to get some sleep because you got to go to the doctor in the morning."

I drove myself to the hospital. Sitting in the lobby to see the doctor is going to be a long wait. After an hour my name was finally called. I went to the desk and this gray-headed lady said, "Walk through that door, the doctor is waiting for you there."

I opened the door and the doctor asked me to follow him into this cold-ass room. He got all my paperwork on this clipboard. After looking at it briefly he said, "I got your brain scans from U.C.L.A. Hospital and, from what I see, you escaped death. The swelling you had has completely diminished, but you are still suffering dizzy spells, and I can tell that your equilibrium is still a bit altered. Let me look inside your ear because, from these x-rays, you still have some bullet fragments in there." He stuck these long narrow tweezers down my ear canal, I can feel it sliding deep inside. Then he slowly withdrew the tool that was grasping onto a bullet fragment. He said, "Aaah, here we go. I got that sucker. See this, Mr. Jones? This is what's throwing off your balance. There's more in there but you are hemorrhaging right now so I'll patch you up and make another appointment. We'll get out more fragments later." He patched me up and gave me my new prescription slip, then said, "Go down the hall to the left of this door and you can get your medication in there. Now don't drive after taking them, they are a bit stronger than the other ones."

"Thank you, doctor. Oh, how much longer I got to wear this cast?" I wanted to know.

"You have about four to five weeks," he replied.

Walking down the hallway brought back memories of when me and Jamala was chasing that crab. I got my pills and my new Medicare card and I'm headed back home.

I'm home alone so I smoked a joint and got high. This is some good weed so I'll wait for Judy to come home before I take my new medication. I don't know the side affects so I don't want to pass out and nobody find me until it's too late.

I'm feeling the weed. I walked to the backyard where I got my lizards. Judy had told me over the phone that some cats killed all of them. She was right, I can see how they did it, it's lizard parts and pieces everywhere, not one is alive out of twenty-five. And them cats even dug up and destroyed all their eggs too. I got to go out and catch some more, I got to have my lizards. Anthony and Paul raise pigeons but I raise lizards as a hobby. Now I got to start over.

I hear a truck pull up, that got to be Judy and her dad. I walked to the front yard and gave her Pops a wave, he waved back. Then I walked Judy into the house. We had made love last night, I couldn't get down like I wanted to with this cast on, but it was still good.

"Did you get your medication?" she asked. "And how was your checkup?"

"Yeah, I got my new meds. I didn't take any yet, I wanted to wait for you to get home. The doctor said that these are much stronger than the others. And I got four to five more weeks with this cast on my arm. I got my new Medicare card too. I'm going to take my pills now that you're home, okay? I got some little red ones for my head and some big white ones for the pain."

"Al, I'm gonna start cooking dinner. I know you said them pills make you sleepy so I'll wake you if you doze off beforehand, okay, baby?"

DRESSED IN BLUE

"Okay. I'm tired. I've been up all day so I'm going to lay down."

The crabs has been putting in work in our hood and other Blood hoods and we have been serving them up too. It's a real war going on in these streets. After getting shot up and my niece getting killed, it's time for them to feel the pain in a real gangsta way.

I got to change my tactic like they did. Sitting in my bedroom thinking how I'm going to do this, it finally came to me. "Mama, I'm going to the swap meet, I need your car."

"Make sure you put gas back in my tank," she ordered.

"Okay, I will," I yelled as I headed out the door. I got on dirty clothes I used to clean the yard.

I drove to the Compton swap meet with my .380 pistol in my pocket. I walked inside and see some crabs, and said, "What's up, cuzz?" and kept moving. I got a stocking cap on my head and my beard is combed out, not in braids. I'm looking just like a crab. I walked to the booth that sells khaki suits, I bought a blue one and a blue rag. Then I went to buy some white Chucks and blue shoestrings.

This Crip was doing his own shopping and said, "Cuzz, it look like you're about to get your party on."

"Yeah, cuzz, I'm going to the homie house on the eastside," I lied but kept moving. I walked out the swap meet, I wasn't nervous at all. I got this crab shit down.

10 TOEZ DOWN

    I pulled up in the driveway, nobody didn't see me come in, that was cool. I went to the backyard and put all the stuff in the patio under the couch. I put Mama keys back in their place and told her that I filled up her tank. Now I'm going to fix my lunch. I got to stay inside until it get dark. I made a peanut butter and jelly sandwich, with chips and a glass of milk. I went in my room and turned on the TV to watch the Loony Tunes. I'm looking at Yosemite Sam with his six-shooters, always busting on Bugs Bunny. I got my laugh on. I took both my guns out to clean them, I don't want them to jam, and I got to wipe off the prints on all the bullets. I'll be taking my .357 magnum with twelve extra shells. When I was ready, I put everything in the patio.

    I still got on my dirty clothes. I walked out the front door then doubled around to the backyard so Mama could say that I'm gone if someone come looking for me. I got the .357 with me. I jumped the back fence to the alley and ran up the hill to the bus stop. If I timed it right the R.T.D. bus will be on its way any second. And it was, the number seven bus pulled up soon afterward and I got on.

    I sat close to the front because I don't want to look like I'm up to something then the bus driver call the one-time on me. But I don't want to be too close to the door because crabs like to jump on and off buses to see if anybody on there don't belong. We do the same thing, but I'm ready if that happen. It's almost three o'clock and a lot of people will be getting off work and on this bus, I got everything timed.

I decided not to go all the way downtown, it's too many polices down there so I pushed the button for the bus driver to let me off. I'm by some factories and it look like they are still at work.

Now I got to find a car that don't have a stick shift. I hate them kind of cars. How can I get my drive on and hold my gun at the same time? That don't mix with me. Ah-ha! I see a little black car that's an automatic. I tried the door and it opened, cool. It was easy to hot wire. I started the car and drove off. I looked to see how much gas it had, there's a full tank. I'm happy to see that.

I got on the freeway and drove back to the hood, I parked on Main Street. I hope no one I know see me. I got out and went back through the alley then walked through the back door. Mama said, "Boy, why is you coming through the back?"

"I just come from Gil house and I walked down the alley."

It's starting to get dark, I'm thinking if I should smoke this fat-ass E.T. joint. Nah, I better not. I will be too high and I can't afford to make no mistakes. I'll smoke it when I return home.

It's eight o'clock and it's dark. Mama is in her bedroom about to go to sleep. I went into the bathroom and put my hair into eight ponytails with blue rubber bands. I took the braids back out of my beard then put on some makeup to cover up the two teardrop tattoos on my face. I went out the front door to the back to the patio and pulled the bag of stuff out. I started putting on all that crab gear and I put the blue rag in my top pocket. Now I'm ready to put in some work. I got the three-five-seven in one pocket with its shells and the other gun with its clip in my back pocket. I got a pack of Camels and my joint in the other top pocket, I got everything together. I look like a crab and I know I can do their ugly-ass walk. I jumped the fence and see that my G-ride is still there. I got in and started it up, I got enough gas to last all night. I took a look in the mirror and seen myself, I look like a crab. I turned on the radio to 1580 KDAY, I got to have some good music to keep my nerves down.

Driving far from the hood I'll get to a point then turn around and put in the work going back toward the house. I did see a few spots that I'm going to stop at. It's a lot of cars on the streets and that's good, because after I'm done, I can blend in with the traffic. I rode down this street and seen about four or five guys hanging out. I parked around the corner and cut the lights off. But I left the engine running because I don't want to hot wire it again. I calculate that I got five minutes or less to do my thang.

I got that crab walk down. I'm smoking on a Camel. My heart is pounding like a jackhammer the closer I get. It's too late to back out now, I'm in too deep. I approach the guys and said, "What's that 'C' like, cuzz? I'm looking for some weed. Do any of y'all have any?"

DRESSED IN BLUE

They just looked at me, no one said a word. Finally this heavyset crab said, "Cuzz, where you from? I don't know you."

"I'm from Westside Compton Crip, cuzz. One of my homeboys told me that y'all got the bomb-ass weed. Cuzz, I'm not the one-time if that's what you're thinking. I want five dime bags. If y'all don't want to sell me none I'll just go on the other street to get some."

"Hold up, cuzz," he said. "I'll go get some." He walked off and I took out five ten-dollar bills from the pocket where I got the three-five-seven. But I know I got to use the nine millimeter. One crab asked me for a smoke, I gave him one. I noticed they had their guard down and I got just a few more minutes to get this done.

Dude came back and said, "Here you go, cuzz, there are five nice-size dime bags. You got to hurry up because one-time is hot around here."

I know that drag, that what we say on the J-Block when we want to sell something not that good.

He handed me the weed. I put it in my pocket and came out blasting with my gun. The first shot went into dude's stomach and the dude that was close to him got it in both legs. One crab yelled, "Cuzz, get the guns, hurry up!"

I hit another one in the back. I'm popping off caps real fast, I got eighteen bullets and they is catching them. One crab got away. I got off nine shots and four crabs is laying on the ground moaning and screaming in pain.

10 TOEZ DOWN

    I took off running and, once I got to the corner, I slowed to a casual walk like nothing ever happen. I got in the car. This only took the five minutes I gave myself and I can see I still got a lot of gas. I rolled the window down and turned the music off. I drove into traffic and got to the first stop sign. I see police cars flying by with their lights flashing and sirens wailing loudly. I got to the next light and can hear the ghetto bird flying overhead. I turned off the street and drove about a mile from where I just left. I know that the yellow tape is getting put up. It's going to be a lot of that tape being used tonight. I got eight shots left in this clip, I got to keep count so I don't get caught slippin'. I reached into my pocket to see what kind of weed I came up with. Nice fat bags. But when I took a sniff I could tell it was some bunk-ass weed. This shit ain't even homegrown! Them busters tried to fuck me but I guess they was the ones that got fucked. I wiped my fingerprints off the bags and tossed them out the window. If someone find them they gonna think they came up on some weed. I should had shot his ass in the head for that bunk-ass shit he tried to sell me. I'm glad I didn't give him my money.

    I'm going through crab hoods and no one is hanging out. Where are the crabs? I got something for them! I drive by this mini-mart and see some dudes, this might be their lucky day. I rode pass and busted a U-turn then parked. I walked toward their car and one dude is pumping gas and the other two is in the store. I got to make this fast. I walked up and said, "Cuzz, where is the party at tonight?"

As he was about to answer me the other two came out the store carrying bags of stuff. The guy replied, "Cuzz, we are going to the house to hang out but there is a party going on two blocks away. We are going to hit it later on. What's your name, cuzz?"

As I was about to tell him, the other crabs walked up on me. That got me so nervous that I instantly pulled out the nine millimeter and shot the one in the chest that was pumping gas. As he fell to the ground the other two dropped their bags. All I hear is forty-ouncers busting as they hit the ground. They must of had at least five of them. I shot at the one that tried to run behind the car. I didn't see him anymore, I know that I hit him. The third one ran toward the back of the store. I chased his ass and, as soon as I turned the corner, I hear "BANG!" "BANG!" I stopped and said, "Damn, that crab is busting back at me and his heat sound like a forty-four, he got a cannon. I stopped pursuit, turned around, and broke for my car. As I was running I looked to see if them other two was still down. They wasn't, one had got on. Now I got to make sure he don't run up on me and let me have it.

I made it back to the car, jumped in, punched the gas petal -- this little car had some getty-up and go. My heart is pounding out my chest. I hit three different streets and now I can hear the ghetto bird and one-time sirens. I got on a busy street and said to myself, "Damn, Ru-al, that was close. I got to cut down on the talking and just let them have it. I need a smoke. That right there go me all juiced up."

I would hate to get smoked in a crab hood. They could get some big-time stripes off me. I put the other clip in the nine millimeter because I'm not done and the car got a half-tank of gas left. I know I can't be out there too much longer because one-time will start pulling over any car they see, then my night will be over. But I"m not going to pull over if that happen, I'll hold court in the streets. I know L.A.P.D. or the sheriff will shoot and ask questions later. I'm getting close to the hood, I got to get one more.

Is that one? Oh, yeah, he got that crab walk. It's about 10:30, it's still early. He's walking by hisself. I'll pull up to see what's up with him. I'm going to wet his ass up, I'll use the .357. I pulled up next to him and parked, but he kept walking. I said, "Hey, cuzz! Check this out. I'm looking for this girl house name Lin. Do you know her?"

He got on some blue 501 jeans and a blue shirt. He is not as big as me but I think I could get a good fight out of him. He said, "Cuzz, I don't know anybody name Lin. Maybe you got the wrong street."

I stepped out the car. He saw the blue rag hanging out my pocket. That made him feel like he was talking to his people. But with lightning speed I socked him hard in the jaw and he fell to the ground. He didn't see it coming, but he

got up real fast. Damn, I hit him good. He must be one of
them dudes that can take a punch because I got him good enough
to T-roll his ass, but he's standing up right now.

He took a swing and almost caught me on the chin, but I
lean back just out of his reach. I came back with a quick
left and then a solid right to his face, but this crab took
all that. Oh hell, nah! I'll fix him. I pulled out my strap
and shot his ass in the shoulder.

"What's up, cuzz?" he said, "I thought we was cool."

I didn't acknowledge him, I just shot him in the other
shoulder. He did a pop-lock move then he fell. I stood over
him menacing and silent.

"Don't kill me, cuzz," he pleaded repeatedly.

I pulled the trigger back just as he closed his eyes. I
said, "Good night, blood," then I just turned and walked away.
I gave him a pass only because he gave me a good fight and he
wasn't a buster. But he will live with that pain he's experiencing right now forever. That .357 got some mean kick to it
and it's loud as fuck too. To see that fire come out this
gun, it's a thing of beauty and I know that crab will see that
flame in his dreams. I drove off, leaving him laying there in
a pool of his own blood. I turned the corner and got on. I
know the one-time will be coming by here real soon.

I checked the gauge, I got enough gas to check out this
last spot where I know some crabs will be hanging out. I
loaded the .357 with fresh shells. There is going to be a lot

of bodies back there, I know I'm pushing my luck. I got shot at once and I could have got knocked out if that crab would have hit me. This will be it for tonight, I want to make it home to smoke this fat-ass joint and forget about everything that happen tonight.

I parked a block away from their alley. This time I got a long walk before I get there. I got to do this right because I know these crabs got straps back there. Okay, Ru-al, lay them down gangsta style, I told myself as I got out the car and took a deep breath.

I thumbed the safety off the nine millimeter and walked down the alley. It's dark and I can see their silhouettes standing by this car. I can hear some music playing too. I'm getting my crab walk on, I got to let them think I'm one of them. As I get closer I see someone drinking on a forty-ounce of Eight Ball. I realized that this is going to take a little more time than I wanted it to. My heart is racing. That deep breath didn't help me none, but I'm in the zone.

"What's up, cuzz?" I said when I knew they could hear me. "I'm Don from Compton Crip Gang and I want to get three-twenty of that bomb-ass weed and two wet daddies (PCP sherm sticks). I got this party to get to."

They all looked at me, then one crab spoke, "Yeah, we got some weed and the wet ones. Cuzz right here got the wet ones and I'll go get the weed."

This dark-skinned crab said, "Cuzz, how did you get over

here?"

That question made me very nervous. The other two dudes had gone to get the dope so it's just three crabs now. I know he want an answer and I better think of something fast. The only thing that came out my mouth was, "Cuzz --" before I pulled out my nine millimeter and shot the one who asked me the question. Then I let the other one have it. The other one got away.

I broke and ran. Out of nowhere I hear "BOOM!" "BOOM!" "BOOM!" -- Oh, hell nah, not this again. I ducked by a car but I still got a little ways to go before I even get out this alley. I shot back. I'm dumping shells on them and they is serving me back. Fuck, I got to get out of here or it's going to get real nasty for me. Have I pressed my luck too far this time? I'm almost out of 9 mm bullets. I'm going all out to get to the car. I stood up and started shooting at them and I made it to my ride. I jumped in, hit the gas, and was gone like a bat out of hell. I kept driving down short streets. I can hear the police sirens growing louder. The ghetto bird is flying somewhere overhead again. My heart is pumping pure adrenaline through my veins, my body feels like it's filled with rocket fuel. Damn, that was some wild shit, and very intense. I better get my ass back home before I come up missing.

I parked the G-ride and unhooked the bare wires hanging from under the dashboard. I took the blue rag and carefully wiped down the entire car. I let the Y.G.'s have it, I know they will use if for the same reasons I did. I jumped the fence and went into the patio where I took off all these crab clothes. It felt good to get out of those filthy mack nasty clothes. I put on my other clothing I had left there. As for the crab stuff, I'll give it to the trash man myself when he comes on Thursday.

Now that my heart rate has slowed down to a semblance of normal I'm sitting on the couch thinking of the crabs that I let have it. I don't know if any of them is ten toes up, but I know this much, they felt the lead from the .357 and the nine millimeter. And that yellow tape was put up tonight in a real way. Now I'll smoke that joint I've been waiting on all night. It will relax and calm me down. Yeah, sitting here in the dark hitting this fatty really hit the spot.

"Al! Al! Get up!" Judy was anxious and confused. "Boy, I don't know what the hell you was saying but you was doing something in your dream that you shouldn't be doing. It must have been some crazy-ass nightmare. I sat there listening to you, I only understood one word, you kept saying, 'cuzz.' Look at you, Al, you got sweat all over your body and the sheets are soaked. Man, whatever you was dreaming about must have been real crazy."

"Baby, I don't remember any dream," I told her. "How long have I been sleep? Them pills knocked my ass out. I'm

DRESSED IN BLUE

feeling pretty good, I don't have any pain right now."

"You been sleep for three hours. Yeah, them pills really did a number on you because you didn't want to wake up. I'm glad they took away your pain though. Now get your stupid face up and get ready for dinner, it's getting cold. I ate already, I'll be taking my bath and, when I'm done, I'll run some fresh bath water for you."

Damn, that dream seem so real! I can't tell Judy about it at all, but I definitely liked it: Dressed In Blue.

*   *   *

CHAPTER FOURTEEN

(The L.A. Riots)

I have been out the pen for three months now, and I'm so frustrated that I can't find a job. This time I'm trying to do the right thing because I don't want to lose Judy by running the streets. I had promised her and my baby that I would do the right thing this time out, I knew that I had to make a change in my life. I have not been going to the hood that much because I know if I did I would get caught up in those streets.

I used up all the money I had looking for a job. I'm driving all around Riverside looking for work, but when I filled out the applications no one would call me for an interview. I knew it was because I'm an ex-con. On all the applications I had to fill out there's that question and the box you have to check: HAVE YOU EVER BEEN CONVICTED OF A CRIME? IF SO, WHAT? I got to tell the truth because if I don't they will look up my name and social security number to find out that way, then they won't hire me. So I would put down armed robbery knowing damn well that I won't get hired. When they see that, a red light goes off and they're like "I'm not hiring that guy. He might rob me and my place of business."

I'm running up the phone bill hunting for a job. I'm doing everything I can to find work, and my parole officer won't help me like he is suppose to either.

This shit is getting to me and Judy knows this. She said, "Albert, don't give up, keep on trying, I got your back. You will find something eventually."

For these three months I have been a house husband, which is cool. I clean up the house, iron her work clothes, fix her lunch, drive her to work then pick her up afterwards. It did feel good to be at home kicking it with her, but I need to make my own money. Every payday she would buy me a carton of Camels, half-ounce of weed, and a handle of gin and socko. She did her part to try to keep me off them streets. I know I can just go to the hood and get my curb sever on, but I'm trying to do the right thing. Judy had told me that she was tired of me in and out of prison. I want to marry her but I want to get off this parole. I don't want to be half hers and half the state's. We can't afford another child, but I sure was trying to put one up in her. She would look at me and take her pill, she made sure there would not be any mistakes. She would say, "You got a girl and I got a boy and that's all we need right now."

I'm enjoying being home with her every day, we had our good times and our bad like any other couple. We are very much in love with each other, our love making is fantastic and happens every night. She is amazing, and she's my Plain Jane.

We went to church every Sunday, Bible studies on Wednesday nights, and cleaned up the church on Saturdays -- I'm loving all of this. Our church isn't that big, we got around twenty-five members there. We have a church in Good Hope in this very little town, one in L.A., and our main church is in Kentucky. We got a lovely first lady, Mother Reynolds. A lot of the members didn't too much like me but she embraced me from day one. Judy had grew up in this church and for her to live with this thug that can't stay out of prison was hard for them to comprehend. But they see that she loves me so they backed off. I had to adjust to her lifestyle and it was cool for a little while, but I'm getting restless.

Judy knew that I was getting frustrated being in the house for three months. She know that I'm a street nigga, that I can't stay in one place for a long period of time. I know where I can make some money and I'll have to do it because these people don't want to give me a job. I'll just become a menace to society once again and, when I'm in that zone, all bets are off in every way, because I won't care about life or the next person outside of my family and loved ones. I told Judy that I'm going to Mama house for a while.

"Al, you know that when you go out there you act a damn fool," she said. "Then I'll get that collect call you telling me that you're in jail and that you didn't do anything wrong, but you're gone for a year or longer. Baby, I know you're trying but don't give up like this."

I said, "You know I tried to find work. I don't want to go back to the pen, but what am I suppose to do?"

THE L.A. RIOTS

The room got real quiet, I see it in her face that she is upset. She said, "Okay, stupid face. If you go back to prison I'm going to be so mad at you."

"I'm not going back to the pen, don't jinks me like that." But I'm knowing damn well I'm about to take another penitentiary chance when I hit these streets. I said my goodbye, but she was not happy about seeing me leave.

I'm on the J-Block getting my curb serve on and I'm making some good money. It's three o'clock in the morning, I'm by myself, I'm bored so I rolled up a premoe. I know I shouldn't because if I do all hell is going to break loose. But I do it anyway. My heart is beating fast. When I light it the first hit tasted too damn good. I slowly let the smoke out and knew right then there was no turning back. Ru-al is on that shit again. I rolled up another and smoked that one too. I walked around the corner to Zell Pop's pad, that's one hangout spot for smokers. We got a few spots in the hood that we call "stadiums" just like a baseball field.

I walked in and it's about six people surprised to see me, but they know that I don't care. I gave Pops a twenty and he went back to his room then returned. I'm at the table with a whole quarter piece on a plate. I cut up what I'm going to smoke and put up the rest. I said, "Batter up." I got the pipe as the bat and the rock is the ball and the lighter is the pitcher -- and I'm trying to hit a home run. That was a good hit. I don't like to get high by myself and the other smokers know that, so I gave everyone a big-ass hit. There are smokers that like to look out the window or walk around all paranoid. That's cool with me because they can keep watch for the one-time for me.

I'm at the point that I don't care about nothing when I'm on this shit. It makes my mind look at everything as something or someone against me if you're not a homie or family member. I never stole from family or sold my stuff for rocks. I have took some dope from a few homies but never to where I looked like I'm a bully. I got to go see my parole officer in the morning and I know I'm going to turn in a dirty piss test. This visit will be my last so I'll go, then I don't have to worry about them getting me for at least two or three weeks, if they can catch me, because I'll be on the lamb. Judy is going to be mad as hell at me when I tell her I'm on the run. I know I got a violation coming if I don't make more before I'm arrested.

Coming from the parole office I know I just turned in a dirty test. Of course when she asked if I was dirty I said no.

On the 60 Freeway back to the hood I got the radio on because the verdict is suppose to come for the pigs that brutally beat up Rodney King. I first seen the beatdown on the TV when I was in Corcoran Prison. If his ass wasn't shermed up they might had killed him. L.A.P.D. put a real beating on him. He was lucky that someone video taped it, or them pigs would have gotten away with it. I'm sure they got away with a

THE L.A. RIOTS

lot of scandalous shit, but this time they are caught. So we wait for the jury to come back with the verdict. They need to lock them pigs up and put them all on the mainline on a level four yard.

I turned off the freeway and rolled down El Segundo when someone ran out their house yelling, "Not guilty! Not guilty! The police was found not guilty!" I heard it simultaneously on the radio too. It was being aired on every media station. I had watched this crab kicking this shit off when he bashed in that white man head with a brick. I got to give it to that crab on that, that was gangsta.

I pulled up to Mom's house and said, "Paul, let's go get paid."

"Let's go, blood, I'm down," he replied.

The streets is crowded with people and cars. We're in Paul's bucket, I got my pistol just in case I need it. We went to the swap meet in our hood on Alvon. Once there it's water ankle high, somebody tried to set it on fire and the sprinklers came on, now everything is wet. We grabbed a lot of clothes and tennis shoes. All the sound systems and music are gone, the homies on the Weakside got to it first. Then we went to Vons supermarket to get all the food we could carry. People got shopping carts full of stuff. It's kids and their mamas running around looting. We dropped off our first load at home and went for more.

Back in Paul's bucket I said, "Let's go to Smart and

Final's big store, they got some good shit." When we got there it was packed with people grabbing whatever wasn't bolted down. The store is across the street from the Ten High School. When we walked in I looked to the left and seen two dudes messing with something. When I got closer I see they is working on a safe that's about three feet high. As I'm about to walk away to let them do their thang, I see it moved. I said, "What's up, blood? Where is y'all from?" I got my hand in my pocket because if they are crabs it's going to get ugly. Paul seen me go in my pocket and gave me that look, like, "Ru-al, don't shoot them if they are crab."

One dude said, "We're from Nickerson Garden Bounty Hunter, blood."

"Bool," I said. "We're from Athens, blood. Let us help y'all with that safe. Come on, Paul, get the other side."

We got the safe to move while one homie went to get a cart. The first time we tried to pick it up we couldn't, it had to weigh four hundred pounds. It took us all to pick it up and set it on the cart. As we started out the door I pulled my gun out so we don't get jacked. B.H. Blood said, "Let's put it in my car and we can go to the projects to open it up."

I know how them Hunters can get so I said, "Nah, blood, Mom's house is just down the street. Plus our car is right here." They agreed without any resistance.

The police passed by but kept on driving, they are not

pulling anybody over, they is not trying to stop this madness.

We got the safe in the front and the front end of the car bottomed out the shocks. The safe is so heavy that the fender is rubbing on the tire. Paul said, "Blood, I hope the fender don't pop the tire before we make it home."

"We will make it. Let me sit on the other side of the car to put some weight over there," I offered. That seemed to work a little bit better. We drove by the dairy, it's on fire. I'm not happy to see that.

We pulled up in the driveway. Paul went to get the dolly to roll the safe to the patio. I told him, "Blood, go get the big boy too." He knew what I was talking about, my chrome long-barrel .357 magnum. I got the .380 but I need the big one to keep the peace. I'm sure they got their strap too, but I'm not taking any chances, it could be a million dollars in this safe, and the homies from Hunters can get scandalous. Paul came back with the gun and a crowbar. We busted the safe open and it's all kinds of money in it. We stacked it up and passed it out. We each got sixteen hundred dollars and everyone is happy. They took the empty safe with them to dump it.

Me and Paul went in the house. I said, "Damn, blood, you seen how we walked up on this come-up?"

"Yeah, I'm cool. Now I'm going over to my son's mother house and chill."

That sound like the best thing to do. I called up John Boy to bring me a quarter piece so I can get high. He came to the house in twenty minutes and I went into the patio and took me a blast. I hid the rest and went to the J-Block.

It's about thirty people out there and somehow they knew that I had the safe. There's trash cans full of ice and beer from the dairy. I got me a Miller Draft and chilled.

Froggy said, "Blood, let's go to the Western Surplus Store, they got guns."

We got into about five cars and everybody got some heat. We get there and it's about seven crabs with big guns standing guard at the door with their blue rags around their mouths. They got a truck parked in the front so we kept driving passed them. I said, "Damn! This is where we should have come first. Now them crabs got more heat to put in work on us."

I hated to see our dairy and Al's Market on fire, that will be a big loss to our hood in so many ways.

We get back to the J-Block, homies is having fun walking around with guns. The one-time better not come around.

I went back home and got the TV on in the patio. I'm looking at Compton, Watts, South Central all burned up. I'm getting my pull on (smoke) when I hear the ghetto bird flying over the hood. I know when I was in the swap meet parking lot the homie had shot at one and they got the fuck on. Now I'm looking at this shit going on, the people has been waiting on something like this for a long time because the tensions had been building up.

I've been getting my pull on all night, looking at TV,

THE L.A. RIOTS

and the riots is still in full force. I found out that the smokers got all the good stuff. I got cases of forty ounces, all kinds of hard liquor, and clothes. I'm buying all their stuff. Some homies was able to get into the Dayton Tire Factory. I wished I could had been in that come-up.

On day three the National Guard are on the streets enforcing a curfew on the city and they are taking people to jail by the hundreds. I'm going to the Nickerson Garden to buy a quarter piece from the homie Rock Berry when I seen about fifteen police cars chasing a Blood from Hunters. He made it inside the projects and the police stopped following because they know it's only one way in and one way out. Plus the homies have been busting on them at every chance they could get. The homie was flying in that caddy. I know I better get my dope and get the fuck out of the hood.

I got to beat the curfew. I had the homie Dundey to drive me to Albanisha house in Chino. I'm leaving my caddy at Mama's house. I got a fresh quarter piece and a lot of stuff from the riots; two cases of forty-ounces, all kind of hard liquor, and an ounce of some bomb-ass weed. I'm cool to hide out for a few weeks, and I get to spend some time with my baby, Albanisha.

I knocked on the door and Wanda opened it, then said, "Come in." I had called her earlier to let her know I was going to stay for a while.

When I walked in Albanisha cheerfully yelled, "Daddy!

Daddy! You're home!" She jumped into my arms and it felt so good to hug my baby girl. Her big sister came to give me a hug too. Me and Dundey went to get my things out his car and then he left. I also had bags of candy for the kids and they was happy to get them.

Sitting on the couch I was watching the news and Rodney King is about to speak. He walked up to the bank of microphones and said, "Can we all just get along, and stop all the rioting and hurting each other?"

I looked at this dude and said, "Buster, hell nah, we can't get along. We done already tore up our hoods over your punkass, now you want us to stop?" Wanda started laughing at my comment. I didn't tell her that I had some rocks. She didn't smoke them but she do smoke weed so we got our smoke on. I did my rock smoking outside where she didn't know about it. I found a spot to hide my gun that I never told her about either. The last time I was here I saw some crab. I just hope they don't start tripping because, if they do, I got to do what I got to do.

Me and Wanda has been getting our sex on, we had our fuck song "Knocking Them Boots." She must had that song on both sides to play over and over and we kept going. This girl know that she got some good pussy. We kicked it for three weeks then I went back to Mama house once the National Guard had left and the pigs stopped locking people up.

When I got back to the hood I heard that Blood and crab

hoods are having these block parties.

I'm chillin' on the J-Block when one Y.G. said, "Ru-al, are you going to the park? Because the homie Bone got Jim Brown to come and they are having a Stop The Violence and Start The Peace get-together with all hoods."

"Yeah, I'll roll up there to check it out but I'm not with that peace shit with them crabs. I don't have any problems with the ones that want to do that, but not me, I'm banging too hard to trust them crabs," I told him.

I get to the park and it's packed with people and I do see some crabs, they are closer to the front where Jim Brown is speaking. The homies is flamed up red everywhere, I think most of everyone is here to see the Hall of Fame football player and doing their peace thang.

This Crip dude got up dressed all in blue, he said, "There will be block parties and I want every hood to welcome anyone that want to come. These are all our streets."

I'm like, "This crab is trippin', I'm not going to any of them block parties and get smoked. They had their chance to get me, I'm not going to invite myself to them." I left after about fifteen minutes.

I get back to the J-Block and see Luna Tick. He said, "Big homie, I know you're not with that peace shit with them crabs."

"Hell nah, blood, you know and I know if them crabs can

catch one of us they won't pass up a chance to smoke us. So I'm bool on that. I'm not letting my guard down because a few want peace, which I know is not going to last long. Them same people that's getting on that stand will be banging in a week or two."

Clone said, "Blood, we are going to the Pueblos and party at their little spot. You want to go, Ru-al?"

"Yeah, let's go. I've been to a lot of their parties and I know they is not with this peace-treaty shit. Plus I got to holla at my boy, Loney Man, and Big Snaps. While we're there I'll walk across the tracks to the Pueblo projects to see my niece Shamika."

K-Dae and Tay rolled up, K-Dae got on all red and her flag on her head. I'm glad that she is not banging like some of the homegirls her age. Tay got on all blue and her blue rag on her head, she's claiming 59 Hoover Crip. Tay and her sister, Teasa, grew up over there and still live there. They was never out there banging but that's their hood. Their brother Jerome never banged, he made his money and was a player.

K-Dae said, "Albert, we are about to hit some of these block parties and have some fun." Tay got this big-ass joint in her mouth. K-Dae don't get high or drink but she do know how to party.

I said, "K-Dae, y'all be careful because everybody is not with this peace-treaty thang. I'm one of them that's not with it. And whatever you do, don't tell any of them crabs that I'm

THE L.A. RIOTS

your brother, okay?"

"Why not?" she asked.

"Because I had a lot of encounters with a lot of them crabs on the streets and in prison so if they can't get me they will hurt you, so don't say you know me. There is no peace in them for me, they got a green light on me."

"Okay, we're out of here," K-Dae said as they took off.

I was wearing all black with some red tie-up Vans, a red belt, red and black hair ties in my ponytails with two in my braids hanging on my beard, I got my red flag hanging out my right back pocket and one wrapped around the neck of my fifth of Thunderbird with red bool-aid. Luna Tick got his big red flag that wraps around his whole body that got to be made out of about twenty smaller red flags. Every Blood hood is here, it got to be over two hundred Bloods and the music is loud. These Eba heads is getting at me, they are digging my gangsta style. Me and Jamala is not together so I get to fuck all the Eba heads I want and not worry about her running them off. A lot of these Bloods I seen in the Blood module in prison. I ran into Loney Man, we gave each other some love and kept it pushing. I walk to where everyone has gathered to see what is going on.

I get over there and it's P.T. (Pimpen Tim) from the J-Block and that's his car with the monster-ass beats. Everybody is checking out his sounds when P.T. gets into an argument and now they want to take all his shit. We didn't know

Blood was going to be here. He's not one of the homies that put in work on crabs so nobody knows him. He don't even see me or the Y.G.s yet, but we see that he is about to get his ass kicked and robbed.

I walked up and said, "Hold up, bloods. This is my homeboy from my hood, he's bool."

The homie from 52 Villian Hood knew me from 4300 module and said, "Wuzz up, Ru-al? You know this dude? Because he is about to get his ass kicked."

"Yeah, he's from my hood. Why? What did he do?" I asked.

Tate said, "Blood is out here fronting like he's all that and don't nobody know him. But if you say he bool he will get that pass."

Everybody went back to getting their party on. The Eba heads is jocking me. I'm one of the biggest Bloods out here and I'm loving my O.G. status, and all these Bloods is enjoying this party. I know none of these Bloods is with that peace-treaty shit. It's four in the morning and we are about to leave. There was no shootings, this was a good night for us B-Dogs.

The next day I slept until three o'clock in the afternoon, I woke up with this banging-ass hangover, then took a shower. I'm getting ready for my day when K-Dae walked into my room. I said, "So, how was your and Tay block party ventures?"

"They was cool until we got to this party in Compton. I was dancing with this Crip dude and he asked me where I'm from

THE L.A. RIOTS

so I said Athens Park Bloods. Then the Crip said, 'You look like somebody I know from there.' I said, Oh you might know my brother, Ru-al. He stopped dancing and his eyes got big then he said, 'I knew you looked like him. Didn't he have a fight with a dude years ago name Cyclone?' I said yeah, why? He said, 'Everybody heard about that fight. But anyway, I was in the pen with Ru-al and he beat up one of my homeboys. I can't dance with you anymore, you and your cousin got to leave this party.' When they found out I was your sister it was like I had the plague in that house. So me and Tay got the hell out of there as fast as we could."

"I told you not to tell them crabs I'm your brother. I just knew somebody would recognize you as my sista, and someone did. You could had got you and Tay hurt," I told her.

"Damn, what did you do to his homeboy for him to hate you like that?" she asked.

"I beat his crab ass real bad and called out his homeboys and they ate cheese. If you're going to anymore of them block parties don't say you know me, okay?"

"Okay, Albert."

The riots had done a lot of damage to so many hoods. People lost their lives, people went to jail, and some tried to come together with peace-treaty meetings. So many people had so much anger build up that they couldn't wait for an opportunity to explode like this. And it took a buster like Rodney King to get beat down on video tape, and for the pigs to get away scot-free, that is what made me and the community so mad. L.A.P.D., Compton Police, Carson Sheriff, and L.A. Sheriff are some of the most dangerous gangs in our state. They dropped gang members in other gangs' hoods so they could get beat down or killed. Now it was our turn to see the law work for us, but it didn't, they let them dirty pigs go free. So I'm not mad at what we done. I can say that Ru-al was a part of something memorable and pivotal in this country that was seen around the world. The L.A. Riots of 1992.

* * *

CHAPTER FIFTEEN

(Five-Day High)

I'm not on the run anymore, my parole officer is not going to violate me for that dirty test I turned in after all that happened in the riots. But I had to go to rehab class for six months, which I had agreed to because it was better than going back to the pen for a year. Judy was happy, now I'll be at home with her. I like it as well because I'm doing the right thing, I'm on the job hunt again and keeping my mind off the hood. I know I tried this a few other times and it didn't last, but his time I got to make it work.

Two months has passed, still I can't find any work and this P.O. lady is not helping me either. I have been calling her two times a week and she would always say, "I got nothing for you." I would go to my rehab class once a week for three months. Before I leave the house I would smoke a joint and drink a beer, I knew I was only getting tested for cocaine. So I'm in class high with all these other dope fiends, the class was cool for the three months I was there.

Today me and Judy got into this big argument. I was already upset for not being able to find a job, so this was the best time for me to make my excuse to go to the hood. I said, "Judy, I have been trying to find work and now you're finding small things to fuss about, so I'm gonna go to my mama house for a while."

"Okay," she said. "But I know you, Albert. You'll get out there and start acting stupid. And what is 'a while'?"

"I'll just be gone for a few weeks," was my answer.

I know going back to the hood I could start smoking again but I don't want to do that because it increases my chances of retuning to prison -- and I don't want that, either. I know when I smoke that shit the level raises up to nine out of ten for me going back to the pen. If I don't go to the pen my smoking sprees only last two to three weeks.

All hoods got O.G.s and down-ass Bloods that smoke rocks. But most of them like to closet smoke, hiding what they doing so no one else will know. When they do come out the closet they are so smoked out that they are selling all their personal belongings and going on store runs. I knew I would never get like that, I didn't hide and I'm definitely not skinny scary. We got homeboys going out of state to make money and they is coming back buying low-riders and having big-time money. I was asked many of times if I wanted to go to other states, but I would say no because I didn't want to go to jail or get smoked in another state. So I just did my thing right here and kept my ass in Compton.

When I do go on my smoking sprees I keep my hair and clothes fresh. I do have a Blood reputation to uphold and I was still running into a lot of Eba heads and getting my fuck on. I never got skinny scary like most smokers but if you fuck with me you will become a victim. I've seen some of the downest Bloods on this shit turn into punks. When that happens you lose your heart and then you really turn into a punk. Not me, I can't go out like that.

A lot of homies has been hitting pawn shops and gun stores then coming back to the hood famous for their brazen illegal actions. This is the new thing, going miles away from the hoods and putting in work, coming back with ill-gotten gains and incredible stories.

I ran into the homeboy Sick Blood, I said, "S.B., we need to come up on a job."

"Blood, I'm working on something right now with my relative. Give me a few days to check everything out and I'll get back at you."

"Okay, blood."

S.B. is one of them Bloods that you know got your back. I will die for Blood and I know he will die for me. He don't have that name for nothing. He's a true C.K. rider and, when he get on his smoking sprees, he is just like me and I like that about him.

S.B. got at me later. He said, "Ru-al, I got it set up to happen in three days. I got this gun shop we can get, it's about five hours from the hood and it's only me and you that's going to do it."

"Okay, blood. You know if all hell break loose you know the rules," I told him.

"Yeah, I know the damn rules. If we got to get out fast you got one minute to get into the car, and if you're not there I'm gone without you, then you got to find your own way home."

"That's it, blood. No need for both of us to get caught. Somebody got to come back to tell the story."

"Ru-al, why you always say that crazy shit? I know the rules too. I know and you know that we are not running out on anyone. Just be ready in a few days."

I walked on the J-Block and see the Mexican homeboy Reyes got two cars parked in front of his house for sale. He got a 1968 Oldsmobile and a 1976 Cutlass. I said, "I want to buy the Cutlass, how much you want for it?"

"Ru-al, I'll sell it to you for fourteen hundred dollars."

"Okay, but you got to give me three days and I'll have the money."

"Okay, I'll hold it for you, but you only got three days. Where is your caddy?"

"She's at my sister Connie house. I have been pushing her too hard for five years, I got to get her engine re-built. That's why I need another car. Blood, just hold on to the Cutlass for me until I get back."

So I got three days to do my thang. I see my boy G-Rab roll up, I know he want to make some money. He pulls up playing Das EFX "They Want EFX." When I hear him playing that song I know that he want to make some money. I jumped into his car and said, "Blood, I need to make fourteen hundred dollars in three days. So what's up?"

He spoke with a lot of excitement, "Okay, let's get paid."

We drove to the factories and robbed two catering trucks with no problem. People don't know they be having a lot of cash on hand. On the third one me and G-Rab walked up to the window and both asked the cook for cheeseburgers. The Mexican dude that's standing outside asked for our money. I gave it to him then pulled out my gun. I said, "Hand me that money bag and you won't get hurt."

It's lunchtime and most of the people that was there had returned to their jobs so no one seen us. He said, "No, I will not give you my money bag."

G-Rab tried to grab it but the Mexican wasn't giving it up, it was wrapped around his waist.

I said, "Okay, give it up or I'll shoot you." I point my gun at his head and his eyes got big. He's looking down the barrel of the .44 bulldog and I know he can see the hollow-point bullets in the cylinder. Without a word he let the bag drop to the ground. We grabbed it and ran around the corner to the car.

"This was a good come-up," I said. "Did you see that Mexican dude put up a fight? He's lucky he didn't get his ass shot because I was real close to letting him have it." We split the eighteen hundred dollars, then I said, "Blood, I got to take some of this money home so I don't fuck it all off."

G-Rab said, "Okay, but before we go to your house let's

go to the swap meet and buy some fresh gear and then go to the Nickerson Gardens to get a quarter piece. I hear the homie Rock Berry got the bomb dope, then we can jump on the freeway to your house."

We both spent two hundred and twenty-five dollars on a quarter piece. Blood hooked us up. We rolled up some premoes to smoke as we drove out the projects. We ran into the homie H.B., he said, "What's happening, blooooooooood?" We started laughing because the homie got the longest Blood greeting I ever heard a Blood say.

We're on the freeway and I'm getting my pull on. Now G-Rab want to get his on so I grabbed the stirring wheel and he leaned back in the seat. I'm telling him when to give me gas or hit the brakes as he's getting his pull on. We are in the second to the fast lane of traffic so we ain't in nobody's way while we get high.

Finally he sat back up and said, "Blood, Rock Berry got the bomb-ass dope. He got the best in Compton and Watts. That was a bell-ringer."

I had to laugh at Blood, because I heard the bells ring, too! It was an hour drive while we did some crazy-ass shit driving on the freeway getting our smoke on doing sixty miles per hour.

We get to my house and Judy is not there. I called over her mama house and told her that I'm home and G-Rab will be spending the night. She said, "Okay, come get me at eight, I got to go to work in the morning."

"Okay, baby." It's cool that Judy never tripped about me bringing homies to the house. The last homie I brought was Ted and he ate my food, drinked my liquor, smoked my dope, and fucked my neighbor. Blood really enjoyed that night.

When Judy came home and I gave her eight hundred dollars for the car. She took her bath and went to sleep while the homie stayed up all night getting high.

We dropped Judy off at work the next morning. On the way home we hit two liquor stores. One thing about robbing liquor stores is you got to beat them to the draw because they got big guns behind them counters. But we seemed to always beat them. I was good at opening up the cash register on the first try by just hitting one button. I take everything, even the food stamps. When it's time to leave G-Rab grabbed a pint of Hennesy. In each store we came up with their pistols so now we got more guns for us too.

Once off the freeway we stopped at Rock Berry house to get two quarter pieces. We rented a room outside the hood for six hours. We set everything up in the room and then we went to crab hood to get some brand-new pipes. This is the only spot that has the best paraphernalia or gadgets. He would go in the store and I would stand by the door of the car with my pistol out just in case some crab rolled up.

Just a month ago G-Rab got into a shootout with some crabs and got hit in the leg so he got this limp. He came out the store with the pipes and a pint of Bacardi 151 and two pints of Hennesy. We are going to do this right. We picked up two fine looking smokers, we were going to tag-team them. We got our raincoats on and ready to go.

G-Rab said, "Ru-al, why you always act like you're fucking in a porno movie or taking photos with all that posing when we're fucking these girls?"

"This is how I get down, it's fun like this, ha-ha!"

I took the rest of the money home from all the jobs I did. Now I got that out the way and Judy is holding it. I get back to the hood and S.B. is waiting on me. He is not a big dude; he stood five foot nine and weighed about one hundred and fifty pounds. He got a short Juri curl but he can fight and is quick to shoot. He got his 9 millimeter and extra clip, he's my kind of nigga. He said, "Ru-al, are you ready to get famous?"

"Hell yeah, blood! I got the .44 bulldog and ten extra shells. Let's do this."

We got on the freeway. I got to get some sleep because I've been up for two days with G-Rab, I need the rest for this job.

"Get up, Ru-al, we're thirty minutes away and you better be looking just in case you got to drive us out of here."

"Blood, if we come-up on this job I'm going to turn the Cutlass into a low-rider."

"Yeah, I seen the Cutlass and it's tight, you came-up,

blood. But first we got to do this and make it back home safe," S.B. cautioned me.

We pulled up in the parking lot of a shopping center and it's cars everywhere. We got to do this just right because if not we will get seen by somebody. I put makeup on my teardrop then checked my gun and shells. My heart is beating super fast and that's a good thing for me. I'll be ready and alert for this because I know that they got guns and they will be ready for something like this too. So we got to get in and out fast and in one piece. "Blood, let's get famous," I said.

I know it's only two guys in there, I got the rundown on the place. We walked in and there is the two white dudes standing behind the counter. One is very tall, at least six foot four and skinny, and the other one is about five ten with long hair. I approached the counter and asked the tall dude to let me see a Glock 45. While he got the model I a wanted I looked around the store and saw three CK47s hanging on the wall. Them will be the first guns I will grab. We can give them crabs some hell with them pieces. S.B. is talking to the other dude keeping him distracted, we are the only ones in the store at the moment.

I looked over the Glock, handled it before handing it back to the salesman. I asked him if I could look at another gun. When he bent down to grab one out of the display cabinet I pulled out my gun and said, "Put your damn hands up or get your fuckin' head blowed off!"

He looked at me in total shock. Then he ducked so fast I missed when I got off my first shot. I said to myself, 'How the fuck did I miss being so damn close? Shit, it's about to get real ugly in here.'

S.B. started busting his 9 millimeter.

The guy that ducked that I missed got off two shots that were a hundred times louder than our guns. He got to have one of them Clint Eastwood guns with hot loads, that motherfucker got my ears ringing. Now I'm bent down hiding by the counter sucking on this cherry Blow Pop. I looked at S.B. and waved him to get out and get the truck started. I shot one time through the counter and see Blood run out the door. Now I got one minute to get my black ass out of here or I'll have to find my way home, or call it a night in this gun shop because these dudes behind this counter is not joking.

I'm squatting down and smell gunpowder and burnt wood. A bead of sweat came trickling down my forehead. I wipe it off so it don't get into my eye. Time seem to stop and all kind of thoughts went through my mind: my baby, Judy, will this be where Ru-al will have his last stand? Whatever the case, I'm going out shooting.

BOOM! BOOM! Two more thunderous shots shook the room from that big-ass cannon. I'm sure people in the parking lot and next door heard all this crazy shit. I know that my minute is gone now. I got to get out of here and I got to do it fast.

I raised up and shot two more times to let them know I'm

still here, for them not to stick their heads up to try to see me. This .44 bulldog got a loud bark and will leave a giant hole if it hits its mark. I got one bullet left in the chamber and I don't have time to reload. I jumped up and ran for the door, making it outside without being shot in the back of the head. If that were to happen, that's where I want it, in the back of the head -- no pain, just lights out. But, so far, I'm safe and unharmed.

I see S.B. stuck to the plan, he's gone, I don't see the truck anywhere. I started walking through the parking lot and to my surprise I don't see anyone, they must be inside some building hiding from all the gunshots. I'm moving slow so I don't draw any attention or suspicion my way. I walked around the corner when I finally heard the police sirens growing louder in the distance. I thought for sure they would have been here by now. I guess I wasn't in there as long as I had thought even though it seemed like a long time. The sirens are getting louder and closer. I got to get me a car so I can get my ass back to Compton alive and in one piece. I would hate to go to jail in this hick-ass town.

I'm about a half mile from that shootout. I got fifteen dollars in my pocket, I'm hungry as hell. I walked into this sandwich shop to get something to eat. I spent ten dollars on food and drink. I have been getting high for three days and not eating, I could hear my stomach growling during the shootout. That Blow Pop kept my mind off food but now I got to get some fuel in my empty tank.

I got my food and sat close to the window so I can look outside. I'll eat slow until things calm down. I know S.B. is on the freeway going home wondering if I'm still alive. Across the street I see a gas station. I need a car and need one bad. I finished eating then went to the bathroom to wash up and put four fresh bullets in my gun. I flushed the empty shells down the toilet.

I'm smoking a Camel and looking over at the gas station, that's where I'm gonna get my G-ride from. I see this tall black man wearing a suite pull up to the gas pump. I walked across the street straight for him. He is the only black person I seen since coming to this town, I hope his car is an automatic. I glanced inside this car to see it was automatic, cool. I said, "Excuse me, sir. Can I make a dollar by washing your windows?"

He looked at me. I don't have any fresh clothes on but he said, "Sure, why not?"

I took the old squeegee out of the dirty water bucket and started wiping the front windshield. I noticed that he was done pumping his gas and was screwing on his gas cap. When I seen him go into his pocket for the dollar he owed me I pulled out my gun and said in a very soft voice, "I don't want to shoot you, just give me your car keys."

He looked at me again, this time with fear in his eyes. He knew I wasn't joking, so he handed me the keys without any hesitation, without saying a word. I got in the car and drove off. I knew that the freeway is just around the corner. I took the on-ramp and stirred into the fast lane to Compton for the long anxious ride home.

I start thinking about the shootout. We didn't get shit and we're not coming home famous. That gun shop had so many pistols and other guns that we could had filled the back of that truck up, and we might not had got them all because there was so many. Now we'll never know. At least I'm alive.

I didn't go to the hood, I parked the G-ride a mile from my house, wiped all the fingerprints off and walked home. When I entered the house Judy is in the kitchen cooking some dinner for herself. I know she had been mad at me so I gave her a kiss that she reluctantly reciprocated. Her lips tasted good. Just four hours ago I was in a shootout, now I'm home with my lady. It feels good to be home, it feels good to be alive and well.

"How did you get home?" she asked puzzled.

"One of the homies dropped me off. Judy, I need that money so I can buy that car tomorrow."

"Okay, I'll set it out for you before I go to work." We ate a good meal and had some make-up sex. I put it on her good. Her icy demeanor has began to thaw afterwards.

I'm at the Riverside Greyhound bus station, I got to ride it all the way to downtown L.A. I got fifteen hundred dollars and my .44 with ten bullets in my pocket. I slept all the way there. I got off the bus and walked to Seventh and Broadway, I'll catch the R.T.D. bus all the way to my backyard. I have not been on the bus in years, this will be a crazy ride home.

As I'm waiting on the number seven bus to come I see police on foot. I knew they was on foot, but not this many. I hope they don't look at me crazy. I'll just stay seated on the bench and hope the bus hurry up and arrives. I got on some gray khakis, gray sweatshirt and some white Chucks with fat red shoelaces. Judy hooked up my ponytails with red rubber bands last night.

Riding on the bus the driver announced, "Last stop, Centry Boulevard." Everybody that was left on the bus got off. Now I got to walk through three different crab hoods and I know I will get seen and there is no other way around it.

I made it passed two crab hoods. If I get past the next one the park is right up the hill. My heart is beating fast as I get closer to where I know they would be. It's hot today and I got on this hot-ass sweatshirt. I crossed the street and see about four or five crabs hanging out. I made it passed them without them seeing me. I walked up the hill to the park and the homies was surprised to see me.

Mel Dog is the first to speak, "Blood, we heard about the shootout you and S.B. had. Everybody thought you got killed or went to jail."

"Yeah, blood, it was crazy but as you can see Ru-al is alive and well," I told him.

FIVE-DAY HIGH

"Ru-al, what is you doing walking through that crab hood?" Mel asked.

"Blood, the bus dropped me off on Centry Boulevard and I had to walk the rest of the way. Oh, don't get it twisted, I got my strap if I had to shoot my way home. Say Mel Dog, could you take me to Moms house?"

"Come on, I'll take you. Do Moms know that you're okay?"

"Yeah, I called her last night, and somehow she heard about the shootout, too."

When I walked into the house Mama said, "Boy, you better cut out all that crazy shit you're doing out there before something real bad happen to you."

"Mama, I'm okay." I gave her a kiss. I can see the look in her eyes that spoke very loud without words. She was upset. I went into my room and put the gun away.

I hear S.B. pull up. I went outside and he said, "Blood, I'm glad to see you, man. When you told me to get out and your minute was up I just knew that you was in for a big fight because them white boys had some big-ass guns. How the fuck did you get out?"

"I had to shoot my way out, got me a G-ride to get home, and here I am. Say S.B., take me around the corner to Reyes' house so I can buy that Cutlass."

We pulled up and Reyes was standing in the front yard. I said, "Blood, I got the money, go get my pink slip."

He went into his house while I'm looking at my new car.

It's doo-doo brown, clean interior, T-tops, new tires and some bumping sounds. When he came out he gave me the title and I counted out fourteen hundred dollars. I took the T-tops off and jumped in and drove away. S.B. left because he had somewhere else to go.

The next day I was rolling through the hood and everyone is asking me who car is this. I proudly let them know it's mine. I know they are wondering how could I buy a car when I'm smoking and I just had that shootout, but didn't come back famous. They didn't know I was putting away more money than I was smoking. I could have used some money to hook up my caddy but it's time for something new.

I went to Jamala house. She is standing in the front yard, we have been broken up for a few months. I'm looking at her stomach, she's five months pregnant with my baby and her second time pregnant by me. Her mama told her not to give the baby my name or she would disown her. That made me mad.

I got out the car and said, "How's my baby? And I'm not talking about you."

"My baby is doing fine," she told me, then said, "I heard about you in some shootout. And what is you doing with Reyes' car?"

"This is my car and yeah, I was in a shootout. I know your mama and a lot of others wished I got smoked," I told her. Then I got back in my car and drove to the J-Block, I need to smoke something to calm me down.

FIVE-DAY HIGH

I told the homie Belly to give me a twenty. I gave him ten dollars, he knew that I wasn't going to pay the full price. I rolled up a fat-ass premoe and, right before I lit it, his sister came running out the house to give me a hug. Me and Lisa is very close, her and Treci are two cool homegirls.

I put fire to my joint and Anthony B said, "Ru-al, go across the street and smoke that, you know I'm on parole and I could turn in a dirty test with you here doing that."

"Well, you better walk away because I'm smoking it right here and right now, blood. I almost got killed yesterday and I need this."

G-Rab come walking up and he was happy to see me. He said, "Blood, I heard about you and S.B. I knew that you would shoot your way up out of that shit. Say, blood, I know you want to get high, I got a room with two Eba heads already necked and a fresh quarter piece. Let's go, take me to Moms so I can get my car."

We get to the motel room and the girls is necked. I see the table with the gadgets, the pint of Hennesy, and weed for the premoes. I said, "Yeah, this is what I'm talking about, blood!"

After a few hours in the room I had to make some money. I went back to Cook Street and picked up my Y.G. Dexter. I said, "Blood, do you want to make some money?"

"Yeah, big homie, let me go get my strap."

We went about thirty minutes from the hood to this auto

shop where this Mexican guy asked us, "How can I help you?"

"I need an engine for a 1976 caddy," I told him.

He walked into his office to look at some paperwork and we walked right in behind him. When he sat at his desk I gave the Y.G. the nod then I pulled out my gun, and said, "I don't want to hurt you, just give me the money." He looked at me as if I was joking until I cocked the hammer back on the .44, then he went into his pocket and handed me a big-ass stack of cash. The Y.G. got the door covered so no one walks in. I reached over and took the ring off his finger too.

We ran to the car and I jumped in through the T-tops without opening the door. I punched the accelerator and the car took off. I'm like, "Damn, this car got some speed!"

We got back to the hood and I gave the young homie his cut of the six hundred dollars we just stole. This was easy. I went home to let Mama see my new car then I jumped on the freeway to show Judy and take this extra money home so I can start working on getting my caddy back on the streets.

I went to Judy mama house and she was there. When I got out the car everybody asked me if it was mine. I said yeah.

We went home. I took a shower, got out some fresh clothes for tomorrow, and made love to Judy all night long. The next morning I took her to work then I jumped back on the freeway headed to Compton.

I stopped at Rock Berry spot and got a quarter piece. I parked my car in front of the house and walked across the street to G-Baby's place. It's a stadium now, the Timmons been living there for years and now they are gone. I walked in and the first person I see is Valentine. I said, "Damn, girl, I have not seen you in years. Come give me a hug."

She put her pipe down on the table and gave me strong embrace. Then I walked into Glen's old room and set up shop. It's just me and her just like old times. We got our smoke and fuck on for hours.

I've been on the smoking spree for three days. I only had this car for two days and I'm already doing jobs out of it. It's 6:30 Sunday morning and I'm looking for something to get into, but it's nothing open this early in the day. I got my pistol on my lap, and my gadget in my top pocket with a five piece already melted on the screen after my last hit.

I turned on Cook Street and see the homie Ugly Blood, I know that walk anywhere. He's two years older than me, about five nine, weighs one hundred and sixty pounds. He's a rider, and I know that he has been up smoking. I stopped the car beside him. He looked over and said, "Ru-al" what's up, blood? I'm trying to find something to get into."

"Me too. Hop on in, blood."

I turned on 130th to Jarvis Street and went toward Val's house. I'm driving slow thinking of a job we can do. And when I looked in my rearview mirror I see the one-time pull up behind us. I said, "U.B., I got my pistol on me. If they pull us over take the gun and run. I'm going to make them chase me and you know the hood, you can run and get away, okay?"

He didn't say anything at first. I'm watching the pigs get closer and closer. Then he said, "Hell nah, blood. I'm on parole, I'm not gonna run with that hot-ass gun."

Me and him has never done anything together and Blood is being skinny scary right now and I don't like it.

I'm still going up the hill at a slow speed when I see the one-time turn on their red lights. "U.B., are you going to run with the gun or not?" I asked more forcefully.

"No, Ru-al."

I pulled over to the curb, I'm thinking I got to get away, my heart is pumping hard. I'm wondering if this is the end of the line for me? This pistol is hot and I know if Carson Sheriff see it they are gonna do some shooting. I left the car idling but I never put it in PARK. I don't have my foot on the brake either since I'm parked up hill, the car stayed in that one spot without rolling backwards. I looked in the rearview mirror again then to the driver's side door mirror, I see both pigs get out their car. When I seen them walking toward me I stomped on the gas peddle and took off like a cheetah chasing a gazelle. I got the jump on them now. This is just like if I'm running on foot; if I get the jump I should get away.

Reyes sold me a tight-ass ride. I'm picking up speed and the pigs is just getting back in their car. U.B. started screaming, "Stop, Ru-al! Stop, blood, let me out!"

FIVE-DAY HIGH

"You should had ran with the gat. You can jump out if you want, the door is not locked," I told him.

I drove up the J-Block and see one of the homegirls walking down the street. She said, "Ru-al, the police is behind you." I gave her a smile then turned on 132nd. I'm doing eighty miles per hour going toward San Pedro and I know there are two deep dips on both sides of the street. I'm flying, I can see the oncoming traffic on the school side, but I can't see on the other side because the apartments is blocking my view on the left. U.B. see that I'm not slowing down, he is going crazy. He spoke with so much fear: "Ru-al, stop! Blood, it's a stop sign, you're going to get us killed."

"Shut up, blood, stop crying like a bitch. It's too late to stop now," I said being frustrated at him.

When I hit the first dip my whole car went airborne, all four tires are off the ground. The car flew across the entire intersection and landed a foot from the other dip. We missed one car buy inches that was travelling in the opposite direction. When the car landed the rearview mirror was jerked out of position on impact and I didn't have time to readjust it. I looked out the door mirror to see I got a bigger lead on them pigs. They got to stop at the stop signs to avoid collisions with traffic.

I'm flying down 132nd going through the Weakside. U.B. is still screaming like a bitch and he's fucking with my thinking. I should push his ass out the damn car. We're about to hit

10 TOEZ DOWN

Alvon and the light is red. I know I can't stop, I just hope no cars is coming through. Being Sunday, it's not too many people on the streets. I turned right so hard that I'll wrap this car on Blood's side around that pole if I don't do it right. My tires is screeching and my hubcap popped off rolling by like it had an engine of its own. I'm now on Alvon, I put the pistol in my pocket. U.B. is still going crazy, I got Blood on Fright Night. I'm doing a hundred miles per hour now, this car is rolling. We're coming up on another stoplight at 135th Street and, once again, I had to blow right through another red light. God had to be looking over me because I was missing cars by inches, this car isn't wrapped around a pole yet, and me and scary Blood aren't dead.

I got to get out this car real soon because I know the ghetto bird is on the way. And if it comes, and I'm still in this car, I'm going to hold court in these streets. After I blew that last red light I'm now in Westside Piru Hood so I know my way around. I slowed the car down to about thirty-five miles per hour and did a hard left turn on 138th. I could go toward the homie James house, but I want to run back toward my house. I slowed down more to fifteen miles per hour then I jumped out while the car is still rolling. I didn't say shit to U.B. Last I looked, his screaming ass was locked in his seat with the seat belt buckled tightly in a car with no driver. I ran across the street to the back of the apartments then I double back and ran across Alvon just as the police turned on

FIVE-DAY HIGH

138th. I jumped two fences into somebody backyard. I landed in the right one because there were no dogs to contend with. I see this old 1964 Chevy and quietly crawled in and laid down. My heart is beating so hard I can hear the pounding of each beat. I can also hear the thumping roar of the ghetto bird flying above. I hope I made it in time to get away because this is my last stop for awhile.

I'm laying in the back seat of this '64 Chevy and I can hear the ghetto bird right above me. I don't think anybody seen me get into this car. I got my pistol and my gadget still in my top pocket. I'm glad I'm not with that skinny scary U.B. because, if I was, I would have been caught or still running. I know he got to be in the back seat of that police car by now. I took my lighter and my gadget out then smoked my five piece. Aaahh! that tasted so good. After all that running and being up all day and night I fell fast asleep.

I woke up and it was dark outside. I looked at my watch to see it was eight o'clock. Damn, I've been asleep for thirteen hours! I got out of the car and stretched my body, working out all the stiffness and sore joints. Then I jumped the fence to the alley, walked to Burger City and called Paul to come get me.

"I'll be right there," he said. He arrived about three minutes later. On the way home he said, "Blood, Mama heard all about what happened and she know that I'm coming to get you, so be ready, she is very upset."

10 TOEZ DOWN

"Yeah, man, that was some crazy shit."

When I walked in the door Mama was there waiting on me. She said, "Boy, what the hell is you doing out there? Them police is going to kill you or put your ass in prison for life. You better get your act together, Albert. Where is your car?"

"I don't know where it is. All I know is I jumped out while it was still rolling and U.B. was still strapped in with his seat belt on. Mama, I just had a cops-and-robbers chase and, as you can see, I got away."

"Albert, you only had that car three days and now it's gone. Boy, I don't know what I'm going to do with you. I say this much, you're playing with death. Just the other day you was in a shootout that should had been enough for you to see the light." She walked away before I could say another word. I know that she is mad at all the stupid stuff I've been doing.

I called Judy to let her know what happen. She is telling me that same thing Mama just said. I don't want to hear that shit again. I hung up then called Reyes. I got to get him to say that the car was stolen, then I got to make some money to get it out of the impound yard in the morning.

I gave the pink slip back to Reyes and he called the police station to find out if the car was there, and that it cost three hundred and eighty dollars to get it out. I told him I'll have the money in the morning.

It's 2:15 in the morning and I'm at Pops stadium getting high. G-Rab walked in and put five big-ass rocks on the table. He handed me two of them and said, "Dee-L know where we can hit a pawn shop. Is you down?"

I looked at him and said, "You know I'm down, blood. Maybe we can get famous while we at it because we came up short in that shootout with S.B. So, yeah, where is it?"

"It's in Delano. Where he live it's about six to seven hours away. We are leaving in about an hour."

"I'm down for that. I got my .44 on me but I need to get my big tramp five seven. I need to get out the hood for a while, I'm hot as a firecracker right now."

G-Rab spoke with smoke coming out his nose. "What the fuck happen to you and U.B.? I heard that he got skinny scary on you and you had to leave his ass. Well, he's in jail for that shit now."

I said, "Blood, you know how I get down. I think he shitted in my car like he was Fright Night. You would have trip at the way he was acting. Say homie, we got about thirty minutes to leave. I'm gonna go to the hamburger stand real fast to get some fries. I'll be right back, blood. Don't leave without me."

The hamburger stand stay open all night. I walked to the drive-thru and ordered some fries. While waiting on the guy to bring me my food this car pulled up with this girl driving, and she got a dude in the passenger seat. She look fine and she got on lots of jewelry. I'm thinking this will be a quick come-up. I looked at her and said, "Hey, how are you doing, lady?"

She looked at me and said, "I'm doing fine."

When they made their order I leaned in and said to the dude, "What's up, blood?" to make sure I'm not about to jack a homie.

"Nothing much, cuzz," he said. "Just getting some grub."

I leaned back and pulled out my gun. I couldn't believe that this crab just 'cuzzed' me. As I'm pulling out my strap I see he is pulling out his too. I ran to the back of their car and dumped three quick shots to his side then broke and ran down 127th Street. Now I'm running through the homies' yards to get to an old girlfriend's house, Darlene. I hear the ghetto bird above the hamburger stand. Damn, I'm having some of the worst luck right now. Sitting on her back porch I hear police cars flying up and down El Segundo. I got to find a way across that street to get to G-Rab before they leave me. I hope Blood don't go out the house with all these one-times flying around. Shit, I got the hood hot and the way the pigs are acting the yellow tape might be up.

Thirty minutes has passed and I don't hear or see the pigs anymore. I had put the extra shells back in my strap, I got only seven more in my pocket.

I jumped the back fence and ran across El Segundo. I made it. I walked down Carlton and got to Dee-L house. They are parked in the driveway, so I jumped in. G-Rab said, "Ru-al, I knew that was you. We heard the gunshots and, when you didn't come back, that told me that you would be on the run. What the fuck happen?"

"I was ordering my food and this car pulled up. I was going to jack this bitch her jewelry but she got a dude in the car that cuzzed me, so I let them have it. Did they put up the yellow tape?"

"Nope, but they took dude to jail and let the girl go. Let's get the fuck out of here, blood. You got the hood too damn hot."

G-Rab and Dee-L split the driving while I went to sleep. These past five days has been full of terror and nothing is going right for me. I hope this is the one job that makes me famous.

It's seven o'clock, I slept all the way there. Before we get to his house I see this store, and said, "Dee-L, how far are we from your house?"

"It's just around the corner," he replied.

"G-Rab, you want to get an eye opener and hit that store?" I asked.

"I'm down, man," he replied.

We do the job and got $486 and some food stamps. Since this is Dee-L spot we gave him a hundred dollars to go get two fifties in rocks.

G-Rab had went to sleep and I'm watching TV, waiting on Dee-L to come back. Blood been gone for along time. He said it would only take a few minutes but forty-five minutes has passed and he's not back yet. I walked to the window and see two pigs behind their police car pointing guns at this apartment. The apartment is upstairs so I can see them real good from up here. I walked over to G-Rab and shook him awake. He looked up at me and said, "What's up, Ru-al? Is Dee-L back?"

"No, he's not, but the one-time is parked in front and they got guns pointed at us."

He got up, walked to the window and looked out. "Yeah, they are out there. Shit, blood, it's over before it even got started. Where the fuck is Dee-L? They must got him, or he left when he seen the one-time."

We hid the money and the guns. Ten minutes later we hear someone on the bullhorn say, "Albert Ru-al Jones and Derrick G-Rab White, come out of the apartment."

"They got us!" I said.

"Blood, that sound like Dee-L on the loudspeaker."

"Hell nah! He snitched on us? I don't believe this shit. It's going to take them some time to run up in here so let's make sure that everything is hid." We ran around the apartment flushing and stashing all that we had.

Now we are cooking up his food, we ate our last meal, by then an hour has passed. I looked out the window and they got S.W.A.T., news trucks, and a lot of other agencies and people outside. I said, "Blood, we're stuck. Let's just let them kick in the door because, if we just walk out now, they might start shooting at us. So unlock the door so they can just come in."

They got on the bullhorn again and told us that they were coming in. I just hope they don't come in shooting.

Ten minutes later, even though we unlocked the door, they kicked it in anyway. We weren't taking any chances, we were already laying on the floor with our hands and feet spreaded out. I hear one pig say, "Don't move or I'll blow your freaking head off!"

I didn't move a muscle except to tilt my head to see these fools got some nice looking gats. One dude put his knee in the middle of my back with all his weight when he noticed me looking up. I know the homie is going through the same thing. They handcuffed then walked us down the steps. As we were paraded outside I seen some fine-ass girls from the apartment watching the bust.

We get to the police substation but we don't see Lucan. They must have let him go for telling on us.

We're in Kern County Jail, once again I failed to get famous. We did make the five o'clock news for robbery though.

Laying on my bunk I'm thinking about the past five days and how I could had got famous. I made money to get that Cutlass. I had a shootout in a gun shop. The next day I buy the car, then two days later I lose it in a chase with the police. Then I shot at a crab at the hamburger stand. Now I'm in a town where I don't know anybody. They got two Blood modules, I'm in one and they got G-Rab in another. Damn, that was five days of being high.

We took a deal for receiving stolen property, time served off the three months in their jail. While in there Jamala had my baby girl Arica, and Wanda had miscarriaged our son. So I was happy and sad. Jamala didn't give our baby my last name because of her mama. Me and G-Rab both got a violation so we should get out the same day, if neither one of us don't fuck off our release date.

After one year I got out with twenty-one inch arms, I'm bigger than I ever been. I went home first to Judy and she laid down the rules, which I agreed to. I get a ride to Mama house, K-Dae got my car out of the impound. I gave my hugs and told Mama I'll do good this time. I promised.

I jumped in my Cutlass and rolled to see if Jamala is at home with my baby, but she's not. She must knew that I was getting out so she left. Now the only thing on my mind is to find Dee-L. He had a whole year to get ready for this ass kicking I'm going to give him for snitching on us.

Before I got off Cook Street G-Rab rolled up. We both got out our cars and hugged it out. I said, "Blood, have you seen Dee-L? You know I got to beat that ass before I go back home."

"Homie, leave that buster alone. I got this job and it's a good come-up. Do you still want to get famous?" he asked.

"Gangsta, I got to pass on that one. Judy gave me an ultimatum: 'Home or the Streets.' I just came to pick up my car and fuck up Dee-L before I go home. I'm sure it's a nice come-up but I got to pass, blood." He understood so we parted ways.

I'm at Pops' house talking to G-Man and I see Dee-L at the liquor store, so I call him over. He came smiling like everything is bool. He said, "Hey, Ru--"

I socked him in the nose then smashed him in the jaw before he could get out another word. He chipped me with a glancing swing, but before I could continue the beatdown that I wanted, he ran back to the store where his car is parked. He's lucky I didn't pull out my gun and pistol-whip his snitchin' ass. He did get one lucky punch in under my eye but I was able to give him a little of what I waited a whole year to give him. Now the word is out that Ru-al beat up Dee-L.

I got a half-ounce of some bomb-ass weed the homeboy gave me and when I get back to my house Judy sees the little mark under my eye. "What happen, stupid face?" she asked, not really being impressed or caring about the answer. Same ol' same with me.

"I had to beat Dee-L ass and he got a lucky punch in. But I'm home now to be with my Judy everyday."

She smiled which softened her face and appeared to be somewhat forgiving. I know this my last time doing that crazy shit and she still have my back, so I don't want to mess up this good thing I have with her.

Things is going well. I'm back to going to church every Sunday. All is good in the Jones' house. I stopped going to

the hood as much and, when I do, I could only stay one or two
days. But that's cool because I know that's what's keeping me
out of trouble and not wanting to smoke that shit. Most of
all, Judy is happy.

G-Man called to tell me that G-Rab done that job by himself and he got into a shootout with some dude there. Now
he's in jail, taking a deal for fifteen years with a day-for-a
day so he will get out after eight years. I hate that I
didn't go with my boy. He just didn't trust anybody like he
trust me so he went on his own. I see he shot his way out,
and he didn't get famous either.

I have been out for six months and doing good. My parole
officer has found me a job being a welder and I start tomorrow.
Things are beginning to change for me and Judy, we are both
very happy. Now we are talking about having a baby and getting
married. We got her nephew, Alon, staying with us. He's cool
and I like him, he's doing good in school too.

I just got done cleaning up the kitchen from that good
meal that Judy cooked. Everybody took their bath and we're
just chillin' in front of the TV. I got on my red and white
polka-dot pajamas and black corduroy house shoes. Judy got
to work in the morning so she's about to go to bed. Me and
Alon just smoked a fat joint, then the phone rings. Who could
be calling us at this time of the night? I picked up the
phone and said, "Hello?"

"It's your parole officer," came the voice on the other

end of the line. "I need you and Alon to come out of the house with your hands up. Don't ask why, just do it."

"Okay," I said, then I turned to Alon to let him know, "the police is outside, they want us to come out with our hands up, but I don't know why."

Judy is looking at me and I'm looking at her. I don't know what the fuck is going on. She has the look of worry in her eyes. Maybe it could be from something I've done in the past, but I wasn't sure of anything.

We do as instructed and go outside. We get handcuffed and I ask my parole officer what's going on. He said, "You're being arrested for double murder."

"I didn't kill anybody."

We were taken away and I was charged with the crimes. Now I have to fight the system for my life. But I'm still Ten Toez Down Gangstas.

* * *

RU-AL'S KARMA

<u>Karma</u>, by Webster: The totality of one person's actions in each state of his existence. Fate. Destiny.

    I believe in karma. You can do so much bad that it comes back to bite you in the ass in a real way. I got away with so many illegal and bad acts, I hurt so many people and their families over my time on these streets. I didn't care who suffered the pain and agony of my crimes as long as it wasn't Ru-al, family, homeboys and homegirls.

    I ask myself if it was karma that I got shot up and lost my niece, Lil China, in a drive-by because I beat up and shot crabs? Did karma come back on me in that way? Was that karma, or a blessing that I'm still alive?

    What about the crabs? What did they do so bad for them to cross paths with me? Whose karma was that? Mines or theirs? Was I the one to pay them back with my fists or my gun for the wrongdoings that they had done? Was it fate that kept me alive this long?

    There is good karma. You do good and good comes back to you. I have seen that karma and I like it. But somehow I would end up with more bad karma, my scales were always unbalanced and weighed heavily in someone else's favor. When I

RU-AL'S KARMA

tried to find a job and couldn't I went on them smoking sprees. Was that bad karma? Who do I blame for that? Or does it all come back to me because I made that choice on my own? I have so many questions about karma. And now that I sit here on Death Row for a crime I did not commit, is this the good karma or the bad? Unfortunately, I got a lot of time to try to figure it out. But I'm sure before it's all over while I'm Ten Toez Down and still able to breathe, I'll get my answers.

*   *   *

RU-AL'S ANGELS

My angels has been looking over me for many years. Because of all the crazy and dangerous things I did, and the crimes I committed while gang-banging, I had to have some ethereal or spiritual presence looking over me, and I know they were my angels. All the shootouts and getting shot I should have been six feet under, but the Lord is not ready for me to walk through those Pearly Gates yet. The many fights I had with Crips, it could have been me on the other side getting knocked out or shot up. It had to be special angels or spiritual beings looking after me that have my back, keeping me safe.

Over the years I lost family members either from some kind of illness, accident, or gang-related violence. And it hurt the whole family to lose them, they was some good people. God-fearing people. Now they are in heaven looking over the rest of their family on Earth, that's their job now. I send my love and thanks to them every night for keeping me and the rest of their family safe. And thank you God for our many blessings.

Angels, I do feel you in my life. When things get rough you come to my aid and I know that it was one of you up there. I miss your physical presence and radiant smile. When I reminisce on old photos, or things we've done together, I just smile with happiness, I feel your love and protection blanketing me in a specal way. Someday I'll see you again in heaven because I will make it there myself, that's a promise. But for now I still need you watching over me and the rest of your family members and loved ones.

I MISS YOU SO MUCH

Granddaddy Humphery. Grandmama Luella. Daddy Wilbert. Uncle Leon. Brother Leon. Sister Patricia. Aunt Delores. Uncle Arthur. Aunt Maple. Niece Mitchshalae. Relative Jerome. Nephew Relly. Relative Lun-Ye. Relative Debra.

R.I.P. My Angels

*   *   *

PIRUS' and BLOODS' HISTORY

In 1972, the Compton Pirus was started by Sylvester "Puddin" Scott and Vincent "Tam" Owens, who also came into conflict with the Compton Crips. "Pirus and Crips were at odds with each other but quite often socialized together," said Twilight Bay, a social intervention specialist who grew up in the gang-affected Circle City Piru neighborhood. "There was a girl that had been dating a member of the Crips and a member of the Pirus and a fight broke out over that."

The incident led the Pirus' leadership to reconsider their alliance with the Crips. Soon after they became know as the Piru Street Boys. Other neighborhoods were also joining forces against the Crips in an alliance that included Bobby Lavender's the Bishops on Bondera Street, the Bounty Hunters in the Nickerson Gardens housing projects; hoods in Watts, Eddie Watts' the Brims and Jan Brewer's of the Inglewood Families all came together against the Crips.

"We were outnumbered by the Crips and we formed an alliance with the Brims," said T. Rodgers, founder of the Black P Stones. "Eventually we had an alliance with other neighborhoods who felt threatened by the Crips." It was this group of allies that would come to be known as the Bloods. The rivalry between the Crips and the Bloods exploded, resulting in over four hundred murders in the 1970s. By 1978, there were

PIRUS' and BLOODS' HISTORY

about fifteen Blood gangs and forty-five Crip gangs throughout L.A., Compton, and Watts. By 1982, Bloods had grown to forty-six neighborhoods and the Crips had one hundred and nine hoods. Bloods treated each other like real brothers, whereas the Crips had rivalries amongst themselves. Bloods treat each other like family, we are united.

The war intensified during the 1980s so much that the L.A. County Jail system created a separate housing section for the Bloods called 3600, 4300, 4600 -- better known as the Blood Modules. These modules was designed to isolate Bloods from the Crip-laden general population or mainline. Coincidentally, another term for Bloods is "Damu" which means blood in Swahili. Damu arose during this time. The term likely became popular as inmates tried to expand our African consciousness and study the language while incarcerated, because the Mexicans spoke Spanish and the white dudes did sign language.

The Blood modules came about because of the constant rat-packing by Crips on Bloods living on the mainline. So all the Bloods was pulled together and put into one module for the next fifteen years. We are outnumbers eight to one. It's hard to be a Blood in this county jail because the mainline is infested with Crips. So if you made it to O.S.S. (Operation Safe Street) office, you was taken directly to the Blood Module. And the Crips had the entire mainline. Today there are roughly seventy Blood gangs and two hundred and ten Crip gangs in L.A., Compton and Watts. Although the feud between the two rival factions is very strong, the number of internal Crip-on-Crip rivalries has grown dramatically. A large number of Blood hoods were growing in cities like Pasadena, Inglewood, Watts and Compton. But we as Blood hoods are still the minority in the South, West, East and North side of L.A., and there is no Blood gangs in the City of Long Beach.

As the years passed and more youngsters has been claiming Blood, and putting work in on Crips, we also started to set-trip on each other's hoods, and that has given the Blood car a black eye. Something that started off as protecting our neighborhoods from the Crips has turned negative for us. Bloods never "jumped-in" anyone in our gang like the Crips do. You can be an ex-Blood and turn Crip. But no Crip can turn into a Blood and be accepted into the family. We don't let just anyone claim Blood. Most Bloods are homegrown. Crips will accept anyone that want to be a Crip, that's why there are so many. We know the Bloods in our car are down. Being outnumbered is what makes being a Blood so bool. And getting that reputation as a Blood lets the others know that he or she is down because it's so hard to become a Blood. This is not for everyone and if you're not homegrown, stay out of it. If you can't handle the ups and downs that comes with this red flag, and being a Damu Gangsta, step back and let real gangstas handle it. There are a lot of homies that grew up in Blood hoods and wasn't banging, never shot nor ever had

PIRUS' and BLOODS' HISTORY

a fight with a Crip. But they are still from the hood and I know if they seen someone from their hood getting jumped they would help the out. So I still have the utmost love for them as a homeboy, they just chose a different way to claim. I chose to be out there in the thick of it like most on both sides of the streets.

Ten Toez Down Gangstas.

*   *   *

B-DOG HOODS ROLL CALL

J-Block; APB, MGB, DL, BPS, Jungles, IFG, WSP, FTP, 135, 151, BH, NHB, FSK, CMG, VNG, Pueblos, 62, Brims, FTB, PPB, WFP, 456, CAP, CPP, VTP, TTP, LPP, CCP, CBP, BSV, 30 Pirus, 20 Outlaws, BBW, IAP, ESP, Hiecenda ES Pain Pirus, 92 Bishops, P9, Carson BH, BPS Bitty Stone, PDL, HHP, MOB, LHP, Centerview Pirus, NHP, Cabbage Patch Pirus, Elm St. Pirus, Hathorne Pirus, Scottsdale Pirus, UBN, BL, YGB. San Diego; 59 Brims, LPB, Skyline Pirus.

Blood love to all our true allies. Northern Brown Brothers. B.G.F. and all my up north niggas. San Francisco, Oakland, Richmond, Hayward, East Palo Alto, San Jose, Berkeley, Sacramento, Vallejo. Keep that red flag flying, homies.

If I missed your hood don't trip you're always a part of this family that's spread throughout killer Cali, from state to state also prison to prison. No matter what, don't let the small shit break that bond and trust that we built over the years. We are one. We can't be like them crabs and ride on each other, that's not how we get down. Show your fellow rads that true Damu love because we all know that we will not leave or run out on another Blood. So let's put our differences aside and show the young homies that's coming after us that we didn't lay down an ugly foundation for them by feuding with each other. And let's not give them crabs that satisfaction that we as B-Dogs is heading into self-destruction like they did. So Bloods, I say from my heart and through my bullet wounds, stay Ten Toez Down Gangstas.

*   *   *

DAMU SAYINGS

"Bloods rules the streets of L.A. killing crabs all night and day. Bloods, Bloods, how do you feel? Dressed in red and ready to kill!"

"Now I lay that crab down to sleep. I tie my red flag around his feet. If he don't die and try to wake, I will shoot him again with my murder eight."

"Let it rain. Let it drip. Sock a crab in his lip. Stomp his face in mud. This is all gangsta, Bloods."

          *   *   *

RU-AL STREET PRAYER

Dear Lord, I bow down to You and only You. Thank You for keeping me alive on these dangerous streets. It's been many of time I should have been dead, but You saved me without me even knowing that it was You. Lord, I know I've done a lot of wrong, hurt a lot of people and their families. Lord, I ask You to forgive me of my sins. I know You're a forgiving God and that's why You come first. It took some time for me to understand, or see, Your presence in my life. When you spared my life in that drive-by and You brought Lil China to heaven, that should have opened my eyes, heart and soul that it was You that saved me from death. But the devil had a strong hold on me. Lord, it took getting put on Death Row for me to see Your grace, mercy, and Your forgiveness. Lord, I know that I'm truly forgiven, and I thank You, my Father in heaven, for this new look on life. I know that I'm still a Blood but I also know you will find a better way to use me. In Jesus name, amen."

"This is the day the Lord has made; we will rejoice and be glad in it."   (Psalms 118:24)

*   *   *

SUMMARY

On May 29, 1964, I was the seventh child born to Wilbert and Christene Jones. On a sunny day in South Central Los Angeles they brought their son, who they named Albert, home to a three-bedroom house on 59th and Bonzales, just around the corner from her mama place. I don't remember anything about that house. When we moved on Main Street, that's when my life really began. Sister Connie took care of me. When I went to preschool she was there to pick me up and find my lost tennis shoes. And on the way home I held my big sister's hand while we sang my favorite song. I was a happy-go-lucky kid. Five years later Paul was born, and then Katie, and now we have a new home on 117th and Mona. After years living there we moved to Portland, Oregon, with granddaddy. Then we moved to Palmdale. After that, the big move happened, back to the City of Compton.

I met Leo and my life did a 180-degree turn. I knew then that my life would never be the same again. I became a Blood on day one. When I had my first encounter with a Crip I was nervous, but not scared. At that moment that's when I noticed that my heart beats faster filled with adrenaline when I'm in danger or about to get into something that will cause pain to someone. Over the years I learn to take that fast-beating heart and focus on the task that's in front of me. With that rush of hyper energy I'm able to make the right move before the

SUMMARY

next man.

I never been scared. One thing I didn't want to be was skinny scary. Because if you get scared, it could cost you your life, or the life of the person that's with you. You give up your manhood or your masculinity by being scary. You got to have heart in this lifestyle. If not, you could get knocked the fuck out or end up ten toes up on your back. I also learned about dealing with other Bloods, they have their own style on how they do theirs; like the ballers, rappers, actors, and mentors -- they did it their way. And I did it my way. I don't knock them because they chose their own path, as long as they keep it real. I have a big heart. One thing I learned was not to be acting hard or trying to be hard. Don't get me wrong, I've seen and have some hard homies. They are the ones that will step up and not think and be so fast to move, then someone got the bad end of the deal, but that's being hard.

I made sure that my banging with other Bloods and hoods let them know that Ru-al is a down B-Dog. I tried to keep my reputation and my respect for all Bloods 100% pure in this game. If you called on me to ride with you I'll be there and I won't leave until the smoke is clear. You will get my all with no questions asked because I know that you wouldn't put yourself in a bad position. I learn to be a thinker. I'm not the one to just jump into something and not know what I'm getting myself into. I'm not going to let no one get me smoked on some dumb shit. Nine times out of ten I'll ride with you and

10 TOEZ DOWN

I know some homie like to get into some stupid shit. That will be the one percent that make me say, "I'm bool on that, blood."

This lifestyle have something that makes you want to be a part of. Going to a hood party or picnic and seeing so many Bloods in one spot with all the love, I just enjoyed being there with them. We act like superstars. We would sign our autographs on different hoods' walls to let them know that we was there and if you run across me you already know who I am because you seen my ghetto autograph.

I feel if I could have found a job after I got out of Job Corps, or prison, things might have been different. I got a lot of "what ifs" but it all comes back to me, I make the last call on what I do with my life. So I don't blame no one but Ru-al. I grew up in a two-parent household all my life and they showed some good values to all us kids. Most households in my hood has two parents, but we chose our own paths.

For those that read this book and know Ru-al you know that I'm a down Blood and all the B-Dogs I spoke on I'm giving you your utmost respect in this Blood gang. I know I might have forgot to put your name in it but, know this, I know you're a true Blood and down for the cause. And for the crabs that has this book in your hand who don't like what you read, well, it's not for you anyway. This is a B-Dog book and didn't your dumbass read that big-ass red kaution sign on the front cover? But if you think that your feelings was hurt you know what to do, make it happen, but you already know the outcome.

SUMMARY

    I know that some homies don't like the way I do mines and that is okay. But the love I have for all Bloods I know I'm loved by hundreds and hated by a few. And if you're one of the few, what can I do? I know I got my bang on my way and what I considered the right way. I will always respect this red flag and others. When I close my eyes at night I know that I kept it real. I welcome you to my hood, my house and, most of all, to my mailbox. I lived long enough to tell my story to you and I know that most got a story to tell. The best way to do it is put it on paper and know that my prayer is your prayer, too.

    Thanks to all B-Dogs for your love and loyalty. Keep your flags neatly pressed in your right back pockets and always have your white Chuck Taylors with the fat red laces. Now I close this part of the book . . . .

    Ten Toez Down Gangstas.

    *   *   *

MY REDEMPTION

At the young age of 13 years old is when I joined the Jarvis Street Pirus. I really didn't know what I was getting myself into until it was too late because I was in too deep.

In my neighborhood, it has to be at least a hundred young boys and girls growing up together, ages 13 to 18. Each home had anywhere from three to nine kids, including both parents. This is a very tight-knit neighborhood, one could walk into any home at any time and be welcomed. We all went to school together. We went to house parties too. Eighty percent of us joined this gang life and some took it to the extreme, I was one of them. But to me it all seemed normal.

This was the start of a life that I never thought I would live. As I got older, and had that first encounter with a Crip, it was a joy knowing I beat up the enemy. But in all the inner cities in Los Angeles, Compton, Watts and many other towns, the youth are growing up the same way, under the same set of circumstances and influences.

Everyone wanted to earn their "stripes" -- a victory over a Crip. I'm sure the Crips were brought up seeking the same retalitary retribution. I had grew into a lot of anger with them Crips and my life got so out of hand that the violence was as commonplace like any old other day filled with hate.

I wrote this book in 1997 from my small prison cell on

MY REDEMPTION

Death Row. I was able to remember that lifestyle on them streets and as it carried on within other prisons. So here it is, 2018, I have sat on these two books for over 21 years, but I'm now 54 years old with a different way of thinking and it's nowhere close to the way I thought, or the way I lived, when I was 13 to 29 years old. I was very active at that time. So telling this story about my life, and a lot of people that I grew up with, I look back and say "Wow, we was crazy and didn't care about our own lives." Now it's all a part of my legacy so I want to make sure I tell it right.

I have been asked many times, do I have any regrets? I would say no, because that lifestyle seemed like the norm to me. But now I have those regrets for the people I hurt. I can say drugs and alcohol -- most hoods had rock cocaine, weed, sherm stick, PCP -- we did those mind-altering substances everyday. So I know that had an affect on my thinking, because a lot of things we done we would not have done it sober. I regret the way I treated the women that came into my life. I was with four to five women at one time over those years and I did love some of them very much: Lorna, Lisa, Jamala. But Judy, I should have married her. I do feel bad as I look back on my life that I should have treated all them women so much better.

I have been asked, why stay in a gang? I feel that I can get across to the young people on how bad gang life can be. The brotherhood is something that was very much a positive influence in so many ways, but the violence, hurt and pain that occurs because of that membership must be used as a pivotal point of change. By staying in I feel I can help direct the youths to a better, and safer, path in life.

So for my redemption I have done a lot of positive work and soul searching the decades I've been here on the Row. Some of that work has translated into writing six books. Two are death-row autobiographies: "I'm In God's Confinement" and "Put On The Shelf To Die." A street gangsta book: "10 Toez Down," and a prison gangsta book: "Behind These Walls." A death-row cookbook: "Our Last Meals?" And an eight-book series of Christian children books.

So I have to show redemption not just for my gang life but for my three G-Babies: Eugene 3rd, Emeire, Emarih; and my baby girl Albanisha Shunice Jones. These books will show them the ugly side of being in a gang and what it cost me. These books will be with them for their G-Babies to pass on.

When I do get out I'm going to go to as many schools and youth groups as I can to tell my story in hopes I can touch hundreds of vulnerable and impressionable minds -- that will be my mission of freedom.

So if someone says that growing up in the hood didn't have no affect on them, they are not telling the truth. Because I know that they know someone that got injured, or killed, in some kind of gang violence.

1993 is the last time I earned a stripe on a Crip, but

MY REDEMPTION

after being on death row I have found a new enemy -- that's the devil. He had a stranglehold on my life, and so many others, and I'm done working for him. I'm staying prayed-up and I have my spiritual and ancestral angeles faithfully looking over me, and my seeds out there.

I'm not going to stop or give up trying to find a way to get them young people interested in something more than the destructive natural of them gangs. And when it's time for me to hang up my red flag, trust me, I'm going to do it with a new lease on life, with no hate toward anyone. With that I'll have my redemption on this Earth.

Albert "Ru-al" Jones

*   *   *

LOST LOVED ONES

Growing up in this neighborhood the people that came into my life, and all those that have showed real love to me and my family, I realized that love is so real and sincere. So for those people that have left this Earth they have left some kind of legacy behind. If it was from P-Rock's parents, Mr. & Mrs. Sutton's laundry mat, where we could wash our clothes; or walking to school and saying hi to Brother Duke and Mother Rosie; or simply seeing the elders in our hood smile really made our day.

When we sold weed in front of Hawkeye's or Snowden's houses, with all the respect to them not to curb serve when our parents were coming home from work. And everyone loved when my daddy drove by, we laughed when he waved with his big hand; we called him "Hands." Just chillin' in someone's yard at a barbecue, or at Big Val's house partying all night until the sun came up.

So no matter how they passed on, if it was from cancer (C), natural causes (NC), or murder (M), they are loved and being missed so much to this very day.

I know that I might have missed someone's name, so please know you are still loved and not forgotten on your special day when you went to Heaven to be with our Lord. We will always know that your positive energy and bright smiles will continue to be with us throughout our years. And thanks for the memories in our neighborhood.

R.I.P.   P.I.P.   B.I.P.

Jarvis Street Mafia Piru
&
Athens Park Bloods
"Love"

IN MEMORIAM

R.I.P. B.I.P. P.I.P.

Wilbert "Hands" Jones (NC)
Mitchshalae "Lil China" Davis (M)
Jerrel "Too Tall" Harvey (M)
Mr. Hayward "Pops" (NC)
Jerome "Jerry" Brown (M)
Warren "Zell" Hayward (M)
Ronnie "Green Backs" (C)
Mr. Ezell (NC)
Regina Ezell (M)
"Lou" Ezell (NC)
Wilbert "Crip" Ezell (NC)
Mr. & Mrs. Williams (NC)
Greg "Pegleg" Williams (NC)
Michael "Goat" Williams (NC)
Carolyn Williams (NC)
Mr. & Mrs. Henery (NC)
Alberta Timmons (NC)
Glen Timmons (NC)
Young Vickie (NC)
Francis Lay (NC)
Eric "EB" Baker (NC)
"Hawkeye" Gram (NC)
Sam Gram (NC)
Brother Melvin (NC)
Brother Duke (NC)
Mother Rosie (NC)
Darrel Sullivan (M)
Denise Sullivan (NC)
Tony "Smoke Dog" (M)

Savandra Moore (NC)
Mr. King (NC)
"Bo Slim" King (M)
Lisa Adams (NC)
Mr. & Mrs. White (NC)
Valerie "Big Val" Hodge (NC)
Mike White (NC)
Odell White (NC)
Carl White (NC)
Brenda White (NC)
Byron "Ziz Zag" (M)
"Avery Dog" (M)
Kusha "Lil Boo" (NC)
"Cheeso" (M)
Leandra "Lee-Lee" (C)
"D-Loko" (M)
"Hot Dog" (M)
"Mel Lok" (M)
Stone "TD" (NC)
Monty Earl (M)
"Beko" (M)
Clifford Sutton (C)
Mr. & Mrs. Sutton (NC)
Gary Carter (M)
Gregory Jones (NC)
Troy Night (C)
Pee-Wee (M)
Syko Mike (M)
Cupcake (M)

Made in the USA
Las Vegas, NV
03 April 2025